"*The Joy of Mixology* is insightful and entertaining—and it will help you make, serve, and enjoy better drinks. The first edition was fantastic. It's even better now."

—SEAN MULDOON, cofounder of the Dead Rabbit Grocery and Grog and coauthor of *The Dead Rabbit Mixology & Mayhem*

"From a very special soul, Gaz Regan, who sees the barroom as a place to imbibe and celebrate our humanity, this new edition of *The Joy of Mixology* is as irreverent and funny as ever—filled with great recipes for drinks and lessons for life."

—DALE DEGROFF, author of *The Craft of the Cocktail* **and** *The Essential Cocktail*

"Regan writing about bars and bartending is like the suspension cables writing about the bridge that hangs from them. He's more than just an insider—he's essential infrastructure, as every page of this new edition of his pivotal book proves."

—DAVID WONDRICH, cocktail historian and author of *Imbibe!* **and** *Punch*

"Gary Regan has updated what was once an essential read to a required one for anyone who's interested in what it takes to be a great bartender. His knowledge of the guests' experience—its humor, its seriousness, and our role in it—will help mold the front lines for generations to come."

—FRANK CAIAFA, author of *The Waldorf Astoria Bar Book*

THE JOY OF MIXOLOGY

THIS REVISED AND UPDATED EDITION INCLUDES

THE HISTORY OF MIXED DRINKS

COMPLEAT INSTRUCTION ON THE METHODOLOGY OF THE COCKTAILIAN BARTENDER

A THOROUGH EXPLICATION OF THE THEORY OF MIXED DRINKS

A COMPLEAT GUIDE TO MINDFUL BARTENDING

A VERITABLE BAEDEKER OF THE BARTENDER'S TOOLS AND GLASSWARE

PRESCRIPTIONS FOR GARNISH PREPARATION

RECIPES FOR THE PREPARATION OF, AND DISCUSSIONS ON, THE HISTORY AND MAKEUP OF ALL MANNER OF POPULAR COCKTAILS, MARTINIS, SIMPLE SOURS, INTERNATIONAL SOURS, NEW ORLEANS SOURS, ENHANCED SOURS, SPARKLING SOURS, FRENCH-ITALIAN COCKTAILS IN ALL OF THEIR VARIOUS HUES AND GUISES, AND MANY OTHER RECENTLY CREATED COCKTAILIAN MASTERPIECES

VARIOUS CHARTS AND TABLES

AND A BIT OF ATTITUDE

THE

OF

MIXOLOGY

THE CONSUMMATE GUIDE TO THE BARTENDER'S CRAFT

GARY "GAZ" REGAN

CLARKSON POTTER / PUBLISHERS
NEW YORK

Published in the United States by Clarkson Potter/Publishers,
an imprint of the Crown Publishing Group, a division of
Penguin Random House LLC, New York.
crownpublishing.com
clarksonpotter.com

Library of Congress Cataloging-in-Publication Data is available.

ISBN 978-0-451-49902-8
Ebook ISBN 978-0-451-49903-5

Printed in the United States of America

Cover design by Laura Palese
Interior design by Marysarah Quinn

10 9 8 7 6 5 4 3 2 1

FIRST REVISED EDITION

THIS BOOK IS DEDICATED TO

DAVID WONDRICH

a Wise Old Soul with the heart of a Bartender,
a True Gentleman, and a Treasured Friend

ACKNOWLEDGMENTS

Give thanks to God.
After all, it's his language you're cashing in on.
—Danielle Egnew

I HAD SO MANY PEOPLE TO THANK when I originally penned the first edition of this book in 2003, and now, some fifteen years later, I've many more folk to add. If I start to try to list everyone, I know I'll be sorry. The book will go to the printer, and two days later I'll think of a few more people who I forgot to include. So I'm not going to name anyone at all.

I will, though, thank the global bartending community for all the support you've given to me over the years. I've learned much from twenty-first-century bartenders during the past decade or more, so I'd like to thank you all for letting me hang with you, watch you, and feel like one of the gang. Without you, my Bartender Brothers and Sisters, my life could never have been as rich as it's become. God Bless each and every one of you.

And there's no way that this book is going anywhere near a printer before I thank my wonderful new wife, Amy, for showing me what true love is all about. In our next lives, Babe, let's try to meet up sooner rather than later, huh?

CONTENTS

A MESSAGE TO BARTENDERS OF ALL STRIPES

SINCE THE FIRST EDITION of *Joy of Mixology* became required reading for bartenders at many craft cocktail bars around the globe, I thought that I'd take this opportunity to address those of you who are new to tending bar, so you'll know what you're getting yourself into.

Many of us find ourselves called behind the bar so we can be a "startender," complete with tattoos, piercings, and hordes of adoring fans who come back night after night to taste our concoctions. I found out quickly that you have a helluva lot of legwork to get through before you even begin to approach that kind of status. Before you gain the fame, you gotta pay your dues. Big time.

If you're new to bartending, be willing to start out as a barback, lugging ice and cases of beer up from the basement, cutting garnishes, polishing bottles, and doing all of the drudge work while others get the big bucks and walk home with the best-looking girl or guy in the place.

When you finally do get behind the bar, as a bartender or as a barback, your first job is to learn how to watch. Watch the seasoned professionals as they go about their business. Notice how both of their hands are busy at all times. See how they can pour gin with one hand and open a bottle of IPA with the other.

Learn from the pros as they manage the guests at the bar, and listen to their interactions. Learn how to deal with angry customers, how to cope with complaints, how to crack wise, and make people smile as they go about their jobs.

When the time is right, ask questions. Find out *why* the pros do what they do, how they prioritize when faced with multiple tasks, and how they steer potential troublemakers toward the door without an angry word being spoken.

Most important: LISTEN. We don't know it all. We'll never know it all. Be prepared to learn something new every day for the rest of your life.

And if you manage to become a full-time bartender, the rest of your life will surely be interesting, to say the least.

With Lotsa Love,
gaz regan

INTRODUCTION

We have a habit in writing . . . to cover up all the tracks, to not worry about the blind alleys or describe how you had the wrong idea first, and so on. So there isn't any place to publish, in a dignified manner, what you actually did in order to get to do the work.

—RICHARD FEYNMAN

IF YOU WERE TO START WALKING from New York to Los Angeles, and were absolutely determined to get there, there is little doubt that you would eventually walk down Hollywood Boulevard. But you might lose your way a couple of times, and that's what happened when I first wrote this book. I just had to get to Los Angeles, and I think I made it, but I took a few wrong turns along the way, visiting places I had no intention of going to. When the Pacific Ocean was in sight, though, I knew that my meanderings had been worthwhile.

While researching the history chapter of this book, consulting the thoughts and reasonings of the past masters of the craft and reading the words of people who had actually encountered such nineteenth-century superstar bartenders as Harry Johnson, holding forth from behind the bar at Little Jumbo, his joint on the Bowery, I found myself wishing that I could travel back to the Gay Nineties and watch a groundbreaking cocktailian at work. I could visit the old Waldorf Astoria, order a Bronx Cocktail from Johnnie Solon himself, and sit back to take in the antics of Buffalo Bill Cody, a man who never refused a drink. Who knows, I might even find myself standing across the mahogany from Jerry Thomas, the man who wrote the world's first cocktail book, in 1862. What a treat that would be.

Later, though, when working on the recipes, and poring through formulas given to me by today's masters of the craft, I realized just how lucky I am to be living in the twenty-first century. I have watched Dale DeGroff making Blue Blazers at the Rainbow Room; I've been served marvelous creations by Tony Abou-Ganim when he was at Harry Denton's Starlight Room in San Francisco; and I have also had the honor of being served the best Manhattans in Manhattan by Norman Bukofzer at the Ritz-Carlton. I witnessed Audrey Saunders being mentored by Dale when they worked together at Blackbird, and before we knew it, she was a star. And I've bellied up to many a bar where the bartender wouldn't know how to make a Caipirinha if his or her life depended on it—but they were bartenders through and through.

WHAT YOU SHOULD KNOW ABOUT THIS EDITION

I've thought about writing a second edition of this book for quite some time, and I've decided not to do it over and over again, but here I am, penning a new version of the book that I think of as my baby, *The Joy of Mixology*.

The first edition, I believe, did much to cement my place in the cocktail world, and it certainly made my name known by lots more people all over the world than had ever heard of me prior to the book being published. With this edition, then, I have much to live up to.

So much has happened in the bar world over the past ten years, and although I've been here to watch it all happen, I haven't been actually working behind bars while bartenders have been creating new techniques behind the stick, learning how to carve huge blocks of ice, playing with roto-vapors, and perfecting all manner of molecular mixology innovations. In my opinion, then, I haven't actually "lived" the advances that have taken place behind the bars of this wonderful new century.

Alternatively, thanks to liquor companies who have hired me to conduct workshops, to judge competitions, and to visit top-notch cocktail bars all over the world, and thanks to all of the bartenders who have attended my Cocktails in the Country retreats, I have witnessed young bartenders pushing the mixology envelope so hard that it nearly burst open. And on occasion, that envelope has, indeed, burst, scattering incredibly complex formulas to the wind, and leaving Bartender Boffins scratching their freshly shaved scalps and heading off back to the drawing board. And this is what has set the current generation of Ganymedes apart from their forebears: These guys don't give up.

Innovation after innovation has been introduced, studied, criticized, analyzed, and perfected by the women and the men who currently hold forth from behind the stick. And along the way, due in no small part to social media, today's bartenders have embraced their chosen craft totally in a bartender community that has become global in a very short time. The best of the bunch these days could stand very tall indeed next to the masters of yesteryear. It makes my little heart glad.

Read on, then, and I hope you'll find in this edition some things I forgot about last time around, and lots of topics that didn't even exist in the bar world just a decade or two ago. We've spent the past twenty years living in the Second Golden Age of the Cocktail. And it's been a damned fine ride.

THE JOY OF MIXOLOGY

THE HISTORY OF COCKTAILS AND MIXED DRINKS

Variety's the very spice of life,
That gives it all its flavour.

—William Cowper,
The Task, Book II, "The Time-Piece," 1785

THERE'S NOTHING quite like a good cup of tea. But do you prefer Earl Grey, Assam, Keemun, Lapsang souchong, jade oolong, Formosa oolong, or Ti Kuan Yin? Or perhaps English Breakfast is more your cuppa. And how do you take your tea? Plain and strong or with milk and sugar, a slice of lemon, a teaspoon of honey, a tot of whiskey, or a good measure of dark rum? One drink with myriad variations, all dependent on the taste of the consumer. And so it is, and always has been, with mixed drinks: The base ingredient can be consumed neat, but it can also be enhanced by the addition of one or more other ingredients. Why do people choose to adulterate fine wines, beers, and spirits? For variety's sake. It's the very spice of life.

It's more than possible that the world's first mixed drinks were created in order to mask the bad flavors of the base ingredient. Alcoholic potions of our dim and distant past were far inferior to the technologically clean products we enjoy today. Archeological evidence shows that the ancient Egyptians used dates and other fruits to flavor their beer, and that Wassail, a spiced drink originally made with a base of hard cider, dates back to pagan England—it was served to celebrate a bountiful apple harvest. We also know that the Romans drank wine mixed with honey and/or herbs and spices. The practice could have arisen from the inferior quality of the wine, but it probably also had roots in the medicinal, restorative, or digestive qualities attributed to the various ingredients. Mulled wine and spiced beer date back thousands of years and are still enjoyed in the twenty-first century.

In order to see how the cocktails and mixed drinks of more modern times came into being, it's necessary to start in the 1600s, when taverns in New England were serving some creative concoctions. Sack Posset was a mixture of ale, sack (sherry), eggs, cream, sugar, and spices such as nutmeg and mace that was boiled over an open fire, sometimes for hours at a time. When the quaffers wanted their ale hot but didn't want to leave it on the fire, they would use a type of poker, known as a loggerhead, that was heated in the fire and then plunged into the tankard of ale. If a fight broke out in the tavern, these pokers could be used as weapons—the fighters were "at loggerheads" with each other.

It's possible that there were more than a few fights in seventeenth-century taverns, too—the colonists didn't drink in short measure. One description of the daily drinking habits of southern colonists states that they started their day with mint-flavored whiskey, stopped work at 11:00 A.M. in order to partake of Slings, Toddies, or Flips, drank whiskey or brandy with water before and during dinner, and finished their day with a whiskey or brandy without water. But overconsumption wasn't tolerated by all the colonists: In seventeenth-century Connecticut, for example, it was illegal to drink for more than thirty minutes at a time, or to down more than a half bottle of wine at one sitting. And if you dined at the Ship Inn in Boston circa 1634, you would have been allowed no more than one cup of wine with dinner.

Among the drinks consumed during the 1700s were Mulled Wines, sherry sweetened with fruit (such as raspberries), and Juleps. We're not sure whether these were the Mint Juleps familiar to us today since, according to Richard Barksdale Harwell, author of *The Mint Julep,* mention of such a drink wasn't recorded until 1803. All sorts of other mixed or flavored drinks were popular with the early colonists, and some of them, such as Toddies, Slings, and an assortment of Punches and Mulled Wines, are still made today, though probably not according to recipes that our forefathers would recognize.

Other drinks that cropped up in America around this time bear names that recall some of the cocktails we drink today. A potion called Mimbo was merely rum and sugar; Stonewall was a mixture of rum and cider; Black-Stripe was made of rum and molasses; a Stewed Quaker was hard cider with a baked apple dropped into it; and one drink, made from simmered sour beer sweetened with molasses and thickened with crumbs from brown bread, had the wonderful moniker of Whistle-Belly-Vengeance. *Early American Beverages,* by John Hull Brown, details a New York City restaurant built in 1712 and known as Cato's Road House. Cato was a slave who had bought his freedom, opened his own joint, and sold New York Brandy Punch, South Carolina Milk Punch, and Virginia Eggnog to accompany dishes such as terrapin, curried oysters, fried chicken, and roast duck.

Our first president, George Washington, was known to be fond of a drink or two, and sometimes more. He indulged in thirteen toasts—one for each state—during a victory celebration at New York's Fraunces Tavern, and it's said that after he partook of Fish House Punch at Philadelphia's State in Schuylkill, essentially a fishing club, he couldn't bring himself to make an entry in his diary for the following three days. There's even a loose connection to Washington and Grog, the mixture of rum and water that Britain's Admiral Edward Vernon introduced to sailors in 1740. Lawrence Washington, George's half brother, served under Vernon and admired him so much that he named his estate for him. Later, of course, George became the chief resident at Mount Vernon.

By the end of the 1700s people in the newly formed United States were still tippling far more alcohol than we'd tolerate today; it's important to remember that at the time, alcohol was seen not only as a social drink but also as a medicine that would stave off, or maybe even cure, all manner of illnesses. John Brown, a medical professor at the University of Edinburgh in the mid-eighteenth century, prescribed liquor for many ailments. When one of his patients had the audacity to die, Brown simply opened up his body and declared the organs to be "fresh," which was proof that his "medicine" had been working. This, no doubt, was sufficient evidence to encourage a party of eighty people at Boston's Merchant's Club to down 136 bowls of Punch, 21 bottles of sherry, and a "large quantity" of cider and brandy during a dinner in 1792.

The eighteenth century also saw Americans become enamored of iced drinks, something that wouldn't gain favor in Europe for another two hundred years. European immigrants to these shores, unused to the hot summers in America, created a demand for ice from the frozen north to be brought down to the people in the sweltering south. Initially ice was fairly expensive and out of financial reach for many people, but prices gradually dropped, and by the mid-1800s iced drinks were the norm. While ice was becoming popular, though, something else happened behind a bar in America that would change the face of mixed drinks forever: At some point close to the year 1800, somebody created the world's first cocktail.

THE BIRTH OF THE COCKTAIL

On May 13, 1806, the *Balance and Columbian Repository* of Hudson, New York, answered a reader's query as to the nature of a cocktail: "Cocktail is a stimulating liquor, composed of spirits of any kind, sugar, water, and bitters—it is vulgarly called a bittered sling." The cocktail had been born, it had been defined, and yet it couldn't have been very well known by the general populace, or the newspaper wouldn't have considered it a fit topic for elucidation.

Where does the word *cocktail* come from? There are many answers to that question, and none is really satisfactory. One particular favorite story of mine, though, comes from *The Booze Reader: A Soggy Saga of a Man in His Cups,* by George Bishop: "The word itself stems from the English cock-tail which, in the middle 1800s, referred to a woman of easy virtue who was considered desirable but impure. The word was imported by expatriate Englishmen and applied derogatorily to the newly acquired American habit of bastardizing good British Gin with foreign matter, including ice. The disappearance of the hyphen coincided with the general acceptance of the word and its re-exportation back to England in its present meaning." Of course, this can't be true since the word was applied to a drink before the middle 1800s, but it's entertaining nonetheless, and the definition of "desirable but impure" fits cocktails to a tee.

A delightful story, published in 1936 in the *Bartender*, a British publication, details how English sailors of "many years ago" were served mixed drinks in a Mexican tavern. The drinks were stirred with "the fine, slender and smooth root of a plant which owing to its shape was called Cola de Gallo, which in English means 'Cock's tail.'" The story goes on to say that the sailors made the name popular in England, and from there the word made its way to America.

Another Mexican tale about the etymology of cocktail—again, dated "many years ago"—concerns Xoc-tl (transliterated as *Xochitl* and *Coctel* in different accounts), the daughter of a Mexican king, who served drinks to visiting American officers. The Americans honored her by calling the drinks cocktails—the closest they could come to pronouncing her name. And one more south-of-the-border explanation for the word can be found in *Made in America*, by Bill Bryson, who explains that in the Krio language, spoken in Sierra Leone, a scorpion is called a *kaktel*. Could it be that the sting in the cocktail is related to the sting in the scorpion's tail? It's doubtful at best.

One of the most popular tales told about the first drinks known as cocktails concerns a tavernkeeper by the name of Betsy Flanagan, who in 1779 served French soldiers drinks garnished with feathers she had plucked from a neighbor's roosters. The soldiers toasted her by shouting, *"Vive le cocktail!"* William Grimes, however, points out in his book *Straight Up or On the Rocks: A Cultural History of American Drink* that Flanagan was a fictional character who appeared in *The Spy*, by James Fenimore Cooper. He also notes that the book "relied on oral testimony of Revolutionary War veterans," so although it's possible that the tale has some merit, it's a very unsatisfactory explanation.

A fairly plausible narrative on this subject can be found in *Famous New Orleans Drinks & How to Mix 'em*, by Stanley Clisby Arthur, first published in 1937. Arthur tells the story of Antoine Amedie Peychaud, a French refugee from San Domingo who settled in New Orleans in 1793. Peychaud was an apothecary who opened his own business, where, among other things, he made his own bitters, Peychaud's, a concoction still available today. He created a stomach remedy by mixing his bitters with brandy in an eggcup—a vessel known to him in his native tongue as a *coquetier*. Presumably not all Peychaud's customers spoke French, and it's quite possible that the word, pronounced COH-KET-YAY, could have been corrupted into cocktail. However, according to the Sazerac Company, the present-day producers of Peychaud's bitters, the apothecary didn't open until 1838, so there's yet another explanation that doesn't work.

Another theory has it that in England, horses of mixed blood had their tails docked to signify their lack of breeding, and were known as "cocktailed" horses, but since I first wrote that, the term has been clarified. David Wondrich, cocktail historian extraordinaire, has concluded that the word's origins did indeed involve horses and their tails, but with a difference: "cocktail," he found, was a bit of ginger or cayenne pepper that crooked horse dealers would put into tired old horses' bums to make them cock their tails up and act a little more lively than usual. I never argue with David Wondrich unless we're discussing whose turn it is to buy the drinks . . .

ADOLESCENCE

Although the cocktail had been created, not many people of the early 1800s were sipping well-constructed drinks. The name of the drinking game at that time was quantity, not quality. If you divided all the distilled spirits sold in the United States in the year 2000 among every man, woman, and child in the country, each person would be allotted just under half an ounce of liquor a day. Two hundred years earlier, though, when the cocktail was a mere babe in arms, enough spirits were sold to supply every man, woman, and child then in the States with almost two ounces of liquor a day. Thus, in 1800, Americans drank nearly four times the amount of distilled spirits as the good folk at the turn of the twenty-first century. The country was full of jitterbugs.

In the early 1800s liquor was often known as "jitter sauce," and *jitterbug* was the moniker allocated to people who drank too much. One jitterbug in particular had his 1812 tavern bill detailed in *The Drunkard's Looking Glass*, a pamphlet issued by the Reverend Mason L. Weems. It seems that this hardy soul drank three Mint Slings before breakfast, nine tumblers of Grog before dinner, three glasses of wine and bitters with dinner, and two "ticklers" of brandy afterward. The total of the bill was six dollars, and it included breakfast, dinner, cigars, and supper (during which more wine was consumed).

Our nineteenth-century forefathers didn't just drink plentifully; they also gave weird and wonderful names to some of their newer creations. According to Richard Erdoes, author of *Saloons of the Old West*, house specialties became popular in the 1820s, and various inns and taverns offered such drinks as Moral Persuasion, Fiscal Agent, and Sweet Ruination. Drinks were also named for luminaries of the time: In 1824, when the Revolutionary War hero the Marquis de Lafayette returned to the United States from his native France, he not only was treated to Lafayette Punch but was also able to sip Lafayette brandy.

During the first half of the nineteenth century, although few people really cared, a new breed of bartenders started to emerge, and by the time Jerry Thomas wrote the world's first cocktail-recipe book, *How to Mix Drinks, or The Bon Vivant's Companion,* in 1862, he had collected formulas for Cobblers, Cocktails, Crustas, Fixes, Flips, Pousse-Cafés, Sangarees, Toddies, Sours, Slings, and Smashes, among others. Seven years later, when William Terrington published *Cooling Cups and Dainty Drinks* in London, he detailed drinks such as A Splitting Headache, a mixture of ale, rum, lime juice, cloves, cinnamon, ginger, and nutmeg, and Hour Before the Battle, a simple affair composed merely of sherry or madeira with bitters. The cocktail front was starting to pick up steam.

People down in Australia were also quaffing mixed drinks at this time, and during the mid-nineteenth-century gold rush there, at least one drink with a very strange name was being fashioned for the prospectors. *Spiers & Pond: A Memorable Australian Partnership,* a short nonfiction account by Phillip Andrew, details the circumstances:

> *In the early [18]50s there were no licensed inns on the fields. Consequently the sly grog trade had assumed enormous proportions. Weird were the drinks. One famous one, retailed at half a crown a wine glass, was known as "Blow-my-skull-off." It was made of* Cocculus indicus *[a poisonous berry found in Ceylon that was used to increase the potency of ale and porter], spirits of wine, Turkey opium, Cayenne pepper and rum, mixed with five parts of water. One good stir and it was ready for the table. A couple of good swigs and the mounted police turned out, hit everyone they could see, before the brawl reached the proportions of a riot.*

In the United States, the demand for well-constructed mixed drinks grew steadily during the latter half of the nineteenth century until, in the 1890s, the Golden Age of Cocktails arrived. It would last right up to the enactment of Prohibition in 1920, but don't think for a moment that every bar in America was serving masterfully mixed drinks. Luc Sante, author of *Low Life: Lures and Snares of Old New York,* claims that in New York during the late 1800s, you could buy a concoction made from whiskey, rum, camphor, benzene, and cocaine sweepings. No name is given for this potent potable, but it cost only six cents per glass.

Bartenders who worked on the first riverboats enjoyed a decent reputation as cocktailians, but they used odd ingredients, such as a "brandy" made from burnt peach pits, nitric acid, cod-liver oil, and unaged whiskey. And according to *Hell's Best Friend,* by Jan Holden, if you were unfortunate enough to order a Manhattan at the Humboldt in Grays Harbor, Washington, the owner, Fred Hewett (who apparently didn't much care for anyone who drank cocktails), would pour a mixture of whiskey, gin, rum, brandy, aquavit, and bitters into a beer mug, top it up with beer, and stir it with his finger before handing it to you.

Bad liquor could be found in the barrelhouses of New Orleans, and for good measure you might also be treated to a blow or two to the head. *The French Quarter,* by Herbert Asbury, describes these dives as long rooms with a row of barrels on one side and drinking vessels on the other. For a nickel you could fill your glass from any barrel, but if you didn't buy another as soon as you emptied it, you faced the chance of being turned out on your ear. And if you got drunk in these places after drinking too much "brandy" (here made from neutral spirits, sulfuric acid, tobacco, grape juice, and burnt sugar), you ran the risk of being rolled in a back room or in the back alley.

Certain dives on New York City's Bowery offered as much as you could drink from a rubber hose connected to a liquor barrel until you had to stop to take a breath; this would set you back a mere three cents. For two cents more, however, certain places would provide a shot of whiskey and a woman to go with it.

If you stopped by the Cosmopolitan Bar in Tucson, Arizona, in 1880, you could have a cocktail made with equal proportions of whiskey and mezcal that, the proprietor claimed, had had "the snakes strained out first." Various other saloons across the country served "Irish whiskey" made from neutral spirits mixed with creosote, hard cider that they called "champagne," and a medicinal drink, Dr. B. J. Kendall's Blackberry Balsam, which contained five grains of opium in every fluid ounce. Cocktails after work could be quite hazardous back then.

HELL'S HALF ACRE

While some cocktailian bartenders were hard at work creating formulas for drinks that have remained popular for more than a century, and serving them to cigar-puffing sophisticates in elegant surroundings, many of the men holding forth from behind the mahogany during the latter half of the 1800s worked in shot-and-a-beer joints, served hardworking men, and contended with a far different kind of atmosphere. The drinks in these bars would hardly have qualified as "cocktailian," but the ways in which the customers were kept amused were innovative, to say the least.

In New Orleans, for instance, you could visit the Buffalo Bill House and watch two men butting their heads together for as long as forty-five minutes at a time. Nearby residents complained about the rough clientele that this type of activity enticed, but the owner rebutted that their objections were ridiculous, since he had purposefully opened his shop in an area of town where "no decent people lived." Far better, when visiting the Big Easy, to have a drink at the Conclave, a joint where the bartender dressed like an undertaker and the backbar was filled with gravestones, each one bearing the name of a different spirit. The bottles were kept in coffins beneath the gravestones.

In *Faces Along the Bar,* Madelon Powers points out that few bars of the late nineteenth century were owned by women, but those women who did get into the business must have been a little larger than life. Powers mentions Peckerhead Kate's in Chicago, Indian Sadie's in Green Bay, and Big Tit Irene's in Ashtabula, Ohio, as examples of such establishments. And some bars of the period catered to the man who didn't want to waste time when he had some serious drinking to do—for convenience's sake, urinals were installed at the foot of the bar.

A few bars in Ohio were so disreputable that they gained nicknames such as Shades of Death, Hell's Half Acre, Certain Death, and Devil's Den. And in the West, certain bars fell into distinct categories: bug houses, whoop ups, snake ranches, bit houses (where every drink cost a bit, or twelve and a half cents), deadfalls, fandango houses (where dancing took place), and pretty-waiter saloons (the waiters were young girls in short skirts). Bars that were transported from one place to another on the railroad were known as Hell on Wheels.

Nineteenth-century bars also had standard attractions, such as billiards and ten-pin bowling, but gymnasium saloons, where men worked out before quaffing a few drinks, were available, too. Dog fights, cock fights, and both bull- and bear-baiting were attractions guaranteed to draw crowds to a bar in the 1800s, and customers at one West Coast saloon were once treated to the spectacle of a dog killing almost fifty rats in less than five minutes.

Gambling was another form of entertainment in the barrooms of the time, and many a man lost his newly mined gold in the saloons of San Francisco. One such joint had scales, sitting atop a small piece of carpet, on every card table. Nuggets were weighed and the appropriate number of gambling chips exchanged for them, but at the end of the night, when all the customers were gone, those pieces of carpet were carefully combed. The gold dust recovered could be enough to put an extra double sawbuck—twenty dollars—into the dealer's pocket.

Boxing matches were staged in some bars during the latter half of the nineteenth century. One of the most famous pugilists of the time, John L. Sullivan, world heavyweight champion from 1882 through 1892, made his New York debut at Harry Hill's, a halfway respectable bar. (Hill boasted that nobody was ever killed there.) But boxing wasn't the only form of entertainment offered at this bar on the corner of Houston and Crosby streets, and in an article he penned for the San Francisco *Alta California* in 1867, Mark Twain described some of the other spectacles that kept the crowds entertained:

> *Presently a man came out on a stage and sang "'Twas a Cold Winter's Night, and the Tempest was Snarling," and several parties accompanied him upon violins and a piano. After him came a remarkably black negro, whose clothes were ragged, and danced a boisterous dance*

> *and sang "I'm a happy contra band," though all his statements regarding himself would have warranted a different condition, I thought. After him came a man who mimicked fighting cats, and the buzzing of mosquitoes, and the squealing of a pig. Then a homely young man in a Highland costume entered upon the stage and danced—and he ought to have danced moderately, because he had nothing in the wide world on but a short coat and short stockings. This was apparent every time he whirled around. However, no one observed it but me. I knew that, because several handsomely dressed young ladies, from thirteen to sixteen and seventeen years of age, went and sat down under the foot-lights, and of course they would have moved away if they had noticed that he was only partly dressed.*

Theodore "The" Allen ran a similar joint on Bleecker Street, named Bal Mabille after the notorious Second Empire Parisian nightclub that had helped popularize the cancan. Nightlife at Allen's bar was described thus in the *Police Gazette,* a popular tabloid of the time: "The clinking of glasses keeps up a fitful accompaniment to the vocalization of the singers in the hall above, while down in the basement the dancers are rotating in the mazy. The lascivious waltz has become tame and the orchestra, catching the infection of the hour, strikes up the merry measures of Offenbach's cancan music. Lively feet keep time to the witching melody in all its lewd suggestiveness and dance themselves into an abandon till limbs of all shapes and sizes are elevated in dangerous proximity to male physiognomy."

Allen himself wasn't a man to be toyed with—he often started fights by putting his cigar out in his opponent's face—but he probably wasn't quite as feared as the western outlaw Johnnie Ringo, who once shot a man to death for refusing to drink champagne with him. Violence was not uncommon in nineteenth-century bars. Customers at the Tiger Saloon in Eureka, Nevada, bore witness to a knife fight between "Hog-Eyed" Mary Irwin and "Bulldog" Kate Miller, and the owner of a joint in lower Manhattan, Gallus Mag, not only bit the ears off customers who got out of control but she also kept the trophies in jars of alcohol on display behind the bar.

These joints are best described as dives, and indeed the majority of bars in the United States in the late 1800s are neatly summed up by Herbert Asbury in *The Great Illusion:* "[Saloons have] been rapturously eulogized as the workingmen's club, as a refuge of the harassed male, as the scene of wise and witty conversation, and as the home of sound liquor lovingly dispensed by a generous and understanding bartender. All this is mainly nonsense; it could apply only to the comparatively few barrooms, mostly in the large cities, which obeyed the laws and were operated as decently as any other business. . . . The stuff served in many saloons was frequently as vile as any of the concoctions guzzled by Americans during prohibition."

But in those comparatively few barrooms that Asbury mentions, there were men who took the job of mixing drinks very seriously. Even Harry Hill hung a sign outside his joint that read:

PUNCHES AND JULEPS, COBBLERS AND SMASHES,
TO MAKE THE TONGUE WAGGLE WITH WIT'S MERRY FLASHES.

THE SMART SET

The people who went to watch men butting heads at New Orleans' Buffalo Bill House would likely have felt out of place at the Waldorf Astoria Hotel, which opened in the 1890s on the site where the Empire State Building now stands. The bar at the old Waldorf Astoria was the scene of the sort of decadence we often associate with the decade that became known as the Gay Nineties. In *The Old Waldorf-Astoria Bar Book,* Albert Stevens Crockett says that in the bar's heyday, "the air was rent with calls of 'Same here!' and 'Here's how!'" At 8:00 A.M., at least half a dozen customers attended the bar for "breakfast appetizers or something to take away what was left of the jag of the night before," and in the afternoons and evenings, twelve bartenders in white coats were kept busy "ministering to an endless array of thirsts."

Crockett's description of the original bar makes it sound very similar to the recently closed Bull and Bear bar in the Waldorf Astoria on Park Avenue: "The actual bar itself, a large, rectangular counter . . . had a brass rail running all around its foot. In its center was a long refrigerator topped by a snowy cloth and an orderly arrangement of drinking glasses. At one end of this cover stood a good-sized bronze bear, looking as if it meant business; at the other end, a rampant bull. Midway between them was placed a tiny lamb, flanked on either side by a tall vase of flowers." Regulars there joked that the flowers were all the public, represented by the lamb, ever saw after Wall Street's bulls and bears were through with them.

An interesting observation giving us a glimpse into the advanced cocktailian craft at the time is that Crockett lists ten brands of bitters commonly used "in small quantities" to construct cocktails at this bar, and the use of orange bitters exceeded that of Angostura. Even more intriguing is the fact that he mentions the use of Fernet Branca as a flavor enhancer, since this potable style of bitters is often sipped neat—nonpotable bitters such as Angostura and Peychaud's are used only as flavoring agents.

This was also the joint where Bat Masterson—buffalo hunter, railroad worker, army scout, gold prospector, newspaperman, and law enforcement officer—once emptied the bar by grabbing Colonel Dick Plunkett, a fellow U.S. marshal, by the throat and accusing him of "talking bad" about him. The situation came to nothing, though; Plunkett remained calm and offered Masterson a seat, a drink, and the chance to talk things over.

Colonel William F. Cody, otherwise known as "Buffalo Bill," was also a regular at the old Waldorf Astoria, and he was well known for never refusing a drink on another man's tab—when asked, he would say, "Sir, you speak the language of my tribe." The tribes that frequented this bar were fairly well heeled, but not all of them had been that way for long. Henry Collins Brown, author of *In the Golden Nineties,* noted, "The Waldorf began to fill up with recently manicured iron workers from Pittsburgh, loggers from Duluth, copper miners from Michigan, brewers from Milwaukee and St. Louis, and other gentry who thought a cotillion was something to eat, but who could sign checks with numbers on them as long as a Santa Fe freight train."

Across the street from the old Waldorf Astoria was the Manhattan Club: "In its window sat Tammany politicians hob-nobbing with broad-clothed bulwarks of the Solid South over Manhattan cocktails, and blowing the smoke of Henry Clay perfectos toward the frescoed ceiling in a futile effort to turn a stone refrigerator into a human habitation. There was Judge Truax telling Henry Watterson how many bottles of Medoc '69 reposed in the catacombs underneath; and Henry giving the Judge a recipe for mint julep that made the judicial bosom heave like a movie star's, and eye glisten like a bridegroom's," wrote Brown.

New York's Hoffman House Hotel, on Broadway between Twenty-fourth and Twenty-fifth streets, was home to another grand saloon of the late 1800s. George Ade, author of *The Old-Time Saloon,* refers to it as the home of the Manhattan but gives no other details. The Hoffman House regularly hosted luminaries of the day: Sarah Bernhardt kept suites there when she toured the States, and this was another haunt of Buffalo Bill's. Opposite the bar at the Hoffman House hung Bouguereau's *Nymphs and Satyr,* a work depicting naked women playfully teasing a half-human woodland creature of Greek mythology known for his lust and drunkenness. The painting was situated under a red velvet canopy and lit by a large chandelier, so that it could be easily seen in the mirror that hung behind the bar; customers could thus admire it without blatantly staring at the picture itself.

New York's Knickerbocker Hotel opened in the early years of the twentieth century, and the bar there, frequented, according to Ade, by "the convivial members of The Forty-Second Street Country Club," was initially home to another famous bar mural: Maxfield Parrish's *Old King Cole.* This rendering isn't offensive until you hear the story of its origin, but tradition has it that you must hear the tale from a bartender where the painting hangs. You can now find it behind the bar of the King Cole Room at New York's St. Regis Hotel on East Fifty-fifth Street.

In New Orleans during the nineteenth century you could find comfort at the Old Absinthe House, a Bourbon Street joint where you might spot such visiting celebrities as William Makepeace Thackeray, Oscar Wilde, or Walt Whitman availing themselves of a drop or two of the Green Fairy at the marble-topped bar. Even P.T. Barnum is said to have visited this joint, but since he was a teetotaler and temperance advocate, he probably just sipped water from the dripper used by others to dilute their absinthe.

La Bourse de Maspero, or Maspero's Exchange, on St. Louis Street, was another hot spot in the Big Easy in the 1800s. It was here that Andrew Jackson is said to have planned to defend the city from the British after the War of 1812. This joint was taken over in 1838 by James Hewlett, a "well-known sporting man of the period," who completely renovated the place, renaming it Hewlett's Exchange and installing "the finest [bar] in the city," according to *The French Quarter* by Herbert Asbury.

Other high-end bars of the time, mentioned in Ade's book, were "such gilt-edge and exceptional places as the . . . Ramos in New Orleans, . . . the splendiferous Righeimer's in Chicago, . . . the Planters' or Tony Faust's in St. Louis, . . . the Antlers in San Antonio, . . . the Palace in San Francisco, . . . the mint-julep headquarters in the Old White at White Sulphur Springs, [and] . . . the much frequented Touraine in Boston." But one posh joint deserves special mention: The Metropolitan, one of Manhattan's earliest grand hotels, opened in 1852, and an observer described it as standing "at the head of the hotels of the world in all points of elegance, comfort, and convenience." The bar at this hotel was graced by bartender Jerry Thomas—the man generally recognized as being the father of the craft of bartending.

THE COCKTAILIANS EMERGE

Jerry Thomas was born in 1832, and before he was thirty years old he had visited England and France, where he'd demonstrated his skills using a set of solid silver bar tools. Prior to this he had tended bar in New Haven, Connecticut, and served as first assistant to the principal bartender at the El Dorado, the first gambling saloon in San Francisco, which housed a barroom complete with grand chandeliers and curtained booths, where certain ladies of the night plied their trade. One customer described the walls of the El Dorado's bar as being filled with "lascivious oil paintings of nudes in abandoned postures." There were huge mirrors on the backbar—the fixture behind the bar where bottles of liquor are displayed. An ornate backbar might not only be mirrored but also feature drawers, cupboards, and shelves; many barkeeps of the time referred to the backbar as the "altar."

Thomas also held forth for a time from behind the mahogany in South Carolina, where he studied the Mint Julep, and St. Louis, where he is said to have created the Tom and Jerry while serving as principal bartender at the Planter's House. New Orleans was also graced by Thomas's presence, and it was there that he encountered the Brandy

Crusta (page 190), the forerunner of some of today's best-loved cocktails, credited to a man known as Santina. Thomas describes this man as "a celebrated Spanish caterer," and Asbury claimed that in 1840 the same guy ran the City Exchange at Royal and St. Louis streets. From New Orleans, Thomas made his way to New York, and after a stint at the Metropolitan Hotel he traveled to Europe. Less than twelve months later, he was back; he worked in New York, San Francisco, and Virginia City, Nevada, before returning to the Big Apple, where he owned various bars, finally settling downtown at his own joint on Barclay Street.

Ten cocktails are contained in the recipe section of Thomas's 1862 book, and all of them contain bitters. Indeed, it would be decades before anyone dared give the name *cocktail* to a drink made without this ingredient. Various and sundry other drinks still popular today are also detailed in this tome: the Champagne Cocktail (which is erroneously shaken) and the Blue Blazer, a Thomas creation, which is actually more of a pyrotechnical display than a thoughtful mix. It has much in common with many drinks made by today's "flair" bartenders: looks good, tastes—well, okay. Thomas also wrote about the Mint Julep, various Milk Punches, and curiously enough, Punch Jelly. This "drink" must be considered to be a forerunner to today's Jelly Shots, although Thomas served it more as a dessert than a drink. It was rather potent, though—readers were warned, "This preparation is a very agreeable refreshment on a cold night, but should be used in moderation. . . . Many persons, particularly of the softer sex, have been tempted to partake so plentifully of it as to render them somewhat unfit for waltzing or quadrilling after supper."

Although Thomas didn't offer a great deal of advice to bartenders in his first tome, his second book, *The Bar-Tender's Guide, or How to Mix All Kinds of Plain and Fancy Drinks*, published in 1887, made up for his past sins of omission. In it, the great master counseled, "An efficient bartender's first aim should be to please his customers, paying particular attention to meet the individual wishes of those whose tastes and desires he has already watched and ascertained; and, with those whose peculiarities he has had no opportunity of learning, he should politely inquire how they wish their beverages served, and use his best judgment in endeavoring to fulfill their desires to their entire satisfaction. In this way he will not fail to acquire popularity and success." In a similar vein, Thomas's rival, Harry Johnson, wrote in his *New and Improved Illustrated Bartender's Manual*, a 1900 update of his own 1882 book:

> *The greatest accomplishment of a bartender lies in his ability to exactly suit his customer. This is done by inquiring what kind of drink the customer desires, and how he wishes it prepared. This is especially necessary with cocktails, juleps, "sours," and punches. The bartender must also inquire whether the drink is to be made stiff, strong, or medium, and then must use his best judgment in preparing it; but, at all times, he must make a special point to study the tastes of his customers and, strictly heeding their wishes, mix all drinks to their desires and tastes. In following this rule, the barkeep will soon gain the esteem and respect of his patrons.*

Johnson, like Thomas, had also spent time behind the bar in San Francisco, circa 1860; and in Chicago, some eight years later, he opened what he described as a place that was "generally recognized to be the largest and finest establishment of the kind in the country." It was destroyed by fire in 1871. Johnson also worked in Boston and New Orleans, but again like Thomas, he ended up in Manhattan, where he opened Little Jumbo, a cocktail bar on the Bowery, near Grand Street.

Henry Collins Brown recalled the joint well:

> *Harry Johnson's "Little Jumbo" saloon near Grand Street . . . had a sign before the door dating back to the time when a bartender had to serve an apprenticeship of several years. The bulk of the trade was then in mixed drinks, the drinks that carried the fame of American beverages around the world. Bartenders had black moustaches with waxed ends in those delectable days, and wore ornamental elastics on their sleeves to keep their cuffs from getting into the drinks. The sign, aforesaid, was a pyramid about four feet high. On the sides were the names of about one hundred mixed drinks. The pyramid tapered from the long-named mixed drink at the bottom to the*

> *short ones like "Gin Fizz" having fewer letters at the top. Oh, that this pyramid were as those of the Pharaohs, of aye enduring stone! And the legends thereon. Let me muse over them, as fond memory brings their glowing letters once more into view. Many of them are classics of concoctional nomenclature and as a faithful historian I must endeavor to reproduce one side of this pyramid to a generation that knows not the "Little Jumbo."*

Harry Johnson's book sheds much light on the craft of the late-nineteenth-century cocktailian. Bartenders had to know how to reduce the proof of certain spirits properly, since at the time some liquors, especially imported products, were shipped at high proof to reduce the bulk, and therefore save on shipping charges. It was best to be cautious though, as Harry Rice, the owner of the Green Tree in New Orleans, found out in 1864; he was stoned almost to death by a group of sailors who weren't satisfied with the strength of his spirits.

The jigger, spelled *gigger* in Johnson's book, is mentioned as being "used by all first-class bartenders, except only a few experts in the art of mixing drinks who have had such experience and practice that they can measure accurately by eyesight alone, without even using a glass for measuring." He suggests that short-handled bar spoons be served with all drinks containing fruit garnishes so that customers can eat without using their fingers. Johnson also commands, "Bartenders should not . . . have a toothpick in their mouth, clean their fingernails while on duty, smoke, spit on the floor, or have other disgusting habits."

Thomas and Johnson were undoubtedly the two greatest masters of their craft in the 1800s, but they weren't the only ones to take their trade seriously. C. L. Sonnichsen, author of *Billy King's Tombstone*, describes two other professionals who plied their trade in the nineteenth-century Wild West: "Billy King, when he began operating his own saloon in the nineties, had [a white bar jacket] with five dollar gold pieces for buttons, which was considered in the best taste of the period." And Buckskin Frank Leslie, a bartender at the Oriental Saloon in Tombstone, was "a complete dandy. His slender body was erect and shapely, and he loved to adorn it with shiney boots, checked pants, Prince Albert coat, and a stiff shirt with black pearl studs. He had a stovepipe hat for special occasions, too." These were men who meant to be taken seriously—the bartender as an authoritarian figure was beginning to take shape:

> *For a time, the lawyer, the editor, the banker, the chief desperado, the chief gambler, and the saloon-keeper, occupied the same level in society, and it was the highest. The cheapest and easiest way to become an influential man and be looked up to by the community at large, was to stand behind a bar, wear a cluster-diamond pin, and sell whisky. I am not sure but that the saloon-keeper held a shade higher rank than any other member of society. His opinion had weight. It was his privilege to say how the elections should go. No great movement could succeed without the countenance and direction of the saloon-keepers. It was a high favor when the chief saloon-keeper consented to serve in the legislature or the board of aldermen. Youthful ambition hardly aspired so much to the honors of the law, or the army and navy as to the dignity of proprietorship in a saloon. To be a saloon-keeper and kill a man was to be illustrious.*

So wrote Mark Twain in *Roughing It*, a book detailing his adventures in the West.

Some of the western bartenders, often known as Ganymedes (referring to the cupbearer to the gods in Greek mythology), could slide a glass of beer down the bar with the exact force that would cause it to come to a halt directly in front of whoever had ordered it, and it was common practice when serving whiskey for the bartender to grab the bottle with his right hand, a glass with his left, and cross hands before placing them both in front of the customer. The customer could pour as much whiskey as the glass would hold, but it wasn't considered seemly to fill the glass to the brim, lest a neighboring customer might inquire if you intended to bathe in it. (For simplicity's sake, I'm using the spelling "whiskey" generically—for American, Canadian, Irish, or Scotch. When referring only to Scotch or Canadian whiskies, however, the traditional spelling is "whisky.")

Although cities such as New York, San Francisco, and New Orleans sported most of the best cocktail bars, by the end of the nineteenth century mixed drinks were becoming popular throughout the country. *The Wild West Bartenders' Bible*, by Byron A. and Sharon Peregrine Johnson, mentions one Albuquerque, New Mexico, bar that in 1886 offered Whiskey, Gin, Vermouth, Chocolate, and Manhattan cocktails, and topped each with a splash of champagne. The bar menu also featured drinks such as the Charley Rose, Gold Band, Collins, Absinthe Frappé, Whiskey Daisy, Pousse-Café, Dide's Dream, Frozen Absinthe, Egg Nog, Egg Flip, Sherry Flip, Whiskey Flip, Gin Fizz, Silver Fizz, Gold Fizz, Blue Blazer, and Mint Julep.

In Chicago during the Gay Nineties you could order a variation on the Bell Ringer, a long-gone category of cocktails served in a glass rinsed with apricot brandy, from bartender James Maloney. And even in London, if you were fortunate enough to be served by Leo Engel, author of *American & Other Drinks* and bartender at the American Bar in the Criterion Hotel, you could request Alabama Fog Cutters, Connecticut Eye Openers, Thunderbolt Cocktails, Lightning Smashers, Boston Nose Warmers, Magnetic Crushers, Galvanic Lip Pouters, and Josey Ticklers. If you were feeling very brave, though, you might be tempted to try Leo's Knickebein: orange curaçao, crème de noyau, and maraschino liqueur mixed in the bottom of a port glass and topped with an egg yolk, which in turn was topped with the whisked white of an egg fashioned into the shape of a pyramid; the drink was finished off with a few drops of Angostura bitters dashed onto the pyramid. In order to drink the Knickebein you had to follow Engel's instructions:

1. Pass the glass under the Nostrils and Inhale the Flavor.—Pause.
2. Hold the glass perpendicularly, close under your mouth, open it wide, and suck the froth by drawing a Deep Breath.—Pause again.
3. Point the lips and take one-third of the liquid contents remaining in the glass without touching the yolk.—Pause once more.
4. Straighten the body, throw the head backward, swallow the contents remaining in the glass all at once, at the same time breaking the yolk in your mouth.

Leo's Knickebein, quite understandably, didn't catch on, but two drinks from the nineteenth century that did stand the test of time emanated from this side of the Atlantic: the Sazerac and the Ramos Gin Fizz are both New Orleans creations. Accounts vary as to who first created the Sazerac, originally a mixture of brandy, absinthe, sugar, and Peychaud's bitters, but it's fairly safe to say that it originated at the Sazerac Coffee House sometime during the 1850s. (Bourbon is now the preferred base spirit, although straight rye whiskey has recently made a comeback in this drink.) The Ramos Gin Fizz, a sublime drink made with gin, cream, lemon and lime juices, egg white, simple syrup, orange flower water, and club soda, was the creation of Henry Ramos, a New Orleans saloon proprietor from 1888 right through until the enactment of Prohibition in 1920.

William "The Only William" Schmidt, author of 1892's *The Flowing Bowl* and a man who had been "active for a period of more than thirty years in the line of hotel and bar business," offered some early insights into the role of the man behind the stick when he wrote, "The situation of a bartender gives the holder the chance of studying human nature. A man fit for the position, and consequently a keen observer—for one thing cannot be separated from the other—will be able to tell a man's character very soon, as far as conduct, education, language, and general *savoir-vivre* are concerned." He also added a point of view that should be taken seriously by anyone who is tempted to use inferior products when making cocktails: "Mixed drinks might be compared to music; an orchestra will produce good music, provided all players are artists; but have only one or two inferior musicians in your band, and you may be convinced they will spoil the entire harmony."

The nineteenth-century harmony of which Schmidt speaks might strike a discord with cocktail fanciers of today. The majority of the drinks popular at the turn of the nineteenth century were, by and large, sweeter than they would become over the next twenty years. Something else happened, though, in the last decades of the 1800s. Something momentous. Something that left us with a range of drinks that must now be considered the capos of the cocktail family: Vermouth became popular among the cocktailian bartenders of America.

ITALY AND FRANCE LEND A HAND

There is no mention of vermouth whatsoever in Thomas's 1862 book, but in 1887 he detailed five recipes that called for vermouth: the Manhattan, the Martinez, the Vermouth and the Fancy Vermouth cocktails (the Vermouth made with bitters, the fancy version with bitters and maraschino), and the Saratoga, made with equal parts whiskey, brandy, and vermouth and a couple of dashes of bitters. The book doesn't, however, specify sweet or dry vermouth. Which did he use?

It's fairly obvious, when you look at recipes in other books of the period, that sweet vermouth, often referred to as Italian vermouth, for its country of origin, was far more common behind bars than was dry, or French, vermouth. Some cocktail books published in those years referred to both "vermouth," with no descriptor, and "dry vermouth"—which must signify that sweet vermouth was the norm, and dry vermouth a relative newcomer to the scene.

This isn't to say that dry vermouth wasn't available in the United States prior to the late 1800s—it was: Noilly Prat, the originator of dry vermouth in 1800, started shipping French vermouth to the States in 1853, some fourteen years before the first shipment of sweet vermouth, made by the Italian company that would eventually (in 1879) be named Martini & Rossi, landed in America. But according to various sources, around the year 1900 Noilly Prat's sales of French vermouth were less than half of Martini & Rossi's of the Italian variety.

The first cocktail still popular today that called for vermouth was the Manhattan; and the Martinez—a precursor to the Martini made with a sweetened gin known as Old Tom, sweet vermouth, bitters, and maraschino liqueur—appeared shortly thereafter. Some of the early recipes for the Martini, which first appeared in the late 1800s, call for exactly the same ingredients used to make the Martinez, so it appears that the Martini started out as a drink made with sweet vermouth, and dry versions of the cocktail followed.

There can be no doubt that vermouth changed the face of mixed drinks in the twentieth century. The Manhattan, the Martini, and the Rob Roy might be considered to be the Triple Crown of cocktails, and you can't make one of them without vermouth. Indeed, Albert Stevens Crockett noted in *The Old Waldorf-Astoria Bar Book* that over half the cocktails known prior to World War I "had vermouth as an essential [ingredient]."

THE FIRST HUNDRED YEARS

The serious bartenders of the 1800s gave us the mixed-drink bases with which cocktailians still work today. The masters of the craft during the first century of cocktails formulated sours and the majority of other categorized drinks, and they learned to use liqueurs and other sweetening agents as substitutes for simple syrup. These barkeeps understood the importance of bitters, and they knew that balance was the key to any well-constructed drink. What other drinks were commonplace at the dawn of the twentieth century?

Highballs—spirits and soda or water—were consumed before the turn of the nineteenth century, and drinks such as Brandy and Soda and Brandy and Ginger Ale are documented in recipe books of the time. Both the Tom Collins, made with Old Tom sweetened gin, and the John Collins, Tom's genever-based cousin, appeared in the nineteenth century. The Shandy, then called the Shandy Gaff—originally ale and ginger ale—was also available, and by the very early 1900s the Dry Martini had been established as a cocktail. Indeed, in 1907 Heublein's Club Cocktails—Martinis and Manhattans among them—were being offered by the bottle by Park and Tilford, a wholesale wine and liquor company. The price was $10.50 for a dozen bottles (presumably quarts), or $14.40 for 144 individual bottles with presumably smaller capacities.

Modern American Drinks: How to Mix and Serve All Kinds of Cups and Drinks, by George J. Kappeler, detailed the oh-so-naughty Bosom Caresser—brandy, milk, raspberry syrup, and an egg—way back in 1895, and although the formula has changed over the years, the drink is still found in many modern-day cocktail books. Kappeler's book was also one of the first—if not *the* first—to mention the Old-Fashioned Whiskey Cocktail, made with sugar, water, bitters, whiskey, and a twist of lemon.

Kappeler claimed that his recipes were "simple, practical and easy to follow, and . . . especially intended for use in first-class Hotels, Clubs, Buffets, and Barrooms, where, if adopted and concocted according to directions given, they will be entirely satisfactory to the caterer and pleasing to the consumer, the latter of whom will immediately notice a marked improvement in his favorite beverage." He included a couple of drinks in his book that bear somewhat modern sounding names: The Brain Duster was made with whiskey, sweet vermouth, absinthe, and simple syrup, and the Electric Current Fizz was constructed by shaking together gin, lemon juice, sugar, and the white of an egg, straining the mixture into a "fizz" glass, and topping it with seltzer; the drink was served with an egg yolk in the half shell, seasoned with salt, pepper, and vinegar, on the side.

George Du Maurier's *Trilby*, a novel that was first serialized in 1894 in *Harper's New Monthly Magazine* and later spawned the 1931 movie *Svengali*, prompted a town in Florida, northeast of Tampa, to change its name to Trilby, complete with streets named after characters in the work and its very own Svengali Square. Of course, someone also had to create the Trilby Cocktail: whiskey, sweet vermouth, orange bitters, absinthe, and Parfait d'Amour, a violet-flavored liqueur.

Tonic water was first created in 1858, and in the 1870s Schweppes marketed the product, but it would take a while before Gin and Tonics were popular outside of India, where the quinine in the soda helped expatriate Brits ward off the effects of malaria. And although the Stinger wouldn't gain its moniker until the twentieth century, Schmidt's 1892 book details the Judge, a drink made with brandy, crème de menthe, and simple syrup. Someone had put the ingredients of the drink together, but it wouldn't get its sting until the simple syrup was omitted.

Before leaving the nineteenth century, a word or two from a guy who lived in the 1890s and reported on the bartenders who served him is in order: "The American bartender of the 'Gay Nineties' was an institution. His fame spread to the four corners of the globe, and visitors to our shores from the continent bowed before his skill in concocting tempting mixtures of 'liquid lightening.' He was and still is in a class by himself. We may go to Europe for our chefs, but Europe comes to us for its bartenders," wrote W.C. Whitfield in his 1939 book *Just Cocktails*.

TROUBLE AHEAD

As the sun rose on the twentieth century, temperance advocates were fast gaining a foothold in the States, and the movement that would lead to nationwide Prohibition had begun in earnest. When the word *temperance* was first used around the beginning of the nineteenth century by societies dedicated to the cause, it didn't mean abstinence, and many members of such clubs still indulged in an occasional glass of something or other, but they never drank to excess. Some people swore off liquor but still enjoyed beer and wine, and others might enjoy a glass of whiskey with friends, although always in moderation. People who shunned alcohol completely were classed as total abstainers and known as teetotalers. And some folks, of course, even prior to the Civil War, thought that all alcohol was evil incarnate.

Scare tactics were used by these latter-day enemies of John Barleycorn, and a good example of this method can be seen in an article published in *Cold Water Magazine* in 1842: "A wretched mother who had been imbibing strong ale in a dram shop, entered the door of her home with her child on one arm and a bag of flour on the other. By mistake she threw her child in the meal chest in a closet near at hand, and placed the bag of flour in the cradle; then threw herself on the bed to sleep. During the night the mother was occasionally aroused by the cries of the poor child and once or twice she actually got up and rocked the bag of flour. Morning came and with it the discovery of the darling babe dead in the meal chest. Since then that wretched mother has signed the Pledge."

Twenty-five years later, as the movement was gaining momentum, Mark Twain took a glimpse into the future when he wrote, "Prohibition only drives drunkenness behind doors and into dark places, and does not cure it or even diminish it." But it was the Anti-Saloon League, formed in 1893, that would prove to be the force behind the enactment of Prohibition. Just ten years after making its voice heard around the nation, the society had such an impact that H.L. Mencken wrote, "Americans reached the peak of their alcoholic puissance in the closing years of the last century. Along about 1903 there was a sudden and marked letting up."

By 1910 almost half the people in the United States were living in "dry" states or towns, and after America declared war on Germany in 1917, distillation of beverage alcohol was made illegal so that the grape and the grain would be eaten rather than sipped. Two years later, William Jennings Bryan, a politician and keen supporter of the Prohibition movement, said, "Ten years from now hundreds of thousands of men who voted against us and struggled to keep the saloon, will go down on their knees and thank God they were overwhelmed at the ballot-box and this temptation far removed from them."

William E. "Pussyfoot" Johnson, an agent for the Anti-Saloon League, wrote some of the organization's propaganda and lectured for the cause. He was so well known at the time that a nonalcoholic drink, the Pussyfoot, was named for him, but six years after Prohibition was enacted, Johnson admitted that during his campaign against American saloons he lied, bribed, and "drank gallons of [alcohol]."

During the nineteen years of the twentieth century that led up to Prohibition, although drinking was frowned upon by many, cocktails and mixed drinks continued to evolve in certain bars—mainly hotel bars in big cities—and some bartenders of that period detailed the favorite drinks of the time, as well as the idiosyncrasies of the era.

Jere Sullivan, author of *The Drinks of Yesteryear: A Mixology,* tended bar prior to Prohibition, and he had some definite ideas of how things should be done. Among his admonitions, for example, he declared, "A Martini or a Manhattan cocktail should be stirred with a spoon instead of shaken unless the individual cares to have it shaken. (Results cloudy.)" Patrick Gavin Duffy, head bartender at New York's Ashland House for twelve years prior to Prohibition, and the man who claimed to have "first brought the highball to America, in 1895," wrote, "With very few exceptions, cocktails should be stirred and not shaken."

Sullivan described himself as a "wine clerk," a term that he defined as a gentleman who "mixed and served whatever little hearts desired." He worked at "the most epicurean hotel and restaurant east of the Hudson River," where he studied the "applied art of compounding and properly serving 'mixed and fancy drinks' for a clientele of most refined and exacting tastes," and he did us the favor of recording what he claimed were the "most popular and most used formulas when drinking was public and amateur mixers had not gone daft in trying by efforts of their own to approximate the enjoyed standards of the old regime." Included in his list were the Alexander, the Bacardi Cocktail, the Bronx, the Champagne Cocktail, the Clover Club, the Gibson, the Grasshopper, the Jacq [*sic*] Rose, the Manhattan, the Dry Martini, the Stinger, and the Yale Cocktail. It's important to note, though, that Sullivan's Bacardi Cocktail was made with rum, sweet vermouth, and Peychaud's bitters, although he does detail a second version that's nothing more than a Daiquiri. The Bacardi Cocktail that we know today, with grenadine as a sweetening agent, didn't appear until sometime during the years of Prohibition, when Americans first sampled the drink in Cuba.

These drinks would have set you back between fifteen and twenty-five cents at a high-class bar back then, whereas a mug of beer could be had for just a nickel; but many bars at the time offered a free lunch to boot, a tradition that dates back to at least the mid-1800s. Asbury maintains that the practice could have begun as early as 1838 at a New Orleans bar called the City Exchange. It was the brainchild, he claims, of an assistant bar manager named Alvarez, a man Asbury also credits with creating the world's first gumbo by cooking a bouillabaisse in a Creole style.

Free lunches were offered by many more bars when, in the 1880s, some of the bigger breweries acquired many saloons and subsidized the cost of the food. Quite naturally, the quality of the food on the table varied drastically, depending on the type of bar you frequented. Neighborhood saloons might offer stew, bread, ham, ribs, potato salad, and frankfurters, whereas at a high-class bar such as the Waldorf Astoria it was possible to find delicacies such as "Russian caviar, . . . light and savory canapés, thirst-provoking anchovies in various tinted guises, . . . substantial slices of beef or ham, . . . a wonderful assortment of cheeses of robust odors, . . . crisp radishes and sprightly, delicate spring onions."

There were only two problems with the free lunch: Bartenders had to be on the lookout for people who sneaked in for food without buying a drink, and they could never be certain that every customer had good table manners. Bartender Harry Johnson reported having to make sure "that the patrons use a fork and not their fingers in digging out . . . the eatables." But customers didn't get the chance to do that at Righeimer's bar in Chicago just prior to World War I. As writer Charles W. Morton remembered in "When Money Was in Flower," an article that appeared in *The Atlantic Monthly* in 1962, "The free lunch was a ham or roast beef sandwich of extraordinary quality, prepared by an elderly Negro who used a slicing knife in each hand and turned out elegantly thin sandwiches without handling them, offering them to the customer on the extended blade of a knife; the style and dexterity in this operation were as attractive as the sandwich itself."

Attractive sandwiches needed to be accompanied by attractive drinks, and in 1906 Louis Muckensturm declared in his book *Louis' Mixed Drinks with Hints for the Care and Service of Wines* that a cherry was the appropriate garnish for "practically every cocktail, excepting when the cocktail is wanted extra dry. In that case olives can be used." But they had different ideas about garnishes at the old Waldorf Astoria, where pickled rooster's combs were used to adorn their Chanticleer Cocktail, a mixture of orange-flavored gin, dry vermouth, and the white of an egg. Crockett wrote that Martinis were the most popular pre–World War I cocktail at the Waldorf, with the Manhattan running second, and customers at the time would gulp down five or six of either drink in succession.

The quantity of drinks that pre-Prohibition quaffers managed to down sounds quite startling considering that this was during a time when much of the country was behind the Prohibition movement, but Crockett's statement is backed up by Charles Brown, author of *The Gun Club Drink Book*, who wrote, "A man would walk into his club or favorite bar perhaps on his way home from the office. He wants one drink and he needs it. . . . But by all the rules of the game he will find it impossible to get out of the club without taking six or more drinks." It should be noted, though, that drinks at that time were much smaller than today's often gigantic cocktails.

If the Martini was the most popular drink in New York at that time, the Manhattan reigned supreme in Baltimore, where, according to Mencken, it was always the cocktail of choice before a traditional Maryland dinner of oysters, terrapin, duck, and salad with ham. "No Baltimorean of condition ever drank gin," he wrote. And Mencken's fellow journalists were none too enamored of the temperance movement—Mencken claimed that there was only one reporter from the South who abstained from alcohol, and he was considered to be insane. Mencken could recall absolutely no newspapermen in New York City as being nondrinkers; he reminisced about one Christmas Eve when he could find only two people sober at the offices of the *New*

York Herald: "All the rest were full of what they called hand-set whiskey. This powerful drug was sold in a saloon next door to the *Herald* office, and was reputed to be made in the cellar by the proprietor in person—of wood alcohol, snuff, tabasco sauce, and coffin varnish."

The coffin varnish could have come in handy on January 17, 1920, when the beverage alcohol industry was put to death and national Prohibition went into effect.

THE GREAT DROUGHT

Prohibition came in like a lion and left like a lamb, but the lion that roared in 1920 just got louder and louder as the dry years passed. And that lion was none too sober. Three years into the Noble Experiment, humorist Ring Lardner noted that the biggest difference in bars was that because, by law, there weren't any, they didn't have to close at any particular hour.

Speakeasies, illegal drinking establishments that patrons were encouraged to "speak easy" about, lest word spread to the wrong ears, flourished in every major city in the country and by all accounts were fun places to visit. Although it's often said that many modern cocktails were created during Prohibition because all sorts of extra ingredients were added to liquor to mask the flavor of the badly made spirits, there's little evidence to support such a claim.

Speakeasy bartenders used fruit juices, sometimes from canned fruit, as well as ginger ale, cream, honey, corn syrup, maple syrup, and even ice cream to make palatable the harsh flavors of spirits that Mencken described as "rye whiskey in which rats have drowned, Bourbon contaminated with arsenic and ptomaines, corn fresh from the still, gin that is three fourths turpentine, and rum rejected as too corrosive by the West Indian embalmers"; but they did little in the way of creating new drinks.

The fact of the matter is that although speakeasies existed in great number, lots of decent liquor was poured in regular restaurants and nightclubs around the country, and many of the owners encouraged customers to bring their own "atmosphere." These joints made most of their money from cover charges and from their exorbitant prices for setups—a glass full of ice with water or ginger ale on the side.

Customers poured their whiskey from a flask or brought bottles to their favorite haunts. These bottles were kept out of view, labeled with the customer's name, and used for that one customer and anyone he or she chose to treat.

Although there is much evidence that some very bad liquor was sold by disreputable bootleggers, the biggest complaint heard during the era was that the whiskey had been watered down too much. Stanley Walker, author of *The Night Club Era* and city editor of the *New York Herald Tribune* at the time, claimed that less than half of one percent of methyl alcohol—a poison present in small quantities of all liquor—was ever found in bad bottles of booze, and since ethyl alcohol—the "active ingredient" in beer, wine, and spirits—is the antidote for methyl alcohol, this was not very dangerous. Badly made spirits containing large quantities of methyl alcohol were responsible for blindness, and sometimes even death, but these made up just a small percentage of illegal hooch during Prohibition. Bootleggers weren't in the business of killing their customers, after all.

Sidney E. Klein, a union organizer in Manhattan during the twenties, says that cocktails just weren't the point when bibbers of the time went out on the town, and that most people just wanted the "straight stuff." Although this doesn't mean that Martinis weren't made and Manhattans left the face of the earth, it certainly wasn't a period when bartenders could be very creative.

The new drinks that did appear during this era were mostly fashioned in Europe, where at least a few American bartenders fled to pursue their careers. Harry Craddock was one such man. He started work as a bartender at the Savoy Hotel, London, in 1925, and compiled *The Savoy Cocktail Book* (1930), in which he admonished bartenders, "Shake the shaker as hard as you can: don't just rock it: you are trying to wake it up, not send it to sleep!" Craddock is also credited with saying that the best way to drink a cocktail is "quickly, while it's laughing at you!"

The Brandy Alexander made its debut in Craddock's book, although it was named Alexander Cocktail (No. 2) at the time; the original Alexander Cocktail, which called for gin as a base liquor, was created before World War I. The Bacardi Cocktail, a variation of the Daiquiri, a late-nineteenth-century creation, also appears to have made its debut during the dry years in America, and is added as a "stick-in" in the only first-edition copy of *The Savoy Cocktail Book* I have seen. But Craddock didn't forget to detail the Bacardi Special—made like a Bacardi Cocktail but using Beefeater gin as well as Bacardi rum—before the book was typeset; the recipe hides behind the Bacardi Cocktail stick-in.

The first printed mention of the Belmont, Income Tax, and Maurice cocktails that I can find are also in Craddock's book, but he doesn't lay claim to creating any of them, and since he did note that he was the man behind the Leap-Year Cocktail (page 232), we must presume that the others were drinks with which he was familiar, but not the father of.

Of course, Americans did travel to Europe during Prohibition, and Craddock's bar at the Savoy was a popular destination for them. While it's more than likely that some new drinks created in Europe made their way back to the States during this time, one new creation stayed at home in Paris until the bars of America legally reopened their doors. That drink was a significant one.

The Bloody Mary was first made in the 1920s by French bartender Fernand "Pete" Petiot, who first married vodka and tomato juice behind the stick at Harry's New York Bar in Paris. Not until after Prohibition was repealed and John Astor installed him behind the bar at the King Cole Room in New York's St. Regis Hotel would the concoction be introduced to stateside drinkers.

Although there *was* good liquor to be had, at least in the high-class speakeasies of America, and some good cocktails were served there, too, they came at a price. The fifteen-cent drinks of yesteryear would now set you back two bucks, and even in low-end clip joints, if you bought a "hostess" a drink, which was usually a Gin Highball made with water and ginger ale, you could count on spending more than a dollar for the privilege.

Speakeasy drinks varied in price, of course, depending on where you were; you could actually get a Sidecar for as little as sixty cents at one joint in South Carolina, where the owner had thought of a novel way to dispense liquor: He claimed to be giving it away. Printed on the bottom of the restaurant's wine and cocktail list were the following words: "As the sale of intoxicating beverages is prohibited by law, the above prices are for service only and do not include the price of the spirituous ingredients."

You could also buy pints of liquor in many speakeasies—whiskey would set you back about $10, and brandy, purportedly imported, went for $15. The speakeasy owners turned a good profit on this liquor: One bootlegger's price list offered brand-name bottles of bourbon and straight rye for $1.50 per pint, and Scotch—Johnnie Walker and Teacher's included—went for just fifty cents more. Gin was offered by the same guy, "Swift," at a paltry dollar a pint, and if you spent over ten bucks, you could choose between a quart of "Hiram Walker's Canadian Club Rye" or any "High Grade Scotch" as a bonus. Swift also noted, "All merchandise may be sampled before you pay."

Prohibition had been thrust upon America at a time when unemployment had been growing fast. After the conclusion of World War I, in 1918, strikes had hit almost all forms of industry; schools had been closed in some areas because of a lack of fuel (the result of almost half a million miners leaving the pits to protest wages and hours); and other schools had closed because teachers were unwilling to work for the pittance offered. Soldiers returning from the Great War were faced not only with a housing and job shortage but also with wives and sweethearts who were, well, not the same women they'd left at home.

The Lawless Decade, by Paul Sann, cites many symptoms of the new emancipated American women of the day, including a revolution in women's underwear that caused the popularity of the cotton variety to dwindle and silk to be the new fabric of choice. New short hairstyles, or "bobbed" hair, signaled a new freedom for women, and hemlines were rising rapidly. Flappers, "good-time girls" with their stockings rolled down below their knees and flashy makeup, danced and drank their way through the Roaring Twenties, arriving just in time for the speakeasies to open their doors.

In speakeasies, "the young women of the entertainment committee . . . are nearly as naked as can be managed with something ornamental still on. . . . The guests are from everywhere and are clothed . . . [in] every range from grave to gay and every origin from Paris to Podunk. . . . When a girl is doing her dance of contortion, a well-trained waiter at the back may let go a grating cry 'Throw her to the Li-ons!' That is just to make everybody feel at home," wrote H. I. Brock and J. W. Golinkin in *New York Is Like This*. Women had finally taken to the bars, and some of them had opened their own joints.

Mary Louise Cecilia "Texas" Guinan, Broadway chorus girl, musical actress, and star of movies such as *The Hellcat, The She Wolf, The Gun Woman*, and *Little Miss Deputy*, was, without doubt, the toast of the town in Manhattan nightclubs and speakeasies, though she also worked in Miami and Chicago during the dry years. "If [Police Commissioner] Grover Whalen is official host of [New York] . . . Texas is unofficial hostess," wrote one wag.

Although Guinan worked mostly as a hostess, greeting guests with her signature opening line, "Hello, sucker," she owned her own joints, too. Ruby Keeler, who went on to star in Busby Berkeley movies, making her film debut in his classic *42nd Street* in 1933, performed at the Texas Guinan Club, where Guinan could sometimes be spotted wearing a necklace of padlocks. The "Queen of the Night Clubs," who would sometimes encourage men to play leapfrog with her during the course of an evening, claimed that her headwaiter had a concession on all liquor sales in the club and that her money was made on cover and setup charges. In 1928, it cost twenty dollars just to gain access to Guinan's Club Intime, and the joint was very successful.

Guinan wasn't the only female speakeasy owner. Helen Morgan, the torch song chanteuse perhaps most famous for her performance as Julie in Florenz Ziegfield's Broadway production of *Show Boat*, entertained her guests from atop a piano in her "speak," and Belle Livingstone, known in the 1890s as the "chorus girl with the poetic legs," opened a Park Avenue "salon of culture, wit and bonhomie," which closed after being raided by the cops. Not to be deterred, Livingstone then opened a five-story "resort" on East Fifty-eighth Street, complete with miniature golf and Ping-Pong tables. That club, too, was raided, and her attempt to flee over the rooftops was thwarted when agents caught sight of her well-known red pajamas. After Livingstone spent her thirty days in prison, Texas Guinan sent an armored car to bring her back to Manhattan. Livingstone claimed afterward that her morals had not been impaired during her stay behind bars, saying, "On the contrary, . . . if anything, [they have] been improved."

Another woman who was famous during the dry years was Assistant Attorney General Mabel Walker Willebrandt, who said, "The ribaldry of the cocktail shaker . . . and the florid eagerness for false stimulation from what is almost always questionable liquor are rapidly fading from the social hours in Washington." Since the nation's capital was known as being one of the places where good liquor was, indeed, hard to come by, she might have been right. But elsewhere, the florid eagerness for false stimulation was not that easily quelled.

New York was home to speakeasies and nightclubs such as Peter's Blue Hour, the Peek Inn, the Metamora Club, the Crillon, Club Borgo, the Beaux Arts, the Silver Slipper, the Jungle Club, Club Richelieu, the Biarritz, Mouquin's, the Blue Ribbon, the Furnace, the Hyena Club, the Day Breakers, the Jail Club, and, funnily enough, the Ha! Ha! Most of these joints were in midtown or uptown, but down in Greenwich Village a certain Barney Gallant decided to open Club Gallant on Washington Square South. It was one of the swankiest joints in town.

According to Stanley Walker, Gallant had the distinction of being the first person in Manhattan to be jailed under Prohibition laws, an event that took place before national Prohibition went into effect. The wartime Prohibition Act of 1918, prohibiting the sale of alcohol until "the termination of demobilization," went into effect on June 30, 1919, and less than four months later Gallant's Greenwich Village Inn was raided. Gallant was arrested along with half a dozen of his waiters; he agreed to plead guilty providing the waiters were set free. Sentenced to thirty days in jail, he served far less, and about a month before national Prohibition began, his Club Gallant opened its doors.

The club, filled with "youngsters with strange stirrings in their breasts, who had come from remote villages on the prairie; women of social position and money who wanted to do things—all sorts of things—in a bohemian setting; businessmen who had made quick money and who wanted to breathe the faintly naughty atmosphere in safety, and ordinary people who got thirsty now and then and wanted to sit down and have a drink," thrived until 1924, when Gallant opened a new joint on West Third Street. If you wanted to drink at this place, you had to follow some rules:

1. Reserve a table in advance so as to be sure of admittance.
2. Do not offer any gratuities to the head waiter or the captain as soon as you enter the door. If the service was satisfactory tip one of them a moderate sum upon leaving.
3. Bring along your own "atmosphere" with you. It avoids controversy and is much safer all around.

4. Do not get too friendly with the waiter. His name is neither Charley nor George. Remember the old adage about familiarity breeding contempt.
5. Pinching the cigarette girl's cheek or asking to dance with her is decidedly out of order. She is there for the sole purpose of dispensing cigars and cigarettes with a smile that will bring profits to the concessionaire.
6. Do not ask to play the drums. The drum heads are not as tough as many another head. Besides, it has a tendency to disturb the rhythm.
7. Make no requests of the leader of the orchestra for the songs of the vintage of 1890. Crooning "Sweet Adeline" was alright for your granddad, but times, alas, have changed.
8. Do not be overgenerous in tipping your waiter. Why be a chump? Fifteen percent of your bill is quite sufficient.
9. Examine your bill when the waiter presents it. Remember even they are human and are liable to err—intentionally or otherwise.
10. Please do not offer to escort the cloakroom girl home. Her husband, who is an ex-prizefighter, is there for that purpose.

Gallant claimed that his secret to success was exclusivity, and that this was the nightclub's "great and only stock in trade." Other places weren't quite as choosy about whom they let in. Walker noted that customers in various venues would "[complain] about the bill when they had expected to be robbed in the first place, . . . try to drink up the town's booze supply in one night, . . . drink too much and then try to lead the band, . . . lose their [money] and then blame the wrong people, . . . get reeling, blind drunk and try to steal their neighbor's girls, . . . [and] tip so much that they were ridiculous or so little that they would be snubbed. . . . In short, the lower stratum of customers were obstreperous, ill-mannered, unable to hold their liquor, and ripe for the plucking." There was quite a party going on.

In New York, the party stretched all the way uptown to Harlem, where, not long after the end of the First World War, white folk had discovered some marvelous clubs. Jimmie's, Small's, the Capitol, and the Palace Gardens were places where working-class African-Americans hung out, while the Cotton Club and the Exclusive Club catered more to Harlem's social leaders. At various nightspots you could catch acts by "Snake Hips" Earl Tucker, Cab Calloway, or Florence Mills, straight back from her success at Les Ambassadeurs in Paris, but one place that deserves special mention is Gilligan F. Holton's Broken Leg and Busted Bar and Grill, on West 138th Street. Holton described one incident in his speakeasy to journalist Joseph Mitchell:

> *One night the place was crowded, and a man and his wife came in. He looked like a big spender. I decided to use him for a psychological test. A test to determine just how much a human being would stand for.*
>
> *I sat him at a table right near the kitchen where it was so warm it would singe your hair. Then I had the waiters spill soup on him and step on his feet and scrape crumbs into his lap. His wife ordered some wine, and I said to myself, "I'll fix her." I got me some cold tea and I poured some kerosene in it and I dumped a little gin in it and I shook it up. Well, this couple stayed in the place until daybreak and spent $125—which was easy to do, of course—and then the man came up to me. I thought he was going to hit me.*
>
> *But no. He said, "Mr. Holton, I want to thank you for a wonderful night. I never had such an interesting time. I am going to tell all my friends about your place."*
>
> *And then his wife said, "And the wine, Mr. Holton! The most wonderful Amontillado sherry I ever tasted. How do you get such wonderful wine in this beastly prohibition country?"*

If Prohibition-era bars weren't filled with creative bartenders honing their collective craft, there were at least a few cocktailians around. A couple of cocktails that were served at speakeasies are detailed in Michael and Ariane Batterberry's *On the Town in New York*: The Goldfish Cocktail, sort of a Dry Martini with goldwasser (an herbal liqueur speckled with gold flakes), was the specialty of the Aquarium speakeasy that sported a huge fish tank as its bar; and at Zani's speakeasy, you could order a Zani Zaza, a drink made with gin, apricot brandy, egg white, lemon juice, and grenadine. No doubt other nightclubs of the time had bartenders who created cocktails during Prohibition, but the vast majority of drinks detailed in books published after repeal were either created prior to 1920, concocted during Prohibition but first made in Europe, or invented by those bartenders who took their place behind the mahogany on December 5, 1933, when the nation was, once again, allowed to drink in peace.

RESTORATION

On December 6, 1933, Sidney E. Klein looked out of his Times Square office window to see throngs of people standing in line to get schooners of beer from a wagon pulled by eight dray horses. Budweiser hadn't waited long to get back on the street. And neither did anyone else—Prohibition's repeal had been ratified at 5:32 P.M. the previous day, and the nation was ready to party in the open again. Too bad everyone was broke.

The Depression started by the stock market crash of 1929 had resulted in unemployment for over thirteen million Americans by the time Franklin Delano Roosevelt took office in March 1933. One of F.D.R.'s remedies for the situation, just one month after he became president, was to legalize near beer; he then made sure that the Twenty-first Amendment to the Constitution, which crushed the Prohibition amendment, was enacted before the year ended. On the following day, the *New York Times* carried such headlines as "City Toasts New Era," "Celebration in Streets," and "Machine Guns Guard Some Liquor Trucks—Supplies to Be Rushed Out Today."

No sooner did the bars of America reopen than the publishers started issuing new cocktail books to jog the memories of those who remembered the "here's how" days prior to Prohibition, and to teach a new generation how to properly mix drinks. A few cocktail guides actually got published prior to the act's repeal, *Shake 'Em Up: A Practical Handbook of Polite Drinking*, by Virginia Elliot and Phil D. Stong, among them. The authors of this tongue-in-cheek party handbook admonished their readers to use nonalcoholic spirits when constructing their drinks, or to boil the alcohol off real spirits if that was all they could lay their hands on.

Sullivan's 1930 book *The Drinks of Yesteryear*—in which he claimed never to have served a flapper, saying that "her hiplash" was unknown to him—details, as the title suggests, pre-Prohibition drinks, not new cocktails. And even Patrick Gavin Duffy's 1934 *Official Mixer's Guide* isn't full of new American drinks, although the recipes suggest strongly that Duffy had read, and thoroughly digested, Craddock's book from the London Savoy.

Apart from the fact that Duffy categorized his recipes by the base liquor, whereas Craddock used the alphabetical approach, many instances point to Duffy referring to Craddock's work, at least as a guide; the one major difference lies in the use of absinthe, which was, and still is, legal in England but had been outlawed in the States. Duffy simply substituted Bénédictine in drinks such as the Monkey Gland Cocktail, and since that time various books have listed one or the other recipe, depending on which book was used for reference. In America, of course, absinthe is, once more, legal again, and substitutes such as Herbsaint, Absente, or Pernod are seldom used these days. Indeed, some absinthe substitutes have been restored to their original formulas to once again be "the real thing." (As it turns out, the law that we all believed to have outlawed absinthe did no such thing. It outlawed spirits with too much thujone—a ketone that we used to believe was responsible for absinthe's alleged psychedelic effects—and no absinthe ever contained enough thujone to make it illegal.)

Perhaps the most important aspect of drinking during the years that followed repeal, right up through the 1970s, is that overconsumption of beverage alcohol was rarely, if ever, mentioned. Drinking was fun. Being drunk was funny. Very few people took the role of the cocktailian too seriously, and some books of the era reflect the nation's attitude.

The Drunk's Blue Book, written by Norman Anthony and O. Soglow in 1933, for instance, details what the authors call the Drunk's Code:

1. Free lunch.
2. Free speech.
3. Free cheers.
4. Five-day week.
5. Every third drink on the house.
6. Lower curbstones.

7. Overstuffed gutters.
8. More lampposts.
9. Rubber nightsticks and rolling pins.
10. More keyholes for every door.
11. More farmers' daughters.
12. Colder ice.
13. Two cocktails for a quarter.
14. Bigger and better beers.

These wags also suggest that if you find yourself lying on the floor in front of a bar, it is improper to rest your elbows on the brass foot rail, and they recommend that if you discover you're driving the wrong way up a one-way street, you should keep to the right side of the road. A whole section of this book is devoted to "How to Get into Fights" and advises such activities as sitting on the curbstone shouting derogatory names at truck drivers, and approaching a couple at a table and, "chucking the lady in question under the chin, say[ing], 'Hello baby. Who's your funny-looking friend?'" Anthony and Soglow wouldn't have many twenty-first-century friends.

Some people, though, *were* interested in mixing a good drink, and Charles Brown noted that sweet drinks such as the Alexander—gin, white crème de cacao, and cream—had come into vogue in the thirties. There's no getting away from the fact that, in general, more women than men enjoy sweeter drinks. In contrast with pre-Prohibition nightlife, women were now every bit as important as men in bars across the country, and they were also throwing cocktail parties at home.

Charles Brown's 1939 *Gun Club Drink Book* noted: "Due to the speakeasy architecture of the Prohibition era, our own cocktail bars now look like . . . foreign imitations, and with their highly cushioned stools and female patrons they are quite different from the barrooms of preceding generations; but then too the women themselves have changed. . . . In the so called 'good old days' a woman's place was the home while the men frequented the bars; nowadays there is no sex discrimination in any sport and almost every home has its own bar."

In 1936 Harman Burney "Barney" Burke, an American bartender who had plied his trade in London, Paris, Berlin, and Copenhagen before returning to America after repeal, listed what he considered to be the fifteen "most popular conventional drinks in the Western world" in *Burke's Complete Cocktail & Drinking Recipes*:

1. Martini Cocktail (Dry or Sweet)
2. Manhattan Cocktail (Dry or Sweet)
3. Bronx Cocktail (Dry or Sweet)
4. Old-Fashioned Whiskey Cocktail (Sweet)
5. Sidecar Cocktail (Sweet)
6. Clover Club Cocktail (Dry)
7. Gin Rickey (Dry)
8. Gin Fizz (Sweet or Dry)
9. Bacardi Cocktail (Dry)
10. Alexander Cocktail No. 1 (Sweet)
11. Rock and Rye (Sweet)
12. Whiskey Cocktail (Dry)
13. Sherry Cocktail (Sweet or Dry)
14. Dubonnet Cocktail (Sweet)
15. Champagne Cocktail

A little confusion arises here, since he lists the Bronx as being either dry or sweet but his recipe calls for both varieties of vermouth. Also, although he suggests that people enjoyed dry Bacardi Cocktails, his recipe calls for as much grenadine as citrus juice, so it couldn't have been very dry.

Burke's Dry Martini contained twice as much gin as vermouth, as well as a couple of dashes of orange bitters, a formula that would last in many cocktail books until well into the forties; and his Manhattan, which could be made with either rye or Irish whiskey, followed a similar path except that while he included bitters in the dry version, he used simple syrup in his Sweet Manhattan, and both Italian and French vermouths were called for.

The Old-Fashioned in Burke's book requires a slice of orange and a lemon twist to be "mulled" with bitters and sugar before the whiskey is added to the glass, and this method of preparing the drink caused many arguments among Old-Fashioned aficionados in the years to come. In the introduction to 1945's *Crosby Gaige's Cocktail Guide and Ladies' Companion*, writer and bon vivant Lucius Beebe wrote about his encounter with a bartender at the Drake Hotel in Chicago when he requested an Old-Fashioned without fruit. Apparently the bartender was so insulted at the thought of anybody imagining that he *might* put fruit in the drink that he admonished Gaige, "Young impudent sir . . . I've built Old-Fashioned cocktails these sixty years . . . and I have never yet had the perverted nastiness of mind to put fruit in an Old-Fashioned. Get out, scram, go over to the Palmer House and drink."

That the Sidecar is included in Burke's list is interesting, since this drink, reportedly created in France during the First World War, was still relatively new to the United States. While it did appear on at least one cocktail menu during Prohibition, "the 'Sidecar' and 'Presidente' cocktails are among the foreign importations that have a considerable following," wrote one mixed-drink fancier in 1934.

Drinks were named for people long before the 1930s. It's possible that the Bobby Burns, for example, was named not for the great Scottish poet but for a cigar salesman who presumably sold the Robert Burns brand of Cuban cigars (no longer on the market) and frequented the old Waldorf Astoria bar. But things got a little out of control when Sterling North and Carl Kroch decided to name drinks after popular books in their 1935 cocktail guide *So Red the Nose, or Breath in the Afternoon.*

The recipes in this lighthearted book were supplied by the author of each work referred to; Ernest Hemingway submitted the Death in the Afternoon cocktail—a simple mixture of absinthe and champagne. His instructions call for the imbiber to "Drink 3 to 5 of these slowly," and the editor's note at the bottom of the page advises, "After six of these cocktails *The Sun Also Rises.*"

Edgar Rice Burroughs submitted the Tarzan Cocktail, made with Bacardi, Cointreau, lime juice, and sugar. Hervey Allen contributed the Anthony Adverse Cocktail, which could help anyone through a little adversity: Barbados rum, lime juice, bitters, brown sugar, and "a strong dash of brandy."

One of the recipes that didn't make it into the main section of the book but was mentioned in the back (presumably because the authors couldn't resist it) came from H. L. Davis, author of *Honey in the Horn.* The drink contained two beer steins of high-proof rum; dark, strained honey; fresh huckleberries; mountain-ash berries; and "best black gunpowder." Davis instructed the bartender, "Mix (at room temperature) and stir savagely until it is no longer streaky in color. Each drink should be served with a toothpick impaling a dead bumblebee, a dead yellow jacket and a dead wasp. These are supposed to be eaten first to give the revelers a notion of what lies in store for them."

On the other side of the Atlantic, Booth's gin compiled a similar collection of cocktail recipes, but these were selected for people such as the Earl of Westmorland, who was assigned the London Buck—gin, lemon juice, and ginger ale—and made it into the book after he allowed them to print his quote: "A cocktail without Booth's is a cocktail under a handicap." The Countess of Oxford and Asquith declared, "It is popular to be liberal with Booth's gin, and then the party will be top of the poll," for which she was awarded the Empire Cocktail, a mixture of gin, calvados, and apricot brandy. And Dame Sybil Thorndike, whose theatrical break came when George Bernard Shaw took her under his wing, was honored with a Trilby cocktail when she said, "A cocktail in which Booth's plays a leading part receives an enthusiastic reception from the most captious critics."

Back in America, high society during the mid- to late thirties had marvelous nightclubs and bars to choose from, some of them being old speakeasies that had gone legit. The Stork Club in New York had been raided and closed on a couple of occasions during the early thirties, but now, in new premises, it was open to anyone with enough money to afford its food and drink. Similarly, El Morocco had been an illegal drinking club, but now people could drink there without fear of raids. On the West Coast, though, a new style of bar started to emerge when Donn "the Beachcomber" Beach started selling pseudo-tropical drinks at his new joint in Hollywood.

Jeff Berry and Annene Kaye detail Beachcomber originals such as the Missionary's Downfall and the Cobra's Fang in their book *Beachbum Berry's Grog Log*, but they noted that the Zombie was his real claim to fame. The Beachcomber's first joint opened in 1934, but in 1937 he moved into bigger and better digs decorated with bamboo, tropical plants, waterfalls, burning torches, and even miniature volcanoes. The American tiki lounge had been born. Victor "Trader Vic" Bergeron copied the style in the late thirties, and he gave us the Mai Tai in 1944.

America didn't truly recover from the Depression until the end of the 1930s, just as the Second World War was beginning in Europe. But bon vivant Charles Henry Baker Jr. must not have been hit too hard by the stock market crash of 1929, since he had been spending his time drinking his way around the world, detailing his adventures in *The Gentleman's Companion*. "Each one of [our experiences that] fetches joyous memory of some friend, place, or adventure . . . is flanked with happy memory of a frosted glass, a smile, the sip of something perfect," he wrote, and went on to describe various and sundry cocktails, some of which he'd encountered at their place of origin.

Baker sipped Singapore Slings at the Raffles Hotel in Singapore, where the drink had supposedly been created in 1915 by bartender Ngiam Tong Boon (since proved to be untrue), and declared it "a delicious, slow-acting, insidious thing." In New Orleans he drank Sazeracs and determined that the best way to enjoy them was to hold the glass under your nose, "inhale the fragrant blend of scents, sip and relax." And he was probably the first to instruct Americans on the ritual of drinking shots of tequila by sucking on a wedge of lemon (not lime), taking a pinch of salt, and shooting the spirit. Baker wasn't afraid to use top-shelf spirits in his cocktails, either; he wrote that it was as impossible to make a fine cocktail with "dollar gin" as it would have been for Whistler to depict his mother using "barn paint."

By the time the 1940s arrived, Americans had been introduced to the Bloody Mary. Vodka was being made in the States, though not many people knew much about it until around the middle of the decade, when Jack Morgan, the owner of the Cock and Bull Tavern in Los Angeles and an executive from the company that was making Smirnoff vodka, got together to create the Moscow Mule. Vodka would never look back.

Rum and Coca-Cola was another drink that became popular in the 1940s, popularized by the Andrews Sisters' version of the Trinidadian calypso by that name penned by Lord Invader. The song was written about, and popular with, the servicemen at the American naval base in Trinidad, where "both mother and daughter [were] workin' for the Yankee dollar." The lyrics sound quite innocent on the surface, but with a little thought . . .

Since the late 1800s, liquor companies have been aware that most of their products are poured into cocktail shakers, and they haven't been shy about bombarding us with "useful" pamphlets to guide us on our way. In 1941, Heublein issued *The Club Cocktail Party Book* to promote its range of bottled cocktails—Martinis, Manhattans, Old-Fashioneds, Sidecars, and Daiquiris—and to teach us how to make such party treats as heart-shaped canapés topped with a crab-flake spread and "your initials in capers."

Cocktail parties in those days were lots of fun, especially if you had Seagram's Magic Age Cards, each one advertising a different whiskey and filled with a "bingo card" of numbers: "Hand the six cards to a person telling him (or her) to return to you only those cards on which [their] age appears . . . simply add together the numbers appearing in the upper right-hand square." Oh, the fun they must have had.

Luckily for us all, some people started to take the subject of cocktails seriously again. In 1945, Lucius Beebe, once called "the outstanding dude among the journalists," wrote, "It is only fitting that the subject of cocktails should be approached with levity slightly tinctured with contempt because, for every good compound, arrangement, or synthesis of liquors, wines, and their adjacent or opposite fruits and flavors chilled and served in a variety of glasses, there are approximately a million foul, terrifying, and horrendous similar excitements to stupefaction, cuspidor hurling, and nausea." Beebe wasn't the only one putting a little thought into the subject—even James Beard, later to become the dean of American cookery, submitted a cocktail recipe for publication in 1945's *Crosby Gaige's Cocktail Guide and Ladies' Companion.*

But if Beebe, Beard, and others took the fine art of mixing drinks seriously, they were mere amateurs compared to David Embury, author of *The Fine Art of Mixing Drinks* (first published in 1948 and revised in 1952 and 1958) and the only true amateur among them. Embury was the first true cocktailian of the modern age, and he took time to analyze the components of a cocktail, breaking them down into a base (usually a spirit, it must be at least 50 percent of the drink); a modifying, smoothing, or aromatizing agent, such as vermouth, bitters, fruit juice, sugar, cream, or eggs; and "additional special flavoring and coloring ingredients," which he defined as liqueurs and nonalcoholic fruit syrups.

Embury taught us that the Ramos Gin Fizz must be shaken for at least five minutes in order to achieve the proper silky consistency, suggested that Peychaud's bitters be used in the Rob Roy, and noted that "for cocktails, such as the Side Car, a three-star cognac is entirely adequate, although a ten-year-old cognac will produce a better drink."

In the second edition of his book, Embury mentioned that he had been criticized for omitting two drinks from his original work: the Bloody Mary, which he described as "strictly vile," and the Moscow Mule, as "merely mediocre." On the subject of Martinis, he explained that although most cocktail books call for the drink to be made with one-third to one-half vermouth, "quite recently, in violent protest of this wishy-washy type of cocktail, there has sprung up the vermouth-rinse method of making Martinis." He describes a drink made from chilled gin in a cocktail glass coated in vermouth. Embury didn't approve of either version, and went on to say that a ratio of seven parts gin to one part vermouth was his personal favorite.

While Embury was taking his drinking seriously, many Americans were quaffing Martinis by the pitcher, and *Playboy* magazine commissioned cocktail maven Thomas Mario and, later, Emanuel Greenberg to deliver cocktail news to a nation of people who drank for fun, and did it on a regular basis.

Esquire magazine issued its *Handbook for Hosts* as early as 1949, detailing drinks such as the Sloe Gin Fizz, the Pan American, the "I Died Game, Boys" Mixture, and the Ginsicle—gin with fruit juice or simple syrup poured over chipped ice in a champagne glass. A cartoon in the book depicts a frustrated bartender mopping his fevered brow and exclaiming, "She ordered it because it had a cute name." The world of cocktails was tilting slightly on its axis, and liquor companies lobbied long and hard to get into the act.

In the fifties, Southern Comfort convinced us to make Comfort Manhattans and Comfort Old-Fashioneds by issuing a booklet: *How to Make the 32 Most Popular Drinks*. By the seventies, when the Comfort Manhattan had become the Improved Manhattan, they were bringing us *Happy Hour Mixology Plus a Primer of Happy Hour Astrology*, presumably so we would have something to talk about at bars: "Oh, you're a Virgo—discriminating, keenly analytical, exacting, and often a perfectionist. Wanna drink?" Even roadside diners were using place mats filled with cocktail recipes to entice customers to have, perhaps, a Dubonnet Cocktail alongside their grilled-cheese sandwich, or a Crème de Menthe Frappé, which they could pour over their stack of silver-dollar pancakes.

Gordon's gin issued a recipe booklet in the late fifties detailing drinks such as the Major Bailey—a sort of gin-based Mint Julep—and the Spriuss Cocktail, "popular at the Hotel Excelsior, Rome," made with gin, apricot brandy, orange juice, and bitters. Monochrome photographs of foreign stamps appear on the pages of this pamphlet, and Gordon's deemed it necessary to warn readers, "All the stamps illustrated have been demonetized and are not valid for postage."

Bars in the last half of the twentieth century were also hit hard by convenience drinks. No need to squeeze lemons or limes anymore; "sweet and sour" is here—it's already sweetened, and you can use it in place of either juice. And the drinks you make with it will take you right back to your childhood—they taste like sherbet. Bloody Mary? Here's a bottle of tomato juice that's pre-seasoned with just enough sauces and spices to let you know they're there, but not enough to offend anyone on the face of the earth. How do you make a Daiquiri? It's easy—the instructions are on the packet. Not all of these drink mixes were terrible, but not one of them rendered potions worthy of the bartenders of yesteryear.

Then in 1965, the Craft Cocktail movement began with a guy in Manhattan who was just looking to get laid. "I lived on 63rd Street between First and York," said Allan Stillman in a 2010 interview with the website *Edible Geography*. "Easy access to the 59th Street bridge meant you could get out of New York quickly, so in that two or three block neighbourhood, there was a pile of airline stewardesses—and for whatever reason, there was also a whole bunch of models. Basically, a lot of single people all lived between 60th and 65th and between York Avenue and 3rd Avenue. It seemed to me that the best way to meet girls was to open up a bar."

It's important to understand that, back in the mid-sixties, there were few, if any, New York bars where single women felt comfortable—bars in New York were mainly beer joints for men. And so, all of those stewardesses and models back then simply partied at, well, house parties. Stillman was about to change all that when he opened a bar called TGI Fridays, which welcomed both men and women, thus creating the first singles' bar—one that felt like a cocktail party.

It's true to say that, in the twenty-first century, we don't think of TGI Fridays as being a chain of craft cocktail bars, but that hasn't always been the case. As detailed in Robert Simonson's book *A Proper*

Drink, when the chain started to get off the ground they used only fresh juices, and the training programs for new bartenders were rigorous, to say the least. To get behind the stick at TGI Fridays back in the day you had to spend the best part of a year bussing tables, waiting on tables, and working as a barback, then you had to memorize a few hundred cocktail recipes, and be able to make a couple of dozen of their drinks while wearing a blindfold. The training at TGI Fridays was second to none, and the chain quickly spread to the United Kingdom, where a legion of serious bartenders were looking to make some serious cash by learning how to tend bar the TGI Fridays' way. As you'll see later in this chapter, this was a turning point for the industry.

In the seventies, although there was a cornucopia of cocktails from which to choose, Martinis still reigned supreme, Manhattans took second place, just as they had at the old Waldorf Astoria bar prior to World War I, and the sweeter drinks that had come into vogue right after the repeal of Prohibition were still popular in American bars. One cocktail was quickly gaining ground on the older classics, though, and it would become a shining star by the 1980s.

The Margarita (page 241) had been around since the thirties, forties, or fifties, depending on whose story you believe, but tequila didn't really catch on in this country until the Swinging Sixties arrived, when hippies and would-be hippies alike heard a rumor that the spirit might act as a hallucinogen. By the seventies all bartenders knew how to fix a mean Margarita, and its popularity grew and grew, until nobody really cared about whether or not there were any mind-altering side effects—it had become a staple drink, and a classic in its own right.

THE NEW COCKTAILIANS

By the mid-1980s the health craze had swept the country, and the cocktail scene was all but dead. Or perhaps it simply lay in hibernation, since something came along that coaxed it out of its cave by screaming loudly, and out of tune: Punk Cocktails hit the scene. Young bartenders who had never been trained in the finer aspects of the cocktailian craft had grown bored of making wishy-washy White Wine Spritzers, tedious Tequila Sunrises, and lackluster Long Island Iced Teas, so they created obnoxious potions with vile-sounding names; you could order an Abortion or a Blow Job in any old bar and nobody would blink an eye. Bars selling dozens of flavors of frozen drinks seemed to spring up overnight, but few of them offered well-constructed Slurpies. And Jelly Shots, made from flavored gelatin and vodka, or sometimes tequila, were being sucked down by underage college kids on campuses everywhere.

Who created these drinks? Nobody seems to know. My friend Stuffy Shmitt learned how to make a drink called Windex at Barney's Beanery in Los Angeles, but he has no idea who first originated it. And it was Stuffy who saw a sign outside a Lower East Side New York joint advertising a cocktail made with NyQuil as a base—but ask him which bar it was, and Stuffy shrugs. Nobody ever bothered to document Punk Cocktails—nobody really cared where they came from. Laughter at the bar, the chance to order a Sperm du Jour—a drink sipped through a straw inserted down the center of a fresh banana—and scantily clad women selling test-tube shooters of relatively harmless concoctions were welcomed, and very much needed, in the bars of America.

For me, this was a very exciting time in the world of mixed drinks; somebody was putting the fun back into drinking. We'd spent much of the 1980s hearing about the hazardous effects of overconsumption, and it seemed as though a whole generation of customers had entered adulthood being warned that they could have a drink providing they didn't have a good time. I dubbed the drinks of this period Punk Cocktails because they seemed to be liquid versions of bands like the Sex Pistols—they certainly didn't harmonize well, but they sure as hell made themselves heard. Bartenders revolted against the elevator-music drinks of their elders and created noisier potions of their own. This phenomenon was exactly what was needed to make potential cocktailians rethink their craft. These cocktails gave bartenders and consumers a license to let loose a little at the bar, opening the path for true cocktailians to once again take an interest in the subject of mixology.

While all this was going down, Dale DeGroff, straight from a six-year gig at the Hotel Bel-Aire in Beverly Hills, started working with restaurateur Joe Baum at Aurora in Manhattan. DeGroff had learned how to make cocktails in the classic style from at least one old-timer in L.A. but he was mostly a self-taught master of the craft. For example, he knew to use cognac, Cointreau, and fresh lemon juice instead of American brandy, cheap triple sec, and sweet-and-sour mix to make a Sidecar. Baum gave him great guidance, recommending old cocktail books for Dale to absorb, but he also left him to figure out plenty of stuff for himself.

Dale DeGroff took over the bar at New York's legendary Rainbow Room in 1987, and a star was born. DeGroff brought us classics such as The Ritz—cognac, Cointreau, maraschino, lemon juice, and champagne—and the Fitzgerald: gin, lemon juice, simple syrup, and Angostura bitters. He worked tirelessly for his well-earned reputation as the consummate craft bartender. His perfectionism caught the eye of the media, and eventually thousands of bartenders would hold Dale up as a shining example of how to tend bar in the classic mode. Now he is probably the best-known American cocktailian of our time.

We should also note that Dale is the man who mentored Audrey Saunders, who went on to open The Pegu Club in New York—one of the world's most renowned craft cocktail bars. Audrey has given birth to such delicious potions as the Gin-Gin Mule and the Old Cuban, both cocktails that have become global phenomena. DeGroff and Saunders have a lot to answer for.

Around this same time period a certain Dick Bradsell was making magic behind the bar in London. Dick's style was very different from Dale's, but they held the same core values of using only fresh ingredients, classical methodology, and stringent work ethics. Dick trained the bartenders at London's Groucho—a fabulous club that caters to the likes of Anthony Bourdain and Stephen Fry; and a couple of members of Britain's Royal Family have been seen there, too. Dick also worked at a bar named for him—Dick's Bar—at The Atlantic, one of the most popular joints in London at the time, and he's rightfully credited with training hundreds of bartenders. And although he wasn't the only prominent bartender in London at that time—I'm looking at you, Chris Edwardes, Nick Strangeway, Doug Ankrah—he was certainly the figurehead. Sadly, Dick died in 2016. His legend lives on.

The scene was set, then, by the time the 1990s rolled around. Dale DeGroff had captured the attention of the bar world in the United States; Dick Bradsell stood poised with a slew of craft bartenders in the United Kingdom, and one last detail completed the scene for the perfect storm that made the Craft Cocktail Revolution spin. The bartenders who had trained at the early incarnations of TGI Fridays on both sides of the Atlantic were well primed to take their places behind the new craft bars that started to open their doors in the 1990s. And to think that it all started in 1965 when a young Allan Stillman opened a bar so he could meet women. Hope he got laid. A lot.

THE INFORMATION SUPERHIGHWAY

Although I was online in the early nineties, it wasn't until halfway through that decade that things really started to flourish on the World Wide Web, and it was around that time that I was contacted by Robert Hess, a computer geek who worked for Microsoft, who geeked out about cocktails after work. Robert, who used the moniker "Drink Boy," had started an online forum for bartenders and cocktail enthusiasts. Now things were really heating up. Bartenders all over the world began adding their two-cents' worth on drink-related topics such as the formula for the original Pisco Punch, the ratios of sugar to water when making simple syrup, and the original base spirit for the Tom Collins—a discussion that spiraled out of all proportion.

Another key figure on the early cocktail web forums was Ted Haigh, a graphic designer in the movie industry who applied his researching skills to uncover all sorts of mysteries, such as the original ingredients used to make Forbidden Fruit liqueur, a product that has been missing from the backbars of the world for quite some time. Under the name "Aging Wino," and later, "Dr. Cocktail," Ted kept us entertained and well informed on the AOL site dedicated to things of that nature. Just as it did with any other industry, the internet quickly advanced the cocktail community by simply connecting bartenders who were eager to share their knowledge with anyone who'd listen.

YOU SAY YOU WANT A REVOLUTION?

In 2003, an event took place at New York's Plaza Hotel that brought together the people who made up a large part of the core of American cocktailian bartenders, and it attracted folk from overseas, too. Allen Katz, then representing Slow Food, New York, pulled everything together after David Wondrich, who would go on to be the author of *Imbibe!*, suggested that "A Tribute to Jerry Thomas" would be a worthwhile venture.

The Plaza's Oak Room was the venue, and the evening saw Dale DeGroff serving Blue Blazers, Audrey Saunders dishing out Tom & Jerrys, Dave Wondrich offering a delightful Arrak Punch, while Ted "Dr. Cocktail" Haigh shook up some Brandy Crustas, Sasha Petraske made Gin Daisies, Robert Hess presented the Japanese Cocktail, George Papadakis stirred up some marvelous Manhattans, and I kept busy mixing up a bunch of Martinez cocktails. The event was a smashing success that made William Grimes proclaim in the *New York Times*, "the Gilded Age lives again." Bartenders from the U.K. attended this event, and it was, to the best of my knowledge, the very first cocktail-centric event to be heralded by the legitimate press in the twenty-first century. "[Jerry] Thomas would have been proud," wrote Grimes.

A few years later, in 2006, I attended the London Bar Show for the first time, courtesy of the Sazerac Company, which had hired me to present a bunch of Buffalo Trace Bourbon drinks to the thirsty crowds there. When I arrived I got a huge surprise. Prior to this I was pretty much unknown in my home country, but unbeknownst to me, things had changed. More than a few London bartenders knew me on sight, and I was pretty flabbergasted by my newfound "stardom." According to all and sundry, it was the first edition of *The Joy of Mixology* that had worked this magic.

Many bartenders, it seems, had latched on to the book, and in some bars it had actually become mandatory reading for the whole bar staff. My baby had learned to walk, talk, and swagger on the duckboards. Thank you, kind world.

Witnessing the beauty that was the 2006 London Bar Show, I realized that the revolution had begun in earnest in the U.K., too—it wasn't until much later that I discovered that the seeds that spawned the movement had been sown many years earlier. My immediate concern back then, though, was how we were all going to keep this going. I should not have worried. Here we are, more than a decade later, and the movement is going strong. How did that happen?

My belief is that it didn't take too very long for the marketing mavens in the big drinks companies to recognize that bartenders are their best brand ambassadors, and since these companies tend to have deep pockets, they quickly started putting their money where it worked best for everyone concerned. They launched competitions with fabulous prizes, flew bartenders around the world to strut their stuff in all manner of exotic locations, and hired bartenders as educators and as marketers.

In my opinion, without the support of the liquor industry, the craft cocktail revolution might well have died early. Bartenders may love to pick on the huge companies that market spirits, and there's nothing wrong with that—keeps them honest and on their toes. However, from where I stand, the industry has been the craft bartenders' little blue pill. Their indulgence has kept us all ready, willing, and able to perform on demand. They subsidized our efforts so we could continue to experiment and evolve our craft.

ONE DAMNED THING AFTER ANOTHER

ICHIGO ITCHIE

Once the revolution started moving, in the early to mid-aughts, certain people started to crop up who would make some massive differences to our craft. One shining example of this comes in the form of Stanislav Kaiholomālie Vadrna, a man from Slovakia who attended my Cocktails in the Country course in 2005 and became a very close friend. I'm not sure how much Stan got from my original course, which was *very* basic back then—it was designed for people who wanted to *become* bartenders rather than for working bartenders who wanted to perfect their craft—but some magic happened 'twixt Stan and me, and we've been bartender brothers ever since. The training he got in Japan, though, had a massive influence on his style.

Roughly translated, *Ichigo Ichie* (ITCHY-GO ITCHY-YAY) means "one meeting, one opportunity," and it forms the backbone of the Japanese philosophy that's applied to the bartending craft in the Land of the Rising Sun. It's so ingrained in Stan Vadrna, in fact, that he had it tattooed onto his forearm one afternoon when I was with him in 2007 in Bratislava. I love this concept, which, to Stan, meant when you meet a new guest at your bar you have only one opportunity to make the right impression. (For more on this mindful approach, see page 80.) There are other Japanese bartending techniques, though, that have entered Western bartending to some extent, and the hard shake might be the most well known.

Kazuo Uyeda, bartender at The Tender Bar in the Ginza district of Tokyo, invented the hard shake, and he'll tell you that he's the only person on earth who does it properly, but that doesn't stop others from trying. The hard shake comprises a series of movements that send the ice colliding with specific parts of the shaker and results in "velvety bubbles that keep the harshness of the alcohol from contacting the tongue," a phrase found on Uyeda's website and mentioned in a 2009 article by Toby Cecchini in the *New York Times*.

I do agree that the hard shake gives a drink a smoother, silkier texture, and I also believe that the same texture can be achieved simply by agitating a drink with lots of gusto. Shake it like you mean it. As far as I'm concerned, the only advantage to the hard shake, with all due respect to Kazuo Uyeda, is that it's great to watch. It's theater. And since tending bar is, to a large degree, performance art, the hard shake has merits all its own.

I contend that it's impossible to tell the difference between a drink shaken using Mr. Uyeda's hard shake and a drink that's shaken very viciously—a method that I tend toward. When I mentioned this in an online forum, Kenji Jesse, the London-based director of the Nomu Consult company, stated that he had asked Mr. Uyeda, "Is the hard shake just a physical motion of body and shaker or is there a state of mind that one must employ to achieve perfection in its technique?" Here's his answer:

> *If the hard shake means how hard you can shake physically, I could never top the younger bartenders! The hard shake is about how to make fine air bubbles: how you can break and change the air into the fine air bubble*

> *pieces that make cocktails mellow and easy to drink. I think there are many valid hard shake techniques. I have my way, but it is not only the way to do a hard shake. I believe there are as many possible techniques as there are bartenders who do the hard shake.*

There's a little problem here with the language barrier, but if I may be so bold, I'd say that when Mr. Uyeda indicated he's the only person who can perform the hard shake, he wasn't boasting at all. He was merely pointing out that no two people will shake a drink in *exactly* the same manner. His hard shake is concerned with the state of mind of the bartender as he shakes a drink. If a bartender concentrates on absolutely nothing else but the shaker and the drink, then he can achieve perfection. It's the Zen of cocktail shaking.

THE LAW OF ATTRACTION

A New Age concept, the Law of Attraction suggests we all have the ability to lure into our lives whatever we are focusing on. Want a peach? Think about peaches and they shall appear. It's not quite that simple, of course, and my version of the Law of Attraction is very different: Show the world a craft that rewards creativity, and creative people will be attracted to it. That, in my opinion, is exactly what has gone down in the past fifteen years or so as the cocktail world has become more democratic.

Bartending in neighborhood joints, in Irish bars, in dive bars, and in various other run-of-the-mill watering holes is exactly the same today as it was way back in the 1970s, and probably earlier, too. Let's take a moment to thank the heavens for that. If there were no joints left that served up pints of Guinness or shot after shot of Jägermeister, our lives would not be complete, as far as I'm concerned. The same applies to the food world—we all love gourmet fare, but don't dare close down any greasy spoons that offer canned corned beef hash and eggs, and the like. Variety's the very spice of life, as we have seen.

The other side of our business, though, the side we see when we enter craft cocktail lounges serving fanciful potions, using molecular mixology techniques, bubbling Maplewood smoke through bottles of bourbon, and other such twenty-first-century bar techniques, has led to a world in which mixology has been upwardly mobile for the past fifteen years or more. The cocktailian craft, in many respects, has become a more widely accessible art form, and as such, artists and entrepreneurs of many hues and guises have been attracted to applying their talents to the world of mixed drinks.

This, in my opinion, has been key to the revolution. People sit up and take notice, and some industry outsiders find themselves strangely attracted to the craft—bankers, lawyers, and even scientists—more so than we'd seen in either the nineteenth or the twentieth centuries. While they may not have started the uprising, our cocktail world would be a far less interesting place without them.

A WALK ON THE WILD SIDE

Let's look at a few people who had "straight" jobs before treading the duckboards and slinging drinks. Take Scottish bartender Andy Stewart, for example. Andy was a bank manager for five years before returning to the business he loved best. "I missed working in hospitality, specifically the creativity and the constant flux of whom you're working with [and who you are] meeting [during] each and every shift," he says. Dealing with spreadsheets and other aspects of the financial side of the bar business came fairly easily to Andy after his experiences in banking, but he's learned more than the obvious tasks during his five years behind a desk. "My customer service skills improved," he says, going on to point out that he'd dealt with people from all walks of life in the banking business. Although Andy is currently a business development manager for the drinks company Berry Brothers & Rudd, he was a celebrated bartender, having worked at The Tippling House, among other spots in Scotland.

Margie Maak, a New Jersey–based VP at a financial advisory firm for around a decade, also upped and quit her job in favor of working behind the bar: "At 39 [years old] this choice has been seen as quite a bit of a silly career [move] by many . . . [but] I've finally fully committed to [doing] what I love," she says. "I can make someone's day better when empathizing with their situation and understanding them. Having lived a life many of my guests still live brings me closer to them. That's why I love this job."

One of my favorite tales of career change comes from Zac Doy, currently a bar owner in Toronto, Canada, who was formerly a "really successful banker specializing in stock trades," complete with the house, car, and all the trimmings. But he wasn't happy. And neither were his clients. Even when he made money for them, they never seemed content. One night, though, a friend asked him to help out behind the bar, and about an hour into his shift he made a cocktail for a woman who, after taking a sip, instantly praised the drink. "I felt so gratified, [and] two months later I quit my job and decided to go into bartending full time. That was seven years ago and I've never looked back since." Some of us are lucky enough to listen to what our gut tells us, I think, and Zac certainly did just that.

Opting out of corporate life in order to pursue a life behind the stick hasn't been happening only in the United States, either. Dutchman Fjalar Goud started his professional life as a car designer and engine developer for Porsche in Germany, but twenty years ago he put down the tools in favor of a life in the bar industry. He now owns a bar academy in Amsterdam, "to spread the love for hospitality and bartending." Part of Fjalar's job in the bar world involves designing cocktail stations; his technical background came in handy in his new career, and that, coupled with his target-oriented background at Porsche, has helped him greatly in setting up his current business, he says.

Scientists have gotten caught up in the cocktail revolution, too, and Darcy O'Neal is a prime example of a scientist turned bartender turned entrepreneur. After studying chemistry for four years, O'Neal took a job researching automotive lubricants for the Esso company in Canada. He did this for seven years, then he spent another seven years working in molecular pathology and histology in London, Ontario. But the bar siren called Darcy. And Darcy heard her. "It all worked out wonderfully," he says, "I get to interact with people who are equally curious about history and drinks, and still get to flex my science muscles every once in a while. All experiments in the lab require precise details," he says, "and that carried over to my cocktail-making jobs. The best compliment I received from customers was that my cocktails were always consistent from month to month."

THE DUST OF DAILY LIFE

If, as Pablo Picasso said, "the purpose of art is washing the dust of daily life off our souls," then the liquid art that some twenty-first-century bartenders have been pouring into our glasses has been responsible for some immaculately clean souls of late.

Let's look at New York City artist Ektoras Binikos, co-owner of Sugar Monk, a Harlem cocktail lounge in New York, as a prime example of this "Art Meets the Barroom" phenomenon. According to Ektoras's artistic website (ektorasbinikosstudio.com), he's an artist with a degree in film direction who works in "multiple mediums, including painting, drawing, installation, video, photography and digital art." On his mixology website, though (ebinikosmixology.com), Binikos says that he believes mixology is alchemy. "It is the chemistry of the most subtle kind which gives the mixologist the ability to transform base spirits into noble elixirs of life," he notes.

In my opinion, minds like this have had the most profound effect on our craft. Let's look at the story of just one of the many weird and wonderful cocktails Ektora has created:

THE MARINA ABRAMOVIĆ COCKTAIL

Marina Abramović is a performance artist who self-mutilates on stage, going to extremes such as almost dying from asphyxiation while lying in "a curtain of oxygen-devouring flames." When Abromović turned sixty years old in 2006, the Guggenheim Museum in Manhattan called on Ektoras to create a drink to serve at her birthday party, and here is the recipe he initially submitted for their approval:

1½ ounces Miller's Gin
½ ounce Amaro Montenegro
½ ounce kümmel liqueur
½ ounce red Verjus
½ ounce blood orange juice (preferably made from Sicilian blood oranges)
½ ounce Yuzu juice (the frozen, not salty kind)
Bitters (2 drops Regan's Orange Bitters and 2 drops Angostura bitters)

2 kumquats
¼ ounce 60-year-old balsamic vinegar
Marina's blood (sterilized and dehydrated), just a minuscule amount in powder form*
*** or Marinas's tears.**

Blood or tears in a cocktail? I wish I could tell you it happened, but I'm afraid the good folks at the Guggenheim insisted he change it, and instead of either blood or tears he settled on red pepper, and he assured me that "Marina slept for seven days with the powder under her pillow so that it would absorb her auratic energy."

As far back as the 1970s I can remember working with actors, writers, painters, poets, and many others with distinct artistic bents, so why am I claiming that artists such as Ektoras have been chiefly responsible for the diversity in the cocktail revolution we've witnessed in recent years? Ektoras, and others of his ilk, uses his talents to create new cocktails. His job behind the bar is part of his grand exhibition. The artistic bartenders of yesteryear seemed to be merely slinging screwdrivers to pay the rent.

More than anything else, I believe, the bartender's job has become so open to innovation that it has propelled the craft cocktail revolution. It's why we are where we are today.

YOU CAN'T GET THERE FROM HERE

Don't ever say that to a bartender. If a bartender wants to go somewhere, she will damned well get there, by hook or by crook. The question is, though, where exactly is our beloved craft heading? What drinks will we be sipping five years from now? There's only one answer to this question: I don't have a clue, and neither does anyone else. If we keep our eyes open, though, we might just glimpse the unicorn of futures past.

As I sat mulling this question in August 2017, I stumbled upon an article on BillyPenn.com, a website centered on Philadelphia, the City of Brotherly Love. "This Philly bartender invented a new way to make drinks," screamed the headline. Oh, really? I thought. This is going to be interesting. I wasn't wrong.

The Fibonacci sequence is a series of numbers that appeared in Sanskrit documents dating to a couple of centuries before the Common Era. It's a fairly simple affair. Each number in the sequence is the sum of the previous two numbers. If we start with the number 1, here's how it goes: 1:1:2:3:5:8:13:21 . . . and so on, and so forth. The sequence, which can be observed in the seeds on a sunflower and the scales on a pineapple (don't ask me how) is used in all sorts of unfathomable—to me, at least—mathematical formulas. Paul MacDonald, head bartender at Philadelphia's Friday, Saturday, Sunday, an eclectic American restaurant, uses the Fibonacci sequence to make drinks.

MacDonald uses five ingredients combined in the ratio of the first five numbers in the famous sequence to make his Fibonacci Cocktails: 1, 1, 2, 3, and 5. Thus, he calls for one part each of the first two ingredients, two parts of the third ingredient, three parts of the fourth ingredient, and five parts of the final ingredient. Phew.

I wrote to MacDonald. "A unified theory of Fibonacci Cocktails is still pretty far off," he told me, "but I've found a few different ways to structure ingredients to achieve balance. Several of the cocktails [I make using this formula] use this same type of bottom-up structure with fortified wines making up the bulk of the drink's volume."

As an example, Paul sent me the formula for his Fire Insurance Cocktail:

FIRE INSURANCE COCKTAIL

¼ ounce Wray and Nephew overproof rum
¼ ounce Don Ciccio Amaro Tonico Ferro-Kina
½ ounce red wine
¾ ounce London Dry Gin
1¼ ounces Cocchi Americano

Stir the ingredients, pour into a coupe glass, and add an orange twist.

Paul explains, "The original idea came from a drink that I wanted to make from five different fortified wines: Tempus Fugit Kina l'Aero d'Or, Rare Wine Co. New York Malmsey Madeira, Cardamaro, Punt e

Mes, and Cocchi Torino. I figured that these wines had diverse enough flavors that they could theoretically be combined in a way that made all of the flavors stand out against each other. After extensive experimentation and tweaking, the winning combination happened to align with a Fibonacci sequence. This fact obviously piqued my interest, so I started tinkering to see what other combinations worked within this framework."

Keep your eye on Paul MacDonald. He's part of our future.

And so, my friends, I close this chapter resting easy in the knowledge that our craft is in safe hands. The hands of geeks. The hands of scientists. The hands of artists. The hands of artisans. The hands of bartenders.

THE BARTENDER:
DO YOU HAVE WHAT IT TAKES?

The average bartender, despite the slanders of professional moralists, is a man of self-respect and self-possession; a man who excels at a difficult art and is well aware of it; a man who shrinks from ruffianism as he does from uncleanliness; in short, a gentleman. . . . The bartender is one of the most dignified, law abiding, and ascetic of men. He is girt about by a rigid code of professional ethics; his work demands a clear head and a steady hand; he must have sound and fluent conversation; he cannot be drunken or dirty; the slightest dubiousness is quick to exile him to the police force, journalism, the oyster boats or some other Siberia of the broken.

—H. L. MENCKEN,
Baltimore *Evening Sun*, May 11, 1911

ALTHOUGH KNOWING HOW TO MIX a variety of good drinks is required of a professional bartender, if you really want to tend bar, other qualities are also absolutely necessary: how to deal with customers, how to deal with waitpersons, how to deal with the boss, and perhaps most important, how to act professionally while keeping the customers happy, comfortable, and, if need be, entertained.

I have worked just about every job in bars and restaurants. I have managed some decent joints, unclogged toilets, cooked, washed dishes, heaved kegs, and in some very unfortunate circumstances, diners have had to put up with my gross inadequacies as a waiter. For some reason, I just never got the hang of waiting tables. Most of all,

I tended bar. I love tending bar. I love the feeling of power supplied by the two feet of waist-high mahogany, I love being in control of the scene, and I love managing the moods of the customers.

Not everyone is cut out to be a bartender. I worked with a guy in the early 1970s who made money hand over fist as a waiter—he was the most popular guy on the floor. But what he really wanted was to tend bar, and when he was finally given a couple of shifts behind the mahogany, all hell broke loose. There was a subtle difference in his attitude that could be attributed only to his change of vocation. When disputes between customers arose and it was imperative that he intervene, I would watch him deliver the same lines he had heard spew forth from my lips in similar circumstances. But instead of taking notice of the all-powerful bartender, customers would become even more belligerent than they had been before he'd entered the fray—something about his attitude after he became a bartender suggested a wee bit of arrogance that was never received well. If you are new to this craft, you will quickly learn whether or not you are cut out for the job. If not, take heart; it doesn't make you a bad person—and maybe you'll be the best waiter in the world. But if you are a born bartender, take pride; it's a craft that deserves respect. And being paid to do a job you adore is a privilege—it's the dream of every sound-minded man and woman in the world.

In 1973, when I started tending bar in New York, there were very few female bartenders in the city. Bar owners justified their hiring practices by claiming they needed men to carry cases of beer, heave garbage pails full of ice, and deal with unruly customers. The times, however, have changed, thank God, and although there are still probably more men than women behind the stick in Manhattan, we've certainly seen much progress on this front. And of course, today's women bartenders carry cases of beer, heave garbage pails full of ice, and deal with unruly customers just as successfully as any man—as long as they are cut out to be bartenders. The same applies to men—if bartending isn't in their hearts, they won't do a good job. The rule of thumb is this: A good bartender, male or female, can handle any given situation at any given time in any given bar.

A WORD ABOUT THE BOSS

Depending on where you work, some of the guidelines detailed herein may be impossible for you to follow. Every bar has its own rules and regulations, and though I am a strong advocate of returning money to unsatisfied customers and a number of other actions that cost owners money in the short term (but save them a fortune in the long term), your boss may not agree with me. Don't risk losing your job for the sake of following my guidelines; you may, however, want to bring them to the attention of your employer by inviting her to read the pertinent sections of this book and mull over my reasons. In short, apply only the guidelines herein that the rules and regulations of your present employer allow. If she disagrees with my tips for dealing with customers and situations, remember: She's signing your paycheck, not me.

HARASSMENT IN THE WORKPLACE

I'd like to address one of the top-of-mind issues today: sexual harassment in the workplace for both women and men. The hospitality industry is no stranger to these issues, and I believe that the current climate presents us with a significant opportunity to play a major role in changing the way society as a whole behaves. If we all make a determined effort to put a stop to sexual harassment in the workplace, I think that we, alongside people in all industries, can stamp it out completely. At least we can try.

It will take the combined effort of women and men to confront the situation and help end this behavior. Be part of the solution by being strong. Call out your colleagues when you spot improprieties. To all of you then, could I ask that:

- If you see something, say something.
- If you hear something, say something.
- If you feel that you are being harassed, shout out loud.

And don't hesitate to report any incidents of sexual harassment to whoever it takes to bring the incident into the spotlight. If that means consulting a lawyer, then consult a lawyer. If we all pull together right now, I believe we can change society and make a better world.

Go to it.

BASIC PHILOSOPHY AND GUIDELINES

My father, a landlord of distinction who ran three successful pubs in his lifetime, taught me that in order to be a good publican—which requires qualities very similar to those of a bartender—you must have "as many faces as the town hall clock." He didn't mean that you shouldn't be true to yourself and speak your mind when need be. What he was saying was that it's often necessary to react to situations in such a way as to guide the outcome to a pleasant conclusion. And that's something nobody can teach you.

It matters not whether you are a professional bartender or simply a person who makes drinks for guests at your home. Your role is the same. It is that of "Mine Host." Your job is to keep things running smoothly by not only mixing drinks but also guiding the ambience of your surroundings, and this is not always an easy task. Though the majority of this chapter is aimed at the professional bartender, amateur cocktailians, too, can gain by learning everything involved in the lot of a bartender.

It starts by being always well groomed and appropriately dressed, but appropriateness depends on the bar at which you work. Most managers or owners will either provide you with a uniform or tell you that you are expected to wear, say, black pants or a black skirt, a white shirt, and a black tie. In some joints, though, you might be expected to wear a T-shirt and jeans. Just follow the rules and regulations, arrive for work in clean clothes with clean hands, nails, and hair, and if you wear an apron behind the bar—which I happen to think looks just dandy—make sure that you change it as soon as anything spills on it.

Since most guests look upon bartenders with reverence, it is up to the bartenders to prove they are worthy of their position, and this is accomplished only with the utmost diplomacy. But diplomacy isn't achieved by words only; attitude also plays a major role.

You must rule the roost from behind the mahogany; you must also be a benevolent dictator who truly cares about the well-being of your guests. If a situation arises that calls for you to, say, ask someone to leave the bar, you must be able to accomplish this task while causing as little upset as possible. It's of no use whatsoever to become angry or to have any sort of superior attitude, although there are times when dealing with truly unruly people when you must lay down the law. On most occasions, it's far better to take the guest in question to one side, explain why you have decided that it's time for him to leave, and assure him that he can return at a later date, providing he promises not to repeat whatever it is he has done to make you take action. You might also choose to talk to one of his friends—pick whoever seems to be either the leader of the group or the one with the most sense. Take that person to one side, explain the situation, and ask for advice on how to handle the fellow in question. Most people enjoy being put into the role of adviser, and often they will take care of the situation for you by departing with their friend.

A phrase that has helped me on countless occasions is, "I need your help," and you might want to think about using it yourself next time you're trying to convince someone to act a certain way. Asking for help seems to disarm people, and the majority of folks become putty in your hand when you ask them for help.

Tricky situations aside, what do guests expect from bartenders? This really depends on what sort of bar you work in, but generalizations can be drawn. People usually come to bars to have a good time. Sometimes people meet at bars to discuss business or to have serious chats with friends, and if that's the case, they are usually best left alone, save for the times when you must converse with them in order to give good service.

Most of the time, though, it is the bartender's responsibility to "feel out" customers, discover whether or not they want to meet other people, to chat to the bartender about almost any subject under the sun, to be left alone to muse, or maybe to read a book or newspaper. It's a good idea for a bartender to be well informed about current affairs and sports, but this isn't an essential quality if she has other attributes, such as being able to tell a good joke or perhaps perform acts of sleight of hand to keep her customers amused.

Politics and religion are two topics that, in the past, have been classically avoided by bartenders, but I don't believe that in this day and age they should be completely verboten, providing the bartender doesn't blatantly offend a guest. If you are completely ignorant about any particular topic—as I am when it comes to sports—you might want to think about playing on that fact in one way or another. When I tended bar in the 1970s and my schedule called for me to be behind the stick when the then usual Monday Night Football Game was on television, I used to ask a fellow bartender for a comment or two that would be appropriate to use during the game. Then when I said something seemingly astute—Bradshaw's throwing well with that bad elbow, huh?—my regular customers would look up in amazement, then burst out laughing. They knew I had no idea what I was talking about.

Similarly, I was always a speedy bartender, mainly because I was well organized, knew where everything was, and had trained my left hand to perform some jobs while my right hand was busy doing something else. But I was never any good at fancy movements behind the bar, and I'd never dare to try juggling bottles, or even catching ice cubes flicked into the air with a bar spoon—something that many other bartenders find easy. To compensate for this lack of hand/eye coordination, I would flick ice cubes into the air then simply walk away without even attempting to catch it. It went down pretty well.

Eavesdropping on guests' conversations is inevitable when you're behind the stick, and this is a good way to figure out how to entertain specific people. Of course, on the one hand, if they are talking about something personal, it's best to leave them alone. If, on the other hand, a couple happen to be talking about, say, a movie they've seen, you can usually jump in and add your comments about it if you've seen it, or about any of the actors in the film if you have something interesting to say. You just have to know when it's appropriate to volunteer your two cents' worth and when it's best to leave people alone.

When you are busy you will have to prioritize, putting specific duties in logical order: The waiter is asking for drinks, the telephone is ringing, new bar customers have just arrived, and a couple of regulars are asking for refills. What do you do first? The golden rule in this situation is: Make sure everyone knows that you are aware they need your attention. Tell your customers and the waiter that you'll "be with them shortly," answer the phone (since it's not going to stop ringing), and make the call as short as possible—"Painter's Gallery Bar, hold please"—and then serve drinks to people in the order in which they were placed. If your regular customers are understanding, they'll sometimes wait patiently while you serve new customers who might otherwise leave in search of a drink elsewhere. And although it might not be the policy for the wait staff to tip you, it's your job to serve them as quickly as possible—they've got to make a living, too, and you must always think about putting as much money in that register as possible in order to keep the boss happy.

Having prioritized that theoretical scenario, though, I should mention that situations vary from one day to another, and a good bartender must be able to assess the situation and act accordingly. For instance, perhaps the regulars at the bar have had enough to drink in your estimation; you might decide to pretend you haven't noticed that they need drinks in the hope that they might decide to go home without your having to confront them. A good bartender should be able to act appropriately in all situations.

In order for you to be able to serve drinks speedily, every bottle and every piece of equipment behind the bar must be in a predesignated spot. That way you know exactly where to go to prepare any drink. Usually the entire team of bartenders at a bar will agree on where to keep what, but some bartenders have specific idiosyncrasies and you might find, when taking over the bar, that a particular tool is not where you usually keep it. To avoid this sort of occurrence, make a thorough check of the bar before you allow your predecessor to leave the area.

If you are the first bartender of the day, make sure you arrive at work in ample time to stock your bar, if necessary, and to ice down bottled beers, cut fresh garnishes, and check that everything is in its place before you open. Daytime bartenders often buy a selection of newspapers for their customers; that always worked well for me, so I highly recommend it.

You should never spend excessive time at the service end of the bar chatting to a member of the wait staff. If you do, neither of you is doing your job properly. However, it's also important to have a good rapport with the servers. They need you to make drinks for them, and you need them to bring food for your customers and various and sundry other items, such as fruit from the kitchen if you suddenly find that you're running low.

Along with being amicable with the wait staff, you should be able to get along well with the manager, the owner, the chef, the line cooks, the dishwasher, the porter, and anyone else who works alongside you. This doesn't mean you need to be best buddies with all these people, but it's imperative that you have a pleasant relationship with all of them. To tend bar properly, you must be a team player.

If you're a professional bartender, in all probability you're going to have to handle cash, and with this in mind, you should remember never to allow anyone other than the manager or owner behind your bar. You are in charge of the register, and you might be required to make up any shortages at the end of your shift. (This is illegal in some states, but if you're consistently short, you probably won't keep your job for long anyway.) Good bartenders, showing an orderly work ethic, tend to keep all the bills in the register facing the same way; they also take responsibility for cash belonging to customers left on the bar. I believe that when somebody's money is stolen, the bartender should replace it from his tip cup.

Consistently walking up and down the bar—mainly to ensure that it's spotless and clear of money—also gives every guest access to you, which is of utmost importance. Bartenders must keep their eyes on glasses, asking guests if they would like a refill when their drinks are getting low. And they must keep their ears open at all times to make sure that conversations are amicable, and that no one guest is annoying another. But remember that, although the woman at the end of the bar has more than half a drink in her glass, and she might seem as though she needs nothing from you at all, there's always a chance she might want to see a menu, or perhaps she needs to ask you where the restrooms are, so you'll want to make yourself available to her, and to every other guest at your bar, as much as possible.

Discretion is another quality that's needed in a good bartender. Guests tend to tell bartenders secrets they wouldn't share with their best friends, and it's imperative that the bartender keep that information to himself. There really should be a law that protects bartenders, the same way that priests and doctors are covered when authorities demand information about their parishioners and patients. And if a telephone call comes through for someone at the bar or at a table, the bartender should always put the call on hold, first saying that he will check to see if that particular customer is in the establishment;

then he must ask whether or not the guest wishes to take the call. Also, if a customer tells you that he was never at the bar on a particular evening, he's right—he was never there (unless, of course, law-enforcement agencies are involved).

In states where it is legal, many bars have a buy-back system wherein the bartender is allowed to give away, say, every fourth drink. It's important that the bartender not abuse this privilege by giving away too many drinks—especially to customers who tip well. This is a common mistake, since it can cause some guests to believe they've "bought you," which can lead to trouble down the line. That said, you should always make sure the customer is aware that the drink is on the house, since it often produces an extra dollar or two in your tip cup at the end of the night.

Unless you know both parties very well, if somebody wants to buy another customer at the bar or at a table a drink, you should always ask the intended recipient whether or not he or she wants to accept the offer. Sometimes people don't want to feel obliged to the buyer. They might not want to enter into a situation wherein they then have to reciprocate, or the buyer could be making advances to someone, and is using the drink as an invitation.

It's the bartender's job to make sure no customer enters into an unwanted conversation with another, and you can do this only by watching body language and/or eavesdropping on conversations. If the seemingly unwanted guest goes to the bathroom, over to the jukebox, or anywhere else out of earshot, take the opportunity to ask whomever you believe he is bothering if you should intervene. Otherwise, you'll have to ask the offending party to step down the bar to a spot where you can talk to him privately and deal with the situation. There are few rules appropriate to every situation. The only advice I can offer here is that you shouldn't approach the offending guest in front of other customers, thereby embarrassing him; and it's usually a good idea to inform another member of staff of what you intend to do, just in case an argument breaks out and you find yourself in need of backup.

Remember, too, that you represent the management and owners of the bar, and therefore you should be prepared to enforce any rules they have set down. If they don't want to serve guests wearing tank tops, then obviously you shouldn't serve people wearing tank tops.

You need to get a feel for what kind of bar the management wants it to be and do your best to make it that way. If you're tending bar in a neighborhood joint, for instance, you will probably greet your guests in a casual manner and use their first names. At a tony restaurant, however, you might be required to say, "Good evening, sir"—or "madam"—when a guest approaches the bar.

Many people are attracted to the life of a bartender because it puts them in close proximity to alcohol. Don't fall into this trap. Although a nondrinking bartender is always desirable, I believe it's useless to tell bartenders not to drink at all while on duty. A good rule of thumb is that you should never consume more than, say, one or two drinks during an eight-hour shift, and then only if this is allowed by the management. The reason I don't think that bartenders should be banned from drinking entirely while behind the bar is that if a bartender wants a drink, he will have one, and if he must wait until the manager's back is turned, he's likely to have, say, a quick shot of tequila. Bartenders who are allowed the odd drink at work are more likely to sip slowly on a beer.

In short, a good bartender should be the captain of his ship; the master of making moods; the dean of diplomacy; as honest as an Arctic summer day is long; as organized as a filing clerk; as punctual as the winter solstice; as neat and tidy as a seasoned librarian; congenial, amiable, and sociable on all occasions; as quick to make decisions as a broker on the floor of the stock exchange; the very soul of discretion; a friend to those who need one (if only while on duty); and a dispenser of sound advice. Ideally, he'll have a little psychic ability, too. And never forget: The demeanor of the bartender is, perhaps, way more important than his cocktailian skills.

THREE WISE BARTENDERS

MANY QUALITIES are needed in a bartender, and some are difficult, if not impossible, to define without simply telling stories about how certain people react to different situations when they are behind the stick. Here I detail three such stories in the hope that they will serve to point out some of the individual traits that go toward making a good bartender great.

CASE STUDY NO. 1

Let's first look at Dale DeGroff, an undisputed cocktailian master, whom I saw in action many times when he ruled the roost at New York's Rainbow Room back in the nineties.

Behind the Promenade Bar at the Rainbow Room, Dale was poetry in motion. His body was fluid, his methodology classic, his demeanor perfect for the environment. When he was behind the bar, usually with other bartenders to back him up, all eyes were always on Dale. His drinks, of course, were always perfect.

Now cut to Dale at work at Bemelman's Bar on February 22, 2002. The room was packed. This was one of the opening-night parties thrown after the joint was remodeled. Dale was consulting with the hotel and had brought in Libation Goddess Audrey Saunders as director of beverages. Audrey was working the floor, and Dale was working the stick with a couple of old-timers who weren't used to the bar being so busy. I watched from a couple of yards back from the bar.

Dale kept his head down. He made no eye contact until he was ready to serve whomever was next. He was quick. Boy, was he quick. And he wasn't behind a bar that he'd worked for years, so his hands couldn't automatically reach out to whatever ingredient he needed next. The moment of truth came when he completed an order and served a drink. For a few short seconds that seemed like an unhurried eternity, Dale's eyes met the customer's eyes. The drink was perfect, and as he added the final touch—usually his signature flamed orange zest—he held the customer in the palm of his hand; then he moved to the next in line. I'd never seen Dale under so much pressure before. He's a consummate sophisticated cocktailian bartender, every bit as much at home when the bar's six deep as he is when he has time to exchange leisurely banter with his customers.

CASE STUDY NO. 2

Early in the year 2000 I found myself outside the Village Idiot, a bar on Manhattan's Fourteenth Street, with about forty-five minutes to kill before an appointment. I'd heard about this joint, so I thought I'd check it out.

Behind the bar was an attractive blond woman in her mid-twenties wearing low-cut jeans and a tiny tank top, and behind her, dozens of bras decorated the backbar. Country-and-western music blared from the jukebox as I yelled for a Manhattan "with bitters." I always order that way since so few bartenders in the twenty-first century know that the drink should always get bitters.

The bartender started pouring the bourbon, then stopped midway through the pour to tell me, "We ain't got no bitters." "Okay," I said, "I'll have it without bitters." She proved herself a little when she then told me that she was quite aware that the drink wasn't as good without bitters, but after pouring the rest of the bourbon into the mixing glass she then informed me that the bar "ain't got no vermouth," either. I told her I'd have a bourbon on the rocks, and she informed me that that was what I'd wanted all along.

Two minutes later, a couple of guys next to me ordered shooters, and the bartender started mixing something over ice, and placed three shot glasses on the bar—she'd decided to join them. Her moment of glory came when she strained the drinks, not through a strainer but through her fingers and into the shot glasses, then clinked her glass with the customers' glasses and shot it back in one.

That bartender was every bit as professional as anyone I've ever seen behind the stick. That's what the Village Idiot was all about. She was representing her bar to the nth degree.

CASE STUDY NO. 3

I first met Norman Bukofzer, the bartender at New York's Ritz-Carlton hotel on Central Park South, in the early 1990s, and I was immediately impressed not only by his cocktailian skills but also by his warm hospitality and his ability to manage the bar and the customers as though he were conducting a symphony orchestra. Our only problem with Norman was that he insisted on calling me Mister Regan. Nobody gets away with that.

I pleaded with Norman to use my first name, and he always agreed to do so: "Okay, Mister Regan, I'll remember in the future," he'd say with a wicked grin on his face. Eventually Norman explained that he had a reputation for remembering all his customers' names, and that if he had to learn first names as well as surnames, his workload would be doubled, so I backed down.

All would have been well with this had I not introduced Norman to Roy Finamore, who was the editor of the first edition of this book, some six months later; Mister Finamore joined the ranks of thousands addicted to Norman's wit and his cocktailian skills. A few months thereafter I was informed that Norman had taken to using Roy's first name at the bar, and I was livid. This called for action. I made the pilgrimage to Norman's bar.

"I hear that Roy Finamore is a regular here now."

"That's right, Mister Regan, he's here three or four times a week."

"And what do you call him, Norman?"

"I call him Roy."

"And why is that, Norman?"

He leaned over the bar until our noses almost met.

"Just to piss you off."

It had taken Norman months to set up this one glorious moment. In my opinion, I was looking into the eyes of Manhattan's best bartender.

A FEW EASY LESSONS

The one rule that all bartenders must learn is this: Nothing is written in stone. Every situation is different, different customers must be treated in different ways, and good bartenders should be able to assess all situations and deal with them appropriately. In the following scenarios, I offer some guidance about how to deal with some specific situations, but the guidelines won't work every time, simply because there's an infinite range of variations. I can only tell you some tricks of the trade that have worked for me in the past.

BEING EARLY FOR WORK CAN REALLY PAY OFF

If you are going to be unavoidably late for your shift, you should let the management know as soon as possible. If you call, explain your situation, and give an estimated time of arrival, the manager will know what to do about the situation, whereas if you don't make contact, he might call another bartender to come in and you could lose your job. Communication is key in all aspects of tending bar. But showing up early for your shift can help in more ways than one.

I was always a "be prepared" kind of bartender. If I was working the day shift, my bar was always completely set up at least fifteen minutes before opening time, giving me a chance to sit down with a cup of coffee and relax before the onslaught. As a nighttime bartender,

I always liked to get a *feel* for the crowd before I set foot behind the stick. It really pays to be prepared.

One bartender I knew in the late 1970s had a wonderful habit of showing up for his evening shift at least half an hour before it began. He would count his bank, make sure the "day guy" had set up his bar properly, and then he would join a couple of customers and buy them drinks before stepping behind the stick. This turned out to be a brilliant ploy. He usually bought drinks for the best tippers at the bar, and after he'd treated them to a drink, they felt obliged to stay for a while after he started his shift. They also felt special because their bartender wanted to socialize with them outside of work hours. His following grew and grew.

IF YOU THINK A CUSTOMER MIGHT HAVE HAD ENOUGH TO DRINK, YOU ARE PROBABLY RIGHT

Oh, the number of times I got this wrong when I first started tending bar. Of course, that was back in the 1970s, when people weren't quite as uptight about "overconsumption," and I was in Manhattan, where most people didn't drive to and from bars. In these more enlightened days, however, it's imperative that you don't serve customers who are already three sheets to the wind. The fact is that you can't afford to serve people who are even slightly inebriated, and it's always best to err on the side of caution.

THE CUSTOMER IS ALWAYS RIGHT—THE FIRST TIME

This is a guideline that sometimes involves swallowing your pride—but always getting the last laugh. Here's a scenario: A guy complains that his hamburger is overcooked; he ordered it medium-rare. You take a look at the burger and see a nice bright pink interior, no sign of overcooked meat at all. This guy is wrong, but do you really want to start an argument? It's only a burger, after all. Here's what to do: Tell the customer that you will order another burger, and inform him that you are going to ask for a rare burger. Explain that the chef always cooks medium-rare burgers to that exact stage of doneness, so if he ever again orders a medium-rare burger in your joint, he should try to remember what to expect. On the first offense, don't ever tell the customer he is wrong; instead, blame the chef, blame the owner, blame the cat if you must, but never argue with the customer.

If, a week later, this guy pulls the same stunt again, it's time to act. You have two choices, and your decision should be based on exactly how much damage this customer is doing to your bar scene. If he is complaining loudly and telling everyone around him about the terrible chef or the lousy bartender, you may just want to get rid of him immediately. Do as a good scout would: Be prepared. Take money from the register or your tip cup to pay him back for his burger and the last drink he ordered, and have it at the ready. Now try to get him off his bar stool and down to the service area, or come out from behind the bar and ask if you can talk to him alone. The important aspect of this act is to make sure this guy isn't losing face in front of others—that will make him feel compelled to save face by creating a scene. Explain that this bar clearly isn't right for him (not that *he* isn't right for the bar), push the money into his hand while telling him that his burger and last drink were on the house, and ask him to leave. Keep in mind that you're probably not the first person to oust him from a bar, so there's a good possibility that he'll be out of your hair quite quickly.

The second option is to wait until this grouse is about to leave of his own accord. Then try to get him out of hearing range of the other customers and explain that, in your opinion, since he isn't happy with your bar, he shouldn't return. If he argues that he wants to come back, you must pull the plug and tell him that you will refuse to serve him again. Whichever tack you take, always make sure other members of staff are around in case the customer makes a scene or turns violent.

HOW TO TREAT A BAD TIPPER

Bad tippers can be really infuriating. You call them sir, you call them madam, you make sure they get a buy-back at the appropriate time, you give them a horse that wins the Belmont Stakes, but still, when it comes time to pay the piper, they leave you next to nothing. How to cure them of this habit? Well, I wouldn't suggest spilling drinks over their best suits, although I've known bartenders who have tried it. You should always keep in mind that even though these ne'er-do-wells don't put any money in your pocket, they are spending some hard-earned bucks at your bar. And those dollars are keeping your boss happy. In turn, your boss lets you keep your job and the bar stays open. It's long-term thinking, but it's better than pounding the pavement looking for a new gig every six months.

This is how you should treat bad tippers: Exactly the same way you treat everyone else. Maybe they'll come around and maybe they won't, but your tip cup is, after all, a result of swings and roundabouts. One guy stiffs you, the next guy leaves you five bucks for pouring him a beer. It all evens out at the end of the shift.

HOW TO DEAL WITH UNWANTED INVITATIONS

I have met some of my favorite people while tending bar, and a few of them have gone on to become true friends. But such occurrences are few and far between. Unfortunately, many bar customers want to be the bartender's best friend, and this can lead to some embarrassing situations. On top of this, the people who want you to come over for dinner or spend the weekend at their country house are very often people with few other friends, and there's usually a good reason for that. You could, of course, invent a house policy that prevents you from socializing with customers, but be sure to inform the boss and the rest of the staff if you do this—the customer is bound to ask about it. It's probably best just to have an automatic excuse for every day of the week: Saturday? Sorry, I have people coming over for dinner myself. Next Wednesday? No, it's my yoga night. Two weeks from Thursday? Let me look in my diary at home and I'll get back to you.

The truth is, there's no really good method of getting these people off your back. Remember, the most persistent ones—those who never take the hint—are probably lonely souls who desperately need some company. Treat them kindly. Let them down gently. They need a little T.L.C. How to deal with unwanted advances: Wear a wedding band at all times—whether you're married or single.

THINGS TO DO DURING SLOW PERIODS

Polish bottles and glassware; write memos to the boss with suggestions for improving service or brands of liquor, beer, or wine that have been requested but your bar doesn't stock; clean the bar and backbar; check your backup inventory; cut garnishes; make Bloody Mary mix; wash the pourers from the liquor bottles. In short, make sure that you've done everything possible to ready the bar for the next shift. (If you don't, it will come back to haunt you.) Things you shouldn't do during slow periods: Read a newspaper or book; sit on the backbar or on a bar stool (I've seen it done); make phone calls; drink.

HOW TO MAKE SURE THAT NEW CUSTOMERS COME BACK

You should always win new customers one at a time, so go the extra yard whenever the opportunity arises. If someone's new to your bar, ask him about himself, get him talking, find out his interests, and, if possible, introduce him to a regular customer whom you think he might get along with.

If a customer asks where the nearest fabric store is, don't say that you don't know; instead, ask other members of staff or other customers at the bar. If you have time, use your phone to find what you need.

If you work in, say, a trendy lounge bar and the customers are new to your neighborhood, tell them about other bars and restaurants nearby: the nearest sports bar, the best Chinese restaurant, the best pizza place. They aren't going to come to your joint every night of the week, but if you help them get to know their new surroundings, they're bound to remember you and what you did for them. And if you know bartenders at any of the other restaurants you recommend, tell these new guys those bartenders' names, adding, "Tell them I sent you." The other bartenders are bound to reciprocate.

You can also advise them about the best dry cleaner, liquor store, locksmith, and myriad other services available in your neck of the woods. Rest assured that you'll see a lot of these new customers in the future.

HOW TO SEAT PEOPLE

Bar customers usually sit wherever they wish, but if you see the opportunity to introduce two people who have similar interests or similar demeanors, there's nothing wrong with saying, "Come sit down here, there's someone I want you to meet." (One bartender did that for me once, but it turned out that he didn't want to introduce me to anyone—he was just making sure that I didn't sit next to the bore at the other end of the bar. I've never forgotten him for that.)

HOW TO DEAL WITH ANGRY CUSTOMERS

If it's at all possible, never allow a customer to leave your bar angry. If somebody complains that there's not enough liquor in his drink, pour a little extra into his glass while explaining that, in the future, you'll only be able to give him your standard pour. He might not return, but he probably won't give you any bad press, either. Whatever the situation, even if it means losing face, you should always try to pacify, not further anger an upset customer. See page 86 for more suggestions about dealing with anger.

HOW TO DEAL WITH PROBLEMS IN THE BATHROOM

From time to time you'll probably hear that someone is ill in the bathroom, and you might have to investigate. *Always* take another member of the staff with you. If the bathroom is reserved for the opposite sex, bring a member of the opposite sex with you. There could be someone waiting to accost you in there, or it could be a scam in which you'll be accused of some impropriety, and if there are no witnesses you'll find yourself in a sticky situation.

HOW TO DEAL WITH MONEY

Nobody wants to be accused of being wrong when it comes to making change or totaling a bill, but mistakes do happen. They must be dealt with in the most delicate manner. If somebody at the bar is paying cash, be it a customer or a waitperson, take the money from his hands and announce exactly how much he owes and how much he is handing to you: "That's fifteen fifty out of a twenty, sir." This way you have both agreed upon how much money is changing hands, and you are giving the customer an opportunity to disagree before you proceed to the register. When you hand back the change, clearly state how much you are giving him: "Four fifty change out of a twenty, sir."

There's an old trick played by grifters (you can see it in the movie *The Grifters*, but I've also had it played on me on more than one occasion) in which a customer will get your attention by waving a twenty-dollar bill in the air, but after you make his drink, he'll hand you a ten. You might make change for a twenty, remembering having seen it previously. If you make change for a ten, the grifter will say, "I gave you a twenty—don't you remember?" And nine times out of ten, you will lose ten bucks. But if you follow the instructions given earlier, the grifter will always lose.

In another moneymaking scheme, a con man at a busy bar will ask to see a menu as soon as he sidles up to the bar. Then, using the menu as a shield, he will steal money from the bar while the customer it belongs to is locked in conversation and you are occupied serving other customers. Keep an eye on anyone who asks to see a menu without first purchasing a drink. Most times the person will turn out to be an innocent prospective customer who merely wants to peruse the bar's bill of fare, but sometimes it will turn out to be a thief.

When people run a tab (ask to pay at the end of the evening rather than paying for each drink when it's served), it's best to ask for a credit card, which you will keep behind the bar until they are ready to leave. The bar in which you work should have rules about this procedure—ask the management about them. A problem sometimes occurs, though, when it comes time to pay and customers disagree about the amount of their bill. Perhaps they forgot that they sent drinks to a couple of friends down the bar, or maybe they just don't realize they had four Margaritas, not three. Whatever the case, the situation must be handled with discretion.

You can start by going back over the evening and trying to pinpoint events that will jog their memory: "Remember, Bill and Jane came in about an hour ago and you sent them drinks" or "You ordered one drink when you came in, another when you got your burger, a third when you were talking to Alice, and I've just served you a fourth." If they still disagree, first check with a manager or refer to the house rules. In my opinion, though, it's best to go along with the customer—but only once. When this happened to me and the situation involved a particularly angry customer, I offered to disregard the bill entirely, but informed the person in question that in the future I would expect him to pay for drinks as he went along. He ended up paying the bill. I don't suggest that you use this tactic every time, but there are occasions when it might come in handy. If you back down and allow the customer to "beat you" over a couple of drinks, when you serve him in the future, inform him how many drinks he's had every time you serve him: "That's your third," and so forth.

MINDFUL BARTENDING

Almost anyone can learn to mix drinks accurately and fast. That is the least of it. I have always believed success behind the bar comes from an ability to understand the man or woman I am serving, to enter into his joys or woes, make him feel the need of me as a person rather than a servant.

—Morrill Cody,

This Must Be the Place: Memoirs of Jimmie the Barman, 1937

You might hear the term *mindfulness* thrown around quite often. It's associated with Buddhism, though atheists, agnostics, Christians, Hindus, Jews, and Muslims practice mindfulness. In fact, plenty of bartenders have been masters of it for years without even knowing it. Though I don't purport to be a qualified teacher of mindfulness, I merely want to pass along what I've been learning in recent years, and inspire bartenders everywhere to begin a personal practice that works for them (see page 83), both behind the bar and as part of your daily life.

The idea of applying mindfulness to the job of a bartender came to me when I was attending mindfulness workshops, and it dawned on me that, since bartenders are very often working in a state of near chaos, and because we constantly have to communicate with guests, servers, kitchen staff, bosses, delivery people, and so many others, anyone working behind the bar would find this practice to be beneficial. I've given mindfulness presentations to bartenders in Moscow, London, Paris, and Beirut, as well as at my Cocktails in the Country workshops in the Hudson Valley and in various cities around the United States; the feedback I've gotten over the past few years has been very positive. I'm pretty sure that every person on the face of the earth, no matter what he or she does to put bread on the table, would benefit from practicing mindfulness, and I'm also sure that it works very well indeed for the men and women who serve drinks for a living.

Mindfulness, in my opinion, is like a tailored suit. The suit has to have lapels, but you get to decide how wide they are. Trousers are mandatory, but cuffs are your call. Similarly, everyone can pick and choose what suits him or her best on the path to mindfulness. Take a look, consider your options, and go with whatever you're comfortable with. A little mindfulness is better than none at all, I believe. It's not easy, and should you decide to try it out, know that you will never achieve 100 percent enlightenment, but that's not the point. Above all, though, no matter what anyone tells you, don't ever take things too seriously. We're here to have fun and you can't be happy and so serious at the same time!

Mindfulness, when applied to tending bar, is an approach to the job that entails being totally aware of everything you are doing, being cognizant of everything that is going on around you, and tuning in to all of your guests' wants and needs. A mindful bartender both trusts his intuition and sets his intentions on being in the service of his customers. He is primarily focused on what the customer in front of him is doing or saying, or upon the drink he is making, but he is also aware of what's going on at the other end of the bar, as well as in the entire restaurant. He keeps tabs on the atmosphere of the place, and he constantly monitors the events, actions, and people that might affect the mood at the bar or within the restaurant. A mindful bartender pays attention to the personal preferences of his guests, and he makes each person's drinks accordingly. The bartender leaves his personal baggage at the door because he knows he can't be fully attentive to customers if he's obsessing about the fight he just had with his sister or if he's making mental notes about everything he needs to do tomorrow morning before his spin class.

TUNING INTO YOUR INTUITION

Do you remember the last time your gut told you not to serve someone another drink but you went ahead and served that person anyway? You regretted it, right? Have you ever walked into a room where a couple has been arguing, and although they "snap out of it" and make like nothing was going down, you could feel the tension in the atmosphere? Have you ever gotten the feeling that someone is looking at you, and when you turned your head, sure enough, you saw someone with his eyes glued to you?

If you answered yes to any of those questions, then I think we can agree that intuition definitely exists, even though it's impossible to measure. Taking notice of how we feel about serving a drink to someone who might have already had enough, and acting on that feeling by refusing service, for instance, will ultimately lead to you feeling happier than you would have felt had you handed him another drink. There might be a bit of a scene if the prospective customer becomes belligerent, but it won't be anywhere near as bad as it could get if he keeps on drinking.

While you're casting your eyes over anyone at the bar on a regular basis, and the tables in the restaurant if you can see them, try to find time to really look at the people there. Not only will you become aware of who needs your attention, but you'll also glean clues to help you understand what's going down at the bar, and in the restaurant. It's fairly easy to understand people's body language, and by trusting the vibes you get as you look around, all sorts of problems can be avoided. The vibes might not be as strong as they are when you walk into a room right after a heated argument, but they are there all the same, and it's not too hard to tap into them.

You can also use your intuition along with your powers of observation to try to empathize with your guests, which can help you better serve them. Sometimes this can be very obvious. Two women talking about hiring a new office manager are at the bar to talk business, while the man buying the bar a drink to toast the birth of his new baby is obviously there to celebrate. But how about the rest of your guests? Why did they come to your bar tonight? If you can discover their motivations for being there, you can treat them appropriately, thus customizing their experience at your bar. You'll probably be protective of the two businesswomen by not trying to make small talk with them, and being on the lookout for anyone who approaches them with that sort of thing in mind. And the man with a new baby will love you for letting him buy the bar a drink, then giving him a nice cognac on the house along with a big smile and hearty congratulations.

A mindfulness practice can help you better tune into your intuition and empathy by clearing all other distractions, so you can hear that inner voice. You must connect to yourself, becoming aware of your thoughts, trying not to judge others, and choosing carefully how you speak with others. If you want to reap the full benefits of mindfulness, treat the dishwasher the same way you treat your guests at the bar, and treat the homeless guy down the street the same way, too. Living a mindful life is a very satisfying venture. Those of you who find this sort of thing difficult, though, needn't fret. Relax, make an effort with the tips that follow, and it is likely you'll find your efforts rewarded.

What is intuition? It is tuition from within. Learn your lessons well.

TEN MINUTES OF HUSH AND WONDER

[The cocktail hour] is the violet hour, the hour of hush and wonder, when the affectations glow and valor is reborn, when the shadows deepen along the edge of the forest and we believe that, if we watch carefully, at any moment we may see the unicorn.

—Bernard DeVoto, *The Hour*, 1948

In 1973, when I first started tending bar in New York, I was more than a little intimidated by my customers. I was a small-town guy from a seaside resort in the northwest of England, and New Yorkers seemed to be larger than life. New Yorkers had so much confidence in themselves. They were far faster on their feet than the customers at pubs in the U.K. that I'd left in order to start a new life in the Big Apple. And of course, once they "sussed out" that I was little cowed by them, they took advantage of that at every opportunity.

Every night, then, when I got to work at Drake's Drum, the joint on the Upper East Side that gave me my first break, I was nervous about interacting with people and having to be in control of the bar. After weeks of dreading work, something had to be done, and so I started to arrive at least an hour before my shift began. I sat at a table, ordered dinner, and refused to let anyone join me. As I quietly ate, I composed myself so that once I got behind the bar, I would be ready to face the crowd. When I finished eating I would continue to sit alone, absorbing the mood of the bar and telling myself that I was going to have a great night.

I was, in effect, meditating and setting my intentions, though I wasn't really conscious of that at the time. I just knew it worked. Customers no longer intimidated me, and as a result, I gained their respect. Soon I loved being the center of attention behind the bar, and although the customers still teased me (and still do, which is how I like to be treated), they did it with love, and I played along, zinging them back whenever it seemed appropriate.

In order to be mindful, then, think about taking a little time—five to ten minutes should do it—to sit quietly on your own and set your intentions for the night ahead. If you can't do this at work, then do it before you leave home. You can set a timer for five, ten, or fifteen minutes to bring you out of your meditation, or you can simply return to the physical world when you feel the time is right. There's no need to sit in a lotus position, though it's easier if you are comfortably seated. Close your eyes and pay attention to your breath, becoming aware of your body and your surroundings. Feel the cool air coming into your nostrils, and the warm breath leaving your mouth or your nose. Think, "I'm breathing in. I'm breathing out."

When your mind drifts, as it inevitably will, and you start fretting, "Oh shit, it's Thursday night and that means that asshole Sam will be at the bar later on," try to avoid holding onto the thought. In your mind's eye, put the thought into a cloud, and watch it float out of view. Then go back to repeating, "I'm breathing in. I'm breathing out." Know that everyone's mind wanders during meditation; the point is to keep bringing it back to the present moment.

When you open your eyes, set your intentions for your shift. While there's nothing wrong with wanting to make lots of money, that end may naturally follow if you focus on helping others and bringing a little sunshine to everyone you interact with while you're behind the bar.

Meditation, or stillness, isn't the only way of anticipating a shift, and if you just can't get your head around the concept, other forms of preparation might work for you. When I've been alone in a bar, setting up for the first shift of the day, I've often found that playing the right playlist at the right volume can help center me. For me, loud music *can be* a form of meditation: the music blocks out that constant conversation in my mind, and I'm able to focus on the night ahead.

With practice, you'll quickly notice that you're better able to cope with whatever comes your way during your hours behind the bar. You'll deal with potentially troublesome customers with more empathy, you'll treat your co-workers with a better sense of camaraderie, and you might even end up understanding why your boss can be so negative at times. (She's just not very mindful, right?) The practice of meditation, no matter how you go about it, and the setting of good, honorable intentions will serve you well. And you'll see a difference in your work and life in a very short time, indeed.

THOUGHTFUL COMMUNICATION

Communication is integral to the bartender's job. It's of the utmost importance that we make a real connection when we interact with others. Try to remember that communication is a two-way street, and listening is every bit as important as talking. Mindful people listen intently to what's being said to them, and they make sure that the person who is talking to them is aware that they are being heard.

When you enter into a conversation with a guest, say, even if the purpose is just to take an order for drinks, always look into the eyes of your guests as they are speaking to you. Even if the guest is looking elsewhere, pay attention to the eyes. More often than not, this will cause the customer to turn her head to look at you as she feels your gaze. When she realizes that you're focusing all your attention on her, your relationship with this customer will change for the better.

Think, too, about how you communicate with your co-workers—not just the other bartenders but also the boss, wait staff, chef, and dishwasher. When you greet your co-workers, providing there's time to do this, look into their eyes, ask them how they are doing, and *wait for a reply.* Listening to people's answers is integral to mindfulness. It's also important to understand that in many cases, people whose hourly rate is minimal at best might feel invisible while they are at work. They are many times taken for granted, with few people giving them the time of day. Mindful bartenders who make an effort to communicate consciously with these people are usually rewarded immediately with a look that tells them *thanks for taking the time to notice me.*

Bartenders who communicate intentionally with their co-workers typically end up fostering healthy work environments. The thoughtfulness becomes infectious, and it soon travels throughout the staff, resulting in a true team of people who care about each other's well-being. And there can be practical, reciprocal advantages to this sort of behavior, too. If a bartender is truly in the weeds, she can perhaps count on the staff to help her out, such as the waiter to bring ice, the dishwasher to the store for lemons, and the line cook to cut twists.

ATTENTIVENESS TO ANGER

Everyone in the world experiences anger, both in themselves and in witnessing other people who are angry. This is true no matter what you do for a living, and anger can occur more easily in bar situations than, say, in coffee shops where no alcohol is involved. In my experience, anger tends to be based in fear. When someone gets angry with someone else, it's possibly because the individual fears that he is powerless in a particular situation. And that might be true, but it's nothing to be afraid of. Perhaps the other person has the upper hand *in this particular situation*, and if that person is allowed to feel like he has won, then the situation will likely deescalate and right itself very nicely indeed. If, for example, you find yourself angry when getting stiffed by a customer, then is it possible that your anger rises from a fear of being disrespected rather than a fear of becoming penniless? After all, more than likely by the end of your workweek your tips will have evened out. Plus, if you can pull yourself back from the anger, guess what? You won't be angry. And not being angry feels real good.

When people do things to upset us, it throws them off balance a little when we don't respond with fire. Next time a pompous asshole treats you like his personal manservant, then, play Jeeves to his Wooster and see how he reacts. I'll bet you he starts to lighten up pretty quickly. And never forget that being angry with someone doesn't hurt the person in the slightest. It just hurts you.

Even if you manage not to get angry, you will most certainly come up against angry customers at work, and you've got to know how to deal with someone else's anger. When one guy accidentally spills a drink onto another guy, the one with the wet shirt will often get very angry. This sort of thing can lead to fights, but if you understand, as I noted earlier, that his anger is a result of his fear that he'll look like an asshole if he doesn't stand up for himself, then you'll find the situation easier to handle. "Excuse me guys, but this sort of thing happens almost every night in here. Think we could put it all behind us if I pay for the dry cleaning?" is the sort of phrasing that works like a charm. Humor works like a charm, too; one Manhattan bartender I know will point a banana at the two people who are about to erupt: "Don't make me use this," he says. Who could stop themselves from laughing at such a silly scenario? Whenever you witness anger, first ask yourself, *What is this person afraid of?* Once you identify the answer, you're way ahead of the game when it comes to quelling the situation.

Finally, it's good to know that there's a secret to never getting angry, and in order to tap into it all you need to understand is this: Just as anger is a result of fear, so is happiness rooted in love. If you approach every situation that goes down in your bar with the intention of seeing past what might appear to be nasty, and understanding instead how love can prevail, then you'll always end up guiding the situation to the happiest ending possible.

THE THEORY OF MIXOLOGY

Cocktail-drinking has a peculiar charm of its own, which lifts it above drinking as otherwise practiced. Your confirmed cocktail-drinker is not to be confused with the ordinary sot.

—*The Living Age*, Volume 155, 1882

WHAT'S IN A NAME?

In the spring of 2000, a contestant appeared on *Jeopardy!* who claimed to have invented chili. Thankfully, he wasn't serious. This man was an amateur chef who dabbled in the kitchen, and one day he had thrown together a few ingredients, thoughtfully marrying spices, meat, beans, and a few other edibles he had lying around until he thought that he'd concocted a flavorful "stew." His wife was called into the kitchen to taste his new creation. Her reaction: "It's good. But it's chili." Such is the way with cocktails and mixed drinks.

The recent past has brought a plethora of new creations to the world of the bartender. It's possible to find the same drink masquerading under different names in different areas of the country, and it's also quite common to discover that a given cocktail is made with different ingredients depending on which bartender you happen to order from on any particular night. Sex on the Beach is a great example, and although it's not ordered these days as much as it was in the '80s, it's one of those drinks every bartender worth his or her salt knows. But do they? I once went through my files to see how many recipes for this drink I'd collected over the years and found no less than twenty-two different versions.

As far as I was concerned, Sex on the Beach was a Highball comprising vodka, peach schnapps, orange juice, and cranberry juice. It's a fairly simple affair, and in its heyday it's possible that it was ordered more for its name than for the quality of the mixture. But I found recipes from bartenders nationwide who were using melon liqueur, raspberry liqueur, and even scotch in their rendition of this drink. Which is the correct recipe? It's impossible to track down.

Only when someone properly documents a new creation can we be certain of the original recipe, and even then there's bound to be a bartender, probably about two thousand miles away, who came up with the same drink at the same time. It might have a different name, but it's the same drink. A good example of this phenomenon is the Blood Orange Cocktail, which was created when a new orange-flavored vodka was introduced to the market back in the early nineties. A Manhattan bartender, John Simmons, decided that it would mix well with Campari. Simmons presented his creation to Bob Camillone, who worked at the company that imported Campari at the time, and Camillone in turn took it to Molly Lynch, brand manager for the Italian aperitif. But Lynch had already thought of this drink. It made sense; Campari marries very well with orange juice, so of course it would be a natural match for orange-flavored vodka.

What can be done to properly record new drinks? Absolutely nothing, as far as I'm concerned. Is this a problem? Well, no. We will have to live with the fact that we might never know who created many cocktails, or the correct ingredients in the original versions.

ACHIEVING BALANCE

Mixed drinks of all kinds should glide down the throat easily, and since most cocktails have a spirit base, the addition of ingredients containing less or no alcohol is needed to cut the strength of the drink and make it more palatable. In most cases, the base spirit, be it gin, vodka, whiskey, or any other relatively high-proof distillate, makes up over 50 percent of the cocktail, and its soul must be soothed if the bartender wants to achieve balance. The other ingredients come in all guises: wines, liqueurs, fruit juices, dairy products, soft drinks, and even water.

Although mixing drinks is akin to cookery in many respects, it is not an exact science. For instance, when you're baking a cake, it's imperative that the ingredients be precisely measured according to whichever recipe is being followed; otherwise the cake might not rise, or it could be too crumbly, too moist, too dry, or simply a disaster. Other aspects of cookery, such as the ratio of flour to butter or oil to make a roux, must also be fairly strictly adhered to. But there are times when liberties can be taken in the kitchen. For instance, you can add extra spices to a jambalaya if you know that the people who will be eating it enjoy extra-hot or more fully flavored dishes.

Cocktailian bartenders are akin to chefs who specialize in sauces, soups, and stews—they should be able to experiment with recipes. Some people enjoy Martinis with just a drop of vermouth; others like Martinis on the wet side, with as much vermouth as gin. And who's to say how much Drambuie belongs in a Rusty Nail? At one time this drink was made with a 50:50 mix of scotch and Drambuie, but it's a far more sophisticated potion when made with less liqueur—80:20 is a good ratio to use. You disagree? Good. We're off to a promising start.

In the cocktail and mixed-drinks recipes in this book, the amounts given for ingredients are guidelines. Prepare a drink exactly according to my instructions and you'll end up with a well-balanced potion; but if you decide that you enjoy the drink more with, say, a tad extra gin, you should feel free to follow your heart. To a point.

The most important aspect of any cocktail or mixed drink is balance, and although guidelines can be set to make, say, a Rob Roy, this drink can vary considerably depending on:

1. **Which bottling of scotch is used?** Scotches vary vastly from one brand to another, and you'll need less sweet vermouth to soothe the soul of a mild-mannered blended bottling than you would to properly balance the drink when made with a bold single malt from Islay, bearing heavy smoke notes and a good dose of iodine.

2. **Which bottling of sweet vermouth is used?** Some vermouths have far lighter bodies than others, and the degree of spiciness can differ enormously from one bottling to another.

3. **Will you add bitters to the Rob Roy?** If so, will you use Angostura, Peychaud's, or orange bitters? Each will bring its own nuances to the drink, but some scotches can be so complex that bitters might not be desirable at all.

Similar options apply to almost any drink you can name, and although it's necessary to follow guidelines such as the recipes in this book, a good bartender will consider all these aspects when preparing any given drink.

So where does this leave you when you're looking for someone to tell you exactly how to make a specific cocktail? As with culinary endeavors, you should initially make the drink according to a standard recipe. Taste it, and if you deem it well balanced, you can continue to use that recipe, providing you employ the same ingredients each time. It's up to you to familiarize yourself with many different bottlings of spirits, and after years of experience you should be able to alter the proportions in the drink when need be in order to create a well-balanced drink every time.

A chef leaves culinary school armed with a good basic knowledge of how to prepare many different dishes, but it could take years before he is able to instinctively add, say, a touch more paprika to a dish because he has bought a new brand that isn't quite as strong as the one he's used to.

The best method of preparing yourself to make any drink is to taste each ingredient before you start. Whenever possible, pour a small amount of the base spirit into a glass; then do the same with all the other liquid components of the drink. Now dip a straw or sipstick into the first glass and, by putting your finger over the top of the straw, capture a tiny amount of the liquid; drizzle this over your tongue by releasing your finger. Repeat the process with each ingredient until you have a clear picture of what all the individual elements are bringing to the party, and you'll be amazed at how easily you're able to make a well-balanced potion.

More than a few bartenders these days also taste the finished drink, using the straw method, before serving it to a customer. This gives you a chance to make sure you've made the cocktail correctly, and adjust it if need be. Would a chef pour sauce over a dish without tasting it first, and maybe adding a little extra salt if he deemed it necessary?

INDIVIDUAL TASTE

It's the job of the cocktailian bartender to take into account the taste of the individual customer. Some folks like sweeter drinks, while others prefer a mouth-puckering sour cocktail. Bartenders must make a habit of finding out about their customer's preferences before making drinks for them. If someone orders, say, a Manhattan, the bartender can politely ask how they like that drink to be made. If the customer isn't sure what's meant by that, the bartender should be able to guide the person through the individual components of the drink, making suggestions along the way.

You start by asking which whiskey the customer wants you to use in the drink; then you describe that bottling, making suggestions as to the ratio of vermouth that you would recommend in order to balance the cocktail. Tell the customer that you recommend bitters in the drink to add depth and complexity, and suggest trying the Manhattan with bitters. If the customer seems to like sweeter drinks, you can even suggest adding a teaspoon or more of juice from the maraschino cherries, even though this strays from the classic formula. If that's what the customer wants, that's what the customer should get. A friend of mine did this recently and was rewarded with the customer's declaring that her Manhattan was the best one she'd ever had in a bar—only her husband had been able to make the drink exactly the way she liked it until then.

Don't think for a moment that you'll automatically be a world-class bartender after reading this book; you'll just be very well armed to handle a job behind the bar. The rest takes time.

INGREDIENTS

The best cocktails and mixed drinks are made with the best ingredients, but that doesn't necessarily mean you must use only the most expensive items. Many bargain bottlings, especially those that aren't advertised extensively, can be of very high quality.

Much to the dismay of many people in the beverage industry, in the early 1990s I started making cocktails with single-malt scotch. Single malts can be rather expensive, but the bold flavors of this style of whisky can transform a great drink like the Rob Roy into a world-class masterpiece. However, a line must be drawn somewhere. In 1998 a forty-year-old bottling of Bowmore single malt was offered to the public at $7,000 per bottle. Would I dare use this scotch in a Rob Roy? Truth be told, as long as someone else was footing the bill, I'd love to try such a drink. But as a rule, although I recommend using only top-quality ingredients in cocktails, I'm more likely to use a $30 to $50 bottling than anything that costs more than, say, $100.

Opting for high quality applies to all the ingredients in any given drink, not just the spirituous items, so it's important to use fresh fruit juices whenever possible. Also, make sure your spices are fresh, that your garnishes are newly cut, and that any other ingredient called for in a drink is of the finest caliber.

IN CONCLUSION

Perhaps you're beginning to realize that to become an accomplished cocktailian bartender you're going to have a long journey ahead of you. Don't despair. The truth of the matter is that if you follow the guidelines in this book, practice, practice, practice, and learn the formulas for the most-requested drinks, you'll be able to mix good drinks in a relatively short time.

You'll quickly discover that the vast majority of drinks called for in any bar are simple Highballs such as Scotch and Soda, as well as Martinis, Manhattans, Margaritas, and other perennial favorites that are quite easy to master. Every bar also has its idiosyncratic cocktails, such as house specialties or weird potions peculiar to that one particular joint. Most bartenders will tell you that it's seldom necessary to know how to make more than a couple dozen drinks in any one bar. And when someone requests a drink a bartender has never heard of, the true professional will either ask the customer how to make it or refer to a good recipe book. Even the most accomplished chefs consult cookbooks before making a dish for the first time, and sometimes they'll refer back to a printed recipe if they haven't made a particular sauce for a while and want to be sure they are using the correct ingredients.

Some bars that have opened in recent years store all their cocktail recipes in an electronic database within their register system so that, if any drinks are ordered that the bartenders aren't sure of, they can easily call up the formulas without guests ever knowing they are referring to written recipes. This is just one of the fabulous aspects of the craft that has emerged only since technology has progressed.

One good way to get a handle on what to expect when you start a job at a particular bar is to go there and notice which drinks are being called for on a regular basis. Situate yourself near the service area, where you can observe not only the drinks being prepared for bar customers but also the cocktails being requested by the wait staff. Watch how the present bartenders make these drinks so you can absorb the house style. Ask questions when you're not sure about specific formulas—you'll probably find that the bartender on duty is more than willing to share his knowledge with you.

You should also be prepared to make mistakes and, as in any other job, to learn from them. In 1973, I arrived in New York from England not knowing how to make anything more complicated than a Gin and Tonic, so I observed bartenders for a full month before even applying for a job. Even then, when I eventually got a position behind the stick, I made more than a few errors. In England, for example, if you order "whisky," you will be served scotch, so I was making Scotch Sours for a while when Whiskey Sours were ordered. It wasn't until a waitress caught me that I learned what I was doing wrong. That's right—not even the customers noticed. Or if they did, they certainly didn't tell me.

A basic knowledge of how to handle bar equipment, a good grasp of a few dozen classic drinks, and a good attitude are really all you need before you set foot behind the stick. Those things, and a true desire to be a bartender, will get you off to a good start.

THE CRAFT OF THE MIXOLOGIST

A bartender in those days was a combination of artist and scientist, who was looked upon with some awe by mere statesmen, bankers and leaders in other professions. To know just how many dashes of lemon juice to introduce into a Manhattan Cooler was no small accomplishment. Great friendships have sprung up therefrom between white jackets and their steady patrons. A bartender who knew the exact proportions of a Supreme Court Judge's tipple might expect any favor from His Honor, short of causing the latter's impeachment.

—HENRY COLLINS BROWN, *In the Golden Nineties*, 1928

ANYONE CAN MAKE a good drink if he puts his mind to it. It's just a case of using the best ingredients in the correct proportions and mixing them according to the prescribed method. No method of mixing a drink—apart from the hard shake, I guess—takes too long to learn or perform. What does take time, however, is becoming a speedy bartender, and anyone new at the job should know from the beginning that speed will come only with practice, and by memorizing the exact location of every bottle and tool behind the bar.

Some bartenders are graceful souls when they mix drinks. They move with extreme fluidity, sometimes flipping an ice cube into the air with a barspoon and catching it in a mixing glass held behind their back. And I saw one bartender in London who did just the opposite: When making a drink his body became robotic, moving in short jolts that reminded me of a character in a silent movie. Personally, I am not a graceful bartender, nor do I turn into a windup toy when mixing drinks. But I quickly learned how to be both precise and speedy when behind the bar.

However you move when you are mixing drinks, try to develop your own personal style and to be consistent. Make customers remember you because of something you do differently from anyone else. I saw that London bartender only once, and that was in the mid-1990s, but since then I've told countless people traveling to London that they must go to Quaglino's to see him if he's still there—he was a joy to behold.

The examples given here—how to hold a shaker and the other meticulous details of how to mix drinks—should be taken as mere guidelines, since personal style is far more important for a good bartender. Take note of specific instructions on such things as how long to stir or shake a cocktail, but feel free to develop your own personal way of actually holding, say, a Boston shaker—just as long as it works well for you and the drink doesn't end up on the floor.

GARNISHES

You will learn how to prepare garnishes in the next chapter, but before you start to actually mix drinks, you should know that certain garnishes are also ingredients. Lime and lemon wedges and any citrus twist (a strip of peel from limes, lemons, oranges, and the like) are the "ingredient garnishes." All too often I see bartenders affix lime or lemon wedges to the rim of a glass, effectively handing the job of squeezing it into a drink over to the customer, who in turn gets sticky fingers. Worse still is the bartender who simply tosses a lemon twist into a drink without twisting it, thereby making the customer fish it out of his cocktail if he wants to enjoy its aromatic essence.

When you add a wedge of lime to, say, a Gin and Tonic, its juices must first be squeezed into the drink. To squeeze the wedge of fruit, take it between your thumb and forefinger and hold it directly above the drink. Use your other hand as a shield, cupping it around the far side of the glass so as to prevent any stray squirts of juice from flying into your customer's face. Now simply squeeze the juice from the fruit, drop it into the drink, add a sipstick, and stir the drink briefly to incorporate the juice.

Citrus twists—strips of citrus zest that incorporate a little of the white inner pith for sturdiness—offer their essential oils to any drink that calls for them, and they can also add a flare of showmanship if the oils are ignited. To properly introduce a twist to a drink, hold it over the glass with the colored side pointing downward. Holding each end of the twist between your thumb and forefinger, turn one end clockwise and the other counterclockwise, releasing the oils from the zest onto the top of the drink. Next, rub the colored side of the twist around the rim of the glass so that any remaining oils are left there, and drop the garnish into the drink.

Many bartenders, for some reason, hate rubbing a twist around the rim of the glass, and some refuse to put the twist into the drink after it has released its secret ingredient. I'm very much in favor of the method just described, which results in a fresh citrus flavor on the rim of the glass and a far prettier drink with the garnish floating on top.

If you wish to flame the oils from a twist, which adds an extra dimension to a drink by caramelizing the oils before they land, a little practice will be necessary. First, when you cut the twist from the fruit—I like to use a paring knife rather than a vegetable peeler so I can include enough of the pith to keep the twist sturdy—you should make it as wide as possible; larger fruits, such as oranges, are best suited to this maneuver since it's fairly easy to cut a twist from them that's almost one inch wide. Have the twist close at hand as you light a match, and hold the match close to the top of the drink. Take the twist in your other hand and grasp it by the sides, using your thumb and first two or three fingers, depending on the length of the twist. (The exterior of the twist should, of course, be pointing toward the drink.) Now position the twist over the match and squeeze it to release its oils. You will see them sparkle as they leap through the flame onto the top of the drink.

TO RIM A GLASS

Very few bartenders know how to properly coat the rim of a glass with sugar (for a Sidecar, for instance), salt (for a Margarita), or other dry ingredients, such as cocoa powder (for a Chocolate Martini). Poor rimming techniques drive me crazy. When a glass is rimmed with one of these items, it's imperative that the dry ingredient stick to the exterior of the glass only. If the salt, for instance, is applied to the interior of the glass, when you add the cocktail it will fall into the drink, thus adding an extra ingredient that doesn't belong in the recipe.

To rim a glass properly, you must first moisten the rim, and this can be accomplished in two ways; you'll need a shallow saucer full of the dry ingredient for both methods. The first technique—my favorite—is to take a wedge of an appropriate citrus fruit (lime for a Margarita, lemon for a Sidecar, for instance) and slot the flesh of the fruit over the rim of the glass. Now, squeezing the fruit gently to release a little juice, slide the wedge around the rim of the glass until the whole perimeter is moist. Take the base of the glass in one hand, holding the other hand vertically for support. Rest the glass on the index finger of your free hand so that the rim faces downward at a 45 degree angle. Allowing the rim of the glass to rest on the surface of the dry ingredient, rotate it until the whole rim is coated. If you have time, you can use a napkin to remove any of the dry ingredient that might have stuck to the glass below the rim—you're trying to achieve a straight line, about one quarter inch deep, around the perimeter of the glass.

The second method is different only in that to moisten the rim, you dip the glass into a saucer full of one of the ingredients in the drink. Triple sec, for instance, works well for both the Sidecar and the Margarita. If the drink contains any liqueur, use that instead of a straight liquor, since the dry ingredient will adhere to it more readily. Admittedly, with both methods a little liquid will make its way into the interior of the glass, but the amount is negligible and the alternative is simply too fastidious to be viable.

If you expect to make large quantities of any drink that calls for a glass with a coated rim, it's best to prepare glasses before your customers or guests arrive. This is also preferable because, given time to air thoroughly, the dry ingredient will adhere better to the glass. Whatever you do, though, don't ever upturn a moistened glass into a saucer of the dry ingredient, coating the inside of the rim as well as the outside. I might just be watching you.

OTHER FANCIFUL GLASSWARE DECORATIONS

It isn't my style to go overboard with garnishes and decorations—quite honestly, I'm just not very good at that sort of thing, and I'd rather spend the time ensuring that my drinks are thoughtfully made and well balanced. However, I've been very impressed by some bartenders who excel at this skill. For instance, I saw one bartender use a zester—more of a kitchen tool than a piece of bar equipment—to cut a very long, very thin spiral of lemon peel. He put one end of the spiral into the drink and draped the rest around the glass a few times until the other end rested on the base of the glass. Very pretty. (His drinks were great, too.)

Another glass garnish that you might see in some antique cocktail books involves cutting a wider spiral of lemon zest with a paring knife, inserting it into a glass, and arranging it so that it coats the interior. In my experience this is viable only when using very slim glasses, such as a champagne tulip—otherwise the spiral simply keeps falling into the bottom of the glass.

WHAT'S ON FIRST?

The old rule of thumb about which ingredient should be poured first when making a cocktail or mixed drink was "Least expensive leads." The reasoning behind this was that if you made the mistake of pouring too much of any one ingredient, less money would have been wasted. However, this isn't a hard-and-fast rule, by any stretch of the imagination. You would never, for example, pour tonic into a highball glass before adding gin or vodka. I'm a great believer in always pouring the base ingredient of any drink first. This way you get a "feel" for how much of the other ingredients to pour. Hence, when making, say, a Sidecar, I will always pour brandy first, followed by triple sec, then lemon juice—precisely the opposite of the rule dictated by price.

Be careful about ingredients that present a freshness issue. Tomato juice, fruit juices, milk, half-and-half, cream, and eggs have a definite shelf life, so these ingredients should be tested before being added to drinks. Fruit juice that has passed its prime can be hard to detect by the nose alone, so it's advisable to shake the container before pouring and observe—effervescence is a sure sign that the juice should be discarded.

Raw eggs, if you choose to use them (see page 128), should be cracked into a receptacle other than the mixing glass and checked for freshness before being added to the drink.

PRECISE POURING

Some bartenders pour by eye. That is, they watch the glass into which they are pouring and judge the depth of the liquid to deem the pour complete. This is an inadequate way of measuring a shot, since it is dependent on the size of the glass and, more important, the ice cubes. If the cubes are small or if the ice is crushed, you will use less liquid to achieve a predetermined depth than you will if the ice cubes are large. If the ice cubes are large, much depends on how they fall into the glass: If one cube wedges against another in such a way as to prevent other cubes from falling alongside them, there will be a large space to fill with liquid before the desired depth is achieved.

I have seen Audrey Saunders pour by eye, but she did this in an empty mixing glass, and she knows how far up the glass to pour for specific measurements. There's nothing wrong at all with this practice, but it wasn't the way I was taught, so I'm going to recommend that you use the method detailed here.

Jiggers and other measuring devices are, of course, very precise and can be used satisfactorily for most drinks. Personally, I prefer the very American free-pour system, wherein the bartender judges, without the use of measuring devises, how much of any ingredient he pours. This gives the bartender a chance to show a little flair in his pouring style and allows him to "feel" his way through a drink—which, in my opinion, is the only way to be a good cocktailian bartender. Also, with drinks that will be served straight up, there's nothing better than seeing a full Martini glass after the bartender drains every last drop from a shaker or mixing glass, thus showing that precision is part of his craft.

Before learning how to free-pour, you should first know about the hidden ingredient in mixed drinks: water. When drinks are properly prepared over ice in a shaker or a mixing glass, one-quarter of the resultant cocktail will be water melted from the ice. This water is a necessary ingredient, since it lowers the alcohol level of the cocktail and thus makes the drink more palatable.

In order to learn how to free-pour you should first practice with a bottle of water fitted with a pourer. When you hold the bottle, be sure to wrap your index finger or your thumb over the base of the pourer. This is a safety precaution. If the pourer is a little loose, you run the risk of it falling from the bottle. Even if you know that a particular pourer has a tight fit, it's imperative that you make a habit of holding bottles in this fashion so that you never make a mistake.

Pour water from the bottle into a measuring device such as a 1½-ounce jigger, and as you pour, count silently in your head. When the jigger is full, stop pouring and remember how far you got in your counting. That's your "shot count." Since people count at different rates, there's no use telling anyone to count to, say, 4 in order to achieve a perfect shot—every bartender should have his own number. You must practice this with a jigger and/or other devices of different measures until you are confident that you can pour any given measurement simply by counting to the appropriate number in your head.

If you are a professional bartender, the management of your bar should give you guidelines about the size of the shot you are expected to serve; this is usually about 1½ ounces. In practice, though, most bartenders pour about 2 ounces of liquor into a highball glass, and however much is needed into a drink that will be served in a cocktail glass. Since cocktail glasses come in many sizes, it's up to you to familiarize yourself with the ones used at your bar or in your home, and to develop a "count" that will result in a drink that fits your glass.

The most difficult aspect of making perfectly sized cocktails is that you're usually dealing with three or more ingredients that must be poured with balance in mind; at the same time, it's imperative that the sum of those ingredients be sufficient to fill your cocktail glass after the ingredients have been shaken or stirred together. How can I possibly teach you to achieve this without being there with you as you work? I can't. It will have to be sufficient for me to tell you that if you have what it takes to be a cocktailian bartender, you will be amazed at how quickly you develop this skill.

Don't, however, fill cocktail glasses to the rim. Why challenge the customer to see if he can get it to his mouth without spilling? And if the drink is being made for a customer at a table, the waitperson must deliver it without the drink sloshing over the side of the glass, which results in a sloppy mess on the serving tray, as well as some pretty sticky fingers for both the server and the customer.

The amount of liquor poured into a drink also varies when it comes to drinks served on the rocks. Unless you are pouring into oversized glasses, these drinks should be filled to within about ½inch of the rim.

TO SERVE A DRINK

All drinks should be served in sparkling clean glasses on a coaster or a napkin that will absorb condensation from the glass. Coasters should also be provided for beer bottles if the whole bottle doesn't fit into the glass or if the customer wishes to pour it himself. Drinks are normally prepared in the small trough on the bartender's side of the bar and then placed in front of the customer, but sometimes a drink such as a Martini straight up is strained into a glass that has already been placed in front of the customer.

It's very important that the customer is able to see you prepare his drink, so don't assemble it out of his view. Ideally you should stand directly in front of the customer whose drink you are mixing, and make sure he is able to see the label on any bottles you use, either before you start to pour or as you are pouring. This way the customer knows that he is getting what he asked for, and he will also enjoy the show as you mix the drink.

If a drink contains a sipstick or other inedible garnishes—plastic mermaids and the like—watch to see when the customer removes these from his drink and sets them down on the bar, and then remove them immediately. You should also keep an eye on coasters and napkins. When one becomes wet because of condensation from the glass or because a customer spilled his drink when picking it up, remove the offending coaster and replace it immediately.

The home bartender should also follow these guidelines, although it can sometimes be difficult to make the drink directly in front of your guests without a real bar. All the other rules, though, are just as important when making drinks for friends.

TEMPERATURE

The temperature of the drink is another important factor to consider when shaking or stirring. Shaking requires approximately half the time in order to reach the correct temperature, as does stirring. As a rule of thumb, you should shake a drink for between ten and fifteen seconds, or stir it for twenty to thirty seconds.

Please note that this information is based on unscientific experimentation, and it doesn't apply to every single drink. I turn to Dave Arnold, who headed up the iconic New York bar Booker and Dax (sadly, it closed in 2016, though Booker and Dax lives on as a "food science development company"). Arnold is the man who constantly delves into matters such as these, for clarification. I encourage you to do the same if you are looking for detailed explanations. For further reading you might want to pick up Arnold's book, *Liquid Intelligence: The Art & Science of the Perfect Cocktail*. You'll find it to be money well spent.

You might hear some people say that Gin Martinis should be stirred rather than shaken in order to avoid "bruising" the gin, but this is a misconception—gin can't be bruised. It's more than likely that the "bruising" referred to here is, in fact, a chill haze—the cloudiness that can occur when certain items get too cold. Martinis used to be made with as much dry vermouth as gin, and vermouth, when well chilled, will develop this haze. There is nothing wrong with a cloudy Martini save for its appearance.

Showmanship is very important when tending bar, and drinkers love to see those ice cubes move up and down and round and round when you prepare their drink in a mixing glass, so this is the receptacle I recommend above all others for preparing a stirred drink.

TO CHILL GLASSWARE

Any chilled cocktail that is served without ice should be poured into a prechilled glass, and the easiest and best way of achieving this is to keep glasses in the fridge or the freezer. But if you don't have room there, a couple of other methods can be used. One way to chill a glass is to keep it upturned or buried in a mound of crushed ice, but this is possible only at bars that have space for a suitable receptacle. Ideally the crushed ice will be held in a bowl or sink fitted with a drain so that melted ice will not become a problem; if this is not viable, you can use a punch bowl or similar receptacle. Be aware, though, that you'll have to drain the bowl periodically, so be sparing with the ice or it will become unmanageable.

The most commonly used method of prechilling glasses is to fill them with ice and water and let them sit while you mix the drink. I recommend that whenever possible you stand the ice-filled glass in a sink and run cold water into it until it overflows—the water that clings to the outside of the glass will help chill it more quickly. Before pouring the drink you must, of course, empty the glass of the ice and water. Holding it by the base or the stem, shake the glass vigorously for a few seconds, allowing the cold water to spill over the outside of the glass; then empty it and once again shake it vigorously to rid it of any last drops of water. When properly chilled, the glass should be frosted on the outside.

TO BUILD A DRINK

Drinks such as the Screwdriver, the Scotch and Soda, or the Gin and Tonic are served in a highball glass and are known as "built" drinks. To build a Highball, simply fill the glass with ice; add the ingredients, liquor first; stir the drink with a sipstick a few times; add any garnish that's called for; and serve it complete with the sipstick. If the garnish is a citrus wedge or twist, it should be added before the drink is stirred, but if it's an ornamental garnish such as an orange wheel, stir the drink and then add the garnish.

Most people drinking highballs will stir the drink a few extra times with the sipstick before discarding it and proceeding to drink. Now you have a wet sipstick on your sparkling clean bar—don't let it languish there. Discard it immediately. Some customers, however, insist on keeping their used sipsticks so they know how many drinks they've had. If this is the case there's not much you can do about it, but you might want to put the used sipsticks on an extra coaster so they don't look quite so untidy. Home bartenders should also be on the lookout for discarded sipsticks—they can end up all over the house—and get rid of them as quickly as possible.

Drinks such as the Black Russian (vodka and Kahlúa) and the Godfather (scotch and amaretto) are often built in the glass in which they will be served, but they are far better when stirred over ice, then strained into an ice-filled old-fashioned glass. This method ensures that the drink is cold before it's poured into the glass, and the ice in the glass will not melt as readily.

TO STRAIN A DRINK

Although some cocktail shakers are fitted with their own strainers, I'm far more enamored of using a spring-loaded Hawthorne strainer or a standard julep strainer in tandem with a Boston shaker when straining drinks. It simply looks more professional. The Hawthorne strainer should be used when pouring from the metal half of the shaker, and the julep strainer is used to strain drinks from the mixing glass. After preparing a cocktail as detailed here, simply fit the strainer firmly onto the mouth of the metal or glass, put your index finger over the top of the strainer to hold it in place, and strain the drink into the serving glass. Once you've emptied the liquid, give the glass a sharp twist in any direction as you return it to an upright position, so that any remaining drops don't fall to the bartop as you remove the mixing glass.

Some bartenders strain shaken drinks by holding a complete Boston shaker horizontally over the glass after "breaking" the two parts, a method similar to one used by bartender William Schmidt in the 1890s. Instead of using a shaker, he put one goblet on top of another and "turned them upside down five or six times," held them up together as high as he could with both hands, and let the liquid drip down into a "tall, fancy glass." When using a Boston shaker for this maneuver, the shaker halves are pulled apart slightly so the liquid pours from the broken seal. I like the showmanship involved in this procedure, but recommend that if you want to adopt this style, you practice with water until you have mastered the maneuver.

WHETHER TO STIR OR SHAKE

Most bartenders will agree that, as a generalization, drinks containing eggs; fruit juices; cream liqueurs, such as Baileys; or dairy products (cream, half-and-half, or milk) should be shaken, while clear drinks, such as the classic Martini or Manhattan, are usually stirred. It's fairly easy to determine why some drinks should be shaken: It's far easier, for instance, to thoroughly combine a spirit with heavy cream or a fruit juice by shaking rather than stirring, whereas the Martini and the Manhattan, made with a spirit and vermouth, are easily mixed when stirred. Bear in mind, however, that there are exceptions to the rule, and that some bartenders choose to stray from classical methods as a matter of personal style.

I prefer to stick to the classical procedures for making drinks as described here when it comes to shaken drinks, but in the case of cocktails that should be stirred I allow certain exceptions. The Stinger, for instance, is a clear drink (brandy and white crème de menthe) that is normally shaken, not stirred. I like the fact that this has become the norm for one particular cocktail, so I, too, use the shaker when making a Stinger. A classic Gin Martini, however, should be stirred as far as I'm concerned, even though some old recipe books prescribe shaking the drink. Some customers, however, will specifically ask for a shaken Martini. Their wish is your command.

TO STIR A DRINK

Before you prepare a drink that calls for stirring as the prescribed methodology, be sure to have at the ready a chilled glass, or a glass containing ice cubes if the drink is to be served on the rocks. You can stir drinks in the base of a cocktail shaker if you wish, but I prefer, by far, to use the mixing-glass half of a Boston shaker. If you choose to use a Martini pitcher to stir your drinks, you'll find that it comes with a long glass rod—which, in my opinion, is a comely but functionally poor substitute for a good barspoon.

The standard barspoon has a twisted shaft, and this isn't merely stylistic; it's a functional part of the design. To stir a drink properly, hold the twisted part of the shaft between your thumb and first two fingers. Plunge the spoon into the mixing glass, twirl the spoon back and forth by twisting your fingers away from, then toward yourself, and simultaneously move the spoon up and down in the glass. This sounds hard but it isn't. Stir the drink for between twenty and thirty seconds to bring the temperature down to between 28 and 38 degrees and to incorporate enough water to make the cocktail palatable. One-fourth of the chilled drink will be water melted from the ice, and this is a highly desirable amount.

TO SHAKE A DRINK

Once again, although I love to look at a beautiful all-metal cocktail shaker, I prefer to use a Boston shaker, with its simple components: two cones, one metal and one glass. There's something about a Boston shaker that makes me think that a bartender means business. It's a serious tool. First, you must prepare the glassware needed for the cocktail, then fill the mixing-glass half of the shaker about two-thirds full of ice. Pour in the ingredients for the drink and place the metal half of the shaker on top of the glass, giving it a sharp tap on the base to ensure that you have formed a watertight seal.

The classic method of holding a shaker involves placing your thumbs on the base of both halves of the Boston shaker with your pinkies intertwined in the middle—which, for me at least, is very uncomfortable. I believe that you should hold the shaker however it feels most comfortable to you, just as long as you keep the two parts together during the shaking. It is important, though, that the glass half of the shaker faces the backbar as you shake, with the metal half pointing toward your customer. In the unlikely event that the shaker breaks apart as you work, the glass will thus fall behind you, and won't fly out into the customer's face.

To chill a drink down to the correct temperature—28 to 38 degrees—it's necessary to shake it for only about ten to fifteen seconds. Then, holding the shaker so that the metal part is on the bottom, tap the metal sharply with the heel of your hand at the point where the two receptacles are joined. This will break the seal and you will be able to lift the glass off the metal container. It's very important to keep the metal on the bottom when breaking the seal—if the glass is on the bottom, sometimes the action of hitting the shaker will cause liquid to spill over the lip of the glass, wetting your hand and the glass, and thus risking the glass slipping to the floor. If the metal is on the bottom, this can't happen. If you have a problem breaking the seal with the heel of your hand—and this happens occasionally to even the most seasoned professionals—tap the metal sharply at the same place on the edge of the bar or another solid surface. Some people worry that this action could break the glass, but I have yet to see that happen. I prefer to transfer the drink from the metal to the glass before pouring—this makes the performance more visually exciting for the customer.

TO ROCK OR ROLL A DRINK

I have heard this method referred to as both "rocking" and "rolling," and it's a way of mixing ingredients without incorporating too much air. Dale DeGroff, a.k.a. King Cocktail, refers to the method as rolling and suggests that the technique is a good one to use when making a Bloody Mary because it won't aerate the tomato juice too much. To rock or roll a drink, simply pour the ingredients into the glass half of a Boston shaker that is two-thirds full of ice. Then repeatedly pour it back and forth between the glass and the metal half of the shaker. To thoroughly incorporate the ingredients in a Bloody Mary, this action should be repeated about half a dozen times, ending up with the drink in the mixing glass; it should then be strained into an ice-filled serving glass.

TO MUDDLE A DRINK

The term *muddling* refers to the action of combining ingredients, usually in the bottom of a glass, by pressing down on them with a muddler—a short wooden pestle, similar in shape to a baseball bat, with one rounded end and one flattened end. The flattened end is used to mix the ingredients.

The Old-Fashioned is probably the most popular drink that requires muddling, but other drinks can also benefit greatly from this.

For instance, you can muddle lemon wedges with granulated sugar to make a Tom Collins or a Whiskey Sour. The sugar abrades the zest of the lemons and produces a far fresher-tasting drink. This phenomenon also occurs in a Caipirinha when granulated sugar is muddled along with lime wedges.

Although muddling can be achieved by using the back of the bowl of a sturdy spoon, I highly recommend that you use a proper muddler. As with the Hawthorne or julep strainer and the Boston shaker, I think the use of a wooden muddler shows that a bartender takes his craft seriously. Muddling is best done on the bar top in front of the customer—it's all part of the performance art that bartenders display from behind the stick.

When muddling ingredients together, be sure to choose a glass that's sturdy enough to hold up to the force of muddling. A double old-fashioned glass without a stem works well if you're preparing a drink suitable for that glass. If you're making, say, a Whiskey Sour or a Tom Collins, muddle the appropriate ingredients in the bottom of a mixing glass, prepare the drink in that glass, and then strain it into the serving glass.

When sugar is called for as an ingredient to be muddled, some liquid will be needed in order to dissolve it. Sometimes the liquid will be produced by the juice of whatever fruit is being muddled; it might also come from a few dashes of bitters. Don't hold back when muddling—squeeze every last drop of juice from fruit wedges by pressing on them firmly and repeatedly with the pestle, and grind the sugar into the liquid until it completely dissolves.

I have witnessed one other form of muddling drinks in just one city, Seattle, and hence have dubbed it the "Seattle Muddle," though I'm sure that bartenders in other cities must sometimes use this method of mixing. In order to perform the Seattle Muddle you must first pour all the ingredients of any given cocktail or mixed drink into a mixing glass two-thirds full of ice. Next, wrap your hand over the top of the glass, and with the other hand insert the pestle into the glass between your thumb and forefinger. Now plunge the pestle up and down, mixing the drink thoroughly before straining it into the serving glass.

The Seattle Muddle is a somewhat messy affair, and it's slightly unhygienic, since the drink splashes against your palm as you mix it, sometimes actually spilling out of the glass if you don't form a watertight seal with your hand. However, this method has the advantage of breaking tiny shards off the ice, and these morsels will remain in the drink after it has been strained. In the case of a cocktail that's being served straight up, these shards will form sparkling little "stars" that float on top of the drink—the visual effect is quite appealing.

TO LAYER A DRINK

Layered drinks are generically known as Pousse-Cafés, and the preparation of these drinks displays the height of showmanship of the bartender. Layering is usually achieved by slowly pouring liqueurs, spirits, and sometimes even cream or fruit juice over the back of a small spoon, or a barspoon, so that the liquid falls very gently onto the previously poured liquid and rests atop it in a new layer. Other objects can be used instead of a spoon; and I first witnessed this in 1993, when New Orleans bartender Lane Zellman poured the ingredients for his creation—the AWOL—over a maraschino cherry. He held the cherry by the stem, and the effect was very entertaining.

In order to ascertain which ingredients will float on top of others you should know the density of each component of the drink. This can be somewhat difficult, however, since liqueurs such as, say, white crème de menthe are made by many different producers, and depending on the formulas used, the density of one bottling is not necessarily the same as another.

Having said that, though, I also add that it can be fairly simple to guess correctly what will float on what, just by knowing the texture of a spirit or liqueur. Cassis, crème de banane, crème de menthe, and crème de cacao, for instance, are all fairly heavy, syrupy liqueurs, so it stands to reason that lighter products such as triple sec, kirsch, and sloe gin will float on any of these products. Spirits such as brandy, whiskey, rum, tequila, vodka, and gin will usually float on top of almost any liqueur, since they contain no sugar and are, therefore, lighter. And heavy syrups such as grenadine will usually withstand the weight of most liqueurs and so should be considered as one of the first ingredients added to the glass.

TO FLAME A DRINK

Be careful. Be very careful. Flaming drinks can be a hazardous affair at best. Once ignited, if that drink spills, you have a fire on your hands, and if it spills onto a person, you might have a human torch in the bar. You should always have a working fire extinguisher on hand when making flaming drinks; make sure you know how to use it before you show off your pyrotechnical skills.

But a raging fire isn't all you have to worry about when you make these drinks. If a drink is allowed to flame for too long, the rim of the glass will become very hot, and it will stay that way for quite some time. You must warn anybody who insists on a flaming drink of this danger and advise him not to bring the drink to his lips until he can touch the rim of the glass with his finger, and keep his finger there without its being burned.

A few different kinds of drinks can be flamed before service. Straight liqueurs such as sambuca, for instance, are often flamed, and sometimes the top layer of a Pousse-Café is set alight. Other drinks—the Zombie is a good example—have a high-proof spirit, such as 151-proof rum, floated on top, and this can also be ignited to impress customers. To flame drinks such as these, simply touch a lighted match to the surface of the drink until it catches fire, and allow it to burn for approximately ten seconds before extinguishing it by placing a small saucer on top of the glass. It's okay to allow the customer to blow the flame out, although a saucer is the more effective method. The bartender should never blow out the flame on a customer's drink—it's unsanitary behavior.

TO BLEND A DRINK

Making a frozen drink in a blender looks like a comparatively easy affair, but it's a little more troublesome than you might imagine if you want the resultant drink to be as smooth as silk and easy to sip through a straw. If you don't have a frozen-drink machine at hand you'll have to use a blender to make frozen drinks. It's best to buy a sturdy commercial blender with a strong motor to make blended drinks, since crushing ice places a lot of stress on the machine's motor.

After adding ice and the drink ingredients to the blender, set the top in place and run the blender on high speed (many commercial blenders have only one speed: fast) for twenty to thirty seconds. Turn the blender off, wait until you are sure that the blades are stationary, then remove the lid and thoroughly stir the ingredients with a bar spoon. Return the lid to the bowl, start the motor again, and repeat the procedure. You might have to stir the drink more than once in order to achieve a perfect frozen drink, but the results are worthwhile.

You should also use your ears when making frozen drinks in a blender. You'll notice that the sound of the motor changes as the ice is crushed and incorporated into the drink, and that's when it's time to turn off the blender and check the drink's consistency.

The amount of ice needed to make any specific frozen drink is in direct relationship to the size of the serving glass, so if you're in doubt, simply build the drink in the glass and then pour the whole thing into the blender. You'll find that this results in a full glass with a slightly convex dome, which is visually appealing.

If you use fruit such as pineapple, peaches, or strawberries in a frozen drink, cut it into manageable pieces before adding it to the blender. Hull strawberries and cut them in half; pineapples, peaches, and other fruits should be cut into 1-inch cubes. Of course, the pit must be removed from stone fruits, and you shouldn't use the core of a fresh pineapple.

TO INFUSE SPIRITS

The infusion of distilled spirits has gained much popularity in the past decade or so, yet infusion is an ancient practice. According to renowned food scientist Shirley Corriher, ethyl, or beverage, alcohol has the power to boost the flavors of any ingredient with which it is married. "Why do we put vodka into Penne alla Vodka?" she offered as a good example. After all, vodka, for all intents and purposes, is without flavor, so how could it possibly enhance a food dish?

Dairy products and water can also "grab" flavors, distribute them throughout a dish, and enhance them somewhat, but according to Corriher, alcohol does more than those two products combined. With that in mind, it's good to remember that a high-proof spirit will yield better results than one of low proof when it comes to infusion, and you can always bring the resultant flavored spirit down to a suitable drinking proof after it has been infused, using bottled water, simple syrup, or even fruit juices.

I prefer to use neutral grain spirits instead of vodka when infusing. At 95 percent alcohol by volume, it seems to literally suck the flavors out of whatever ingredient you add to it. However, that product isn't available in every state (I have to travel to Connecticut or New Jersey to procure mine), so if you can't find it locally, use 150-proof vodka—which is legal throughout the country.

To infuse a spirit with any ingredient, you must first find a jar with a tight-fitting lid that's large enough to hold the liquor and the fruit (or whatever ingredient you choose) and still have air space at the top so you can shake the jar periodically. Prepare your ingredients (see list on page 114), add them to the jar along with the liquor, tightly screw the lid onto the jar, and give it a good shake. Now place it somewhere away from direct sunlight but where you'll see it at least once a day, preferably twice or three times. Whenever you walk past it, give it another good shake.

You should taste your infusion regularly—at least once a day after the first twenty-four hours, and twice a day if you are infusing hot peppers or similar strong-flavored ingredients, since they tend to take over the drink.

The average amount of time required to infuse spirits ranges from two to five days, depending on the ingredients used and the proof of the liquor. After seven days it's highly unlikely that any more flavor will be extracted from any ingredient.

When the infusion is ready, strain it through a double layer of dampened cheesecloth, preferably into another large jar. The main problem with infused spirits is that it's sometimes difficult to remove from the spirit tiny particles of the ingredient used for the infusion, so it's a good idea to allow it to rest for a day or so after you've strained it, allowing these particles to drop to the bottom of the jar. Then you should carefully decant it into a bottle, leaving the residue in the bottom of the jar just as you would if you were decanting a bottle of vintage port.

PREPARING VARIOUS INGREDIENTS FOR INFUSIONS		
INGREDIENT	AMOUNT PER 750 ML DISTILLED SPIRIT	PREPARATION METHOD
APRICOTS	4–5	Wash well. Remove the stone and cut into 1-inch cubes. Peel can be left in place or removed.
BELL PEPPERS	1–2	Wash well. Remove the top and tail, cut into 6 to 8 pieces, and discard the seeds.
BING OR QUEEN ANNE CHERRIES	1 pound	Wash well. Crush with a pestle, breaking the pits. Don't discard the pits.
COFFEE BEANS	6–8 ounces	Crack the beans using the back of the blade of a large sturdy knife.
FRESH HERBS	1–2 bunches	Wash well and dry. Roughly chop.
GRAPEFRUIT ZEST	4–6 grapefruits	Wash well. Remove the zest carefully, making sure not to cut into the bitter white pith.
HOT PEPPERS	1	Wash well. Wearing gloves, remove the top and tail, cut into quarters, and discard the seeds.
LEMON ZEST	12 lemons	Wash well. Remove the zest carefully, making sure not to cut into the bitter white pith.
LIME ZEST	12 limes	Wash well. Remove the zest carefully, making sure not to cut into the bitter white pith.
ORANGE ZEST	6–8 oranges	Wash well. Remove the zest carefully, making sure not to cut into the bitter white pith.
PEACHES	3–4	Wash well. Remove the stone and cut into 1-inch cubes. Peel can be left in place or removed.
PINEAPPLE	1	Remove top and tail. Peel and core, then cut the flesh into 1-inch cubes.
PLUMS	6	Blanch briefly in hot water. Remove the skin and stone and cut into quarters.
STRAWBERRIES	1 pound	Wash well. Hull and slice in half.
TOMATOES	1 pound	Blanch in hot water. Remove the skins, cut into quarters, and discard the seeds.

If you use a high-proof spirit for infusion, you'll need to dilute it to a drinkable strength when it is decanted. Use bottled still water to do this—I recommend Poland Spring as a brand with very little, if any, flavor of its own. And you'll have to do some math if you want to bring your infusion down to a specific proof. One liter of spirit at 151 proof contains 75.5 centiliters of pure alcohol. Since 200 proof is equivalent to 100 percent alcohol, for 100 proof, the amount of alcohol in the diluted infusion must be equal to 50 percent of the whole; thus here you'll need to end up with 1.51 liters of infused liquor. Therefore, you must add just over half a liter of bottled water to your infusion to bring it down to the right proof.

I recommend that you don't bring infusions down to less than 100 proof. At that level infusions tend to keep a clear appearance, but when they are diluted beyond that, they can become murky when chilled.

Many infusions require the addition of sugar before serving, a good example being Limoncello, the Italian infusion of lemon zest, which needs to be sweetened to become more palatable. Add sugar in the form of simple syrup, which is made by mixing 1 cup of granulated sugar into 1 cup of hot water over medium heat, stirring frequently until the sugar dissolves and the liquid is transparent. Allow the syrup to cool to room temperature before adding it to your infusion.

You can also add honey to your infusions, but be careful to add it in small amounts lest it overcome the other ingredients. Another way of sweetening an infused spirit is by adding a liqueur to it, but again, you should take care not to add too much at once.

FAT WASHING

The method of infusing cocktails with fatty products such as bacon, or even milk, was introduced, I believe, by Eben Freeman in 2007 when he worked at Tailor in New York. He had learned the methodology of fat washing the previous year from Sam Mason, a chef at WD-50, the New York restaurant that was hailed as "a shrine to molecular gastronomy." And to take this one step further, we should note that Mason got the idea from perfume makers who used fat washing to extract aromas that were hard to extract with any other method.

Fat washing is relatively easy inasmuch as it's just a case of infusing something like bacon fat, ham hocks, popcorn, or even butter into a distilled spirit for an hour or so, shaking it a few times during the first thirty minutes, then allowing it to rest for another half hour. Next, pop the container into a freezer for a couple of hours, and strain out the solids, using a coffee filter. This methodology is culled from *Liquid Intelligence*, and Arnold notes that, if you use fats that don't solidify in the freezer, such as olive oil, you might want to use a gravy strainer to separate the fat from the spirit.

FOUNDATIONS OF THE BAR:

GARNISHES, MIXERS, AND SUPPLEMENTAL INGREDIENTS

Fill a mixing glass half full of fine ice; add three dashes of gum syrup, 2 dashes maraschino, the juice of a quarter of a lemon, two dashes Peychaud or Angostura bitters, and one jigger brandy; mix. Take a lemon the size of a fancy sauterne or claret glass; peel the rind from three-fourths of it all in one piece; fit it into the glass; moisten the edge of the glass with a piece of lemon, and dip it into fine sugar, which gives it a frosted appearance. Strain your mixture into this glass, trim with fruit, and serve.

—George J. Kappeler,
Modern American Drinks: How to Mix and Serve All Kinds of Cups and Drinks, 1895

THE ITEMS LISTED and discussed as follows are integral to the cocktailian craft. They can turn a mediocre drink into a masterpiece, whether by adding depth, character, and individual nuances to the drink itself or merely serving as an eye-pleasing garnish. It is of utmost importance that the bartender be intimate with these items, and that he understand what each one looks like, how it tastes, what other ingredients are suitable to mix with it, and the drinks in which it plays an integral part.

BITTERS (SEE PAGE 119)

- Angostura Bitters
- Peychaud's Bitters
- Orange Bitters
- Dale DeGroff's Pimento Aromatic Bitters
- Other Bitters

SAVORY PRODUCTS (SEE PAGE 123)

- Clam Juice and Beef Bouillon
- Tomato Juice
- Tomato Water
- Horseradish
- Hot Sauces
- Worcestershire Sauce

SWEETENING AGENTS (SEE PAGE 124)

- Simple Syrup and Various Other Sweeteners
- Grenadine
- Lime Cordial
- Elderflower Syrup
- Orgeat Syrup
- Various Fruit Syrups
- Coconut Cream

EGGS AND DAIRY PRODUCTS (SEE PAGE 128)

- Eggs
- Milk, Cream, and Butter

FRUIT JUICES (SEE PAGE 130)

- Lime Juice and Lemon Juice
- Orange, Tangerine, and Grapefruit Juices
- Cranberry Juice
- Pineapple Juice
- Tamarind Juice
- Other Fruit Juices and Nectars

VARIOUS AND SUNDRY SUPPLEMENTAL INGREDIENTS (SEE PAGE 132)

- Dry Ingredients, such as Salt, Sugar, and Ground Cinnamon
- Orange Flower Water
- Gelatin
- Food Coloring

TEA (SEE PAGE 133)

SODAS (SEE PAGE 133)

GARNISHES (SEE PAGE 134)

- Lemon and Lime Wedges
- Lemon, Lime, and Orange Twists
- Fruit Wheels
- Pineapple Garnishes
- Maraschino Cherries
- Celery
- Fresh Herbs
- Olives and Other Savory Garnishes
- Chocolate Syrups, Shells, Sprinkles, and Shavings
- Various Other Garnishes

BITTERS

Of all the items listed in this chapter, bitters are the most important, and I'm happy to report that there are now so many varieties of bitters on the market that it makes my head spin. It's important to note, I think, that a mere two drops of bitters added to most cocktails will drastically alter the drinks, giving them an added dimension.

Potable bitters, such as Fernet-Branca, are commonly used as postprandial drinks in Italy because they are believed to aid digestion, but most of the bitters dealt with here are nonpotable, meaning that they are not meant to be consumed neat or on the rocks. Most nonpotable bitters are commonly employed as a flavor enhancer in cocktails and mixed drinks. Usually high in alcohol—between 70 and 90 proof—they therefore have a long shelf life, lasting for twelve months without refrigeration.

ANGOSTURA BITTERS

In 1820, after serving in the Prussian army and tending to the wounded at the 1815 Battle of Waterloo, Dr. Johann Gottlieb Benjamin Siegert traveled to the Venezuelan port of Angostura to help General Simón Bolívar liberate the country from the Spanish. Bolívar succeeded in his mission in 1821 and moved on to liberate Ecuador, Peru, and Colombia. Dr. Siegert stayed on in Angostura (renamed Ciudad Bolívar in 1846) to study native botanicals and determine if they could be used medicinally. By 1824, he had developed a tonic known as *amargos aromáticos,* which he marketed commercially. Now called Angostura bitters, the product is made in Trinidad, and is the best-known cocktail ingredient of its kind in the world.

The Angostura company claims that the product gained worldwide renown when, shortly after its creation, it became a staple of ships' provisions; it was used to treat seasickness, fever, and scurvy. The recipe for this potion, though, remains a well-guarded secret.

Without Angostura bitters, many cocktails are somewhat one-dimensional, but when just a dash or three of Angostura are added, they are transformed into complex, multidimensional potions. This ingredient should be constantly on the mind of the creative cocktailian as a possible item to add to new drinks, especially those made with a base of brown spirits, such as whiskey, or brandy, but these bitters are amazingly adaptable to other spirits, too. If you dash a little Angostura onto vanilla ice cream, you'll understand how versatile this product can be.

Bartenders should also know that Angostura bitters can help cure hiccups. Coat a lemon wedge with granulated sugar and douse it with Angostura bitters. The person suffering from the malady should then bite down on the lemon wedge. You should be aware, however, in case a customer is a strict teetotaler, that this product contains 45 percent alcohol by volume.

Angostura bitters are available in most supermarkets, as well as specialty food and beverage stores, but if you have any difficulty finding them, or need to find out more about the company, you can always check out www.angostura.com.

PEYCHAUD'S BITTERS

The second most important cocktail bitters, Peychaud's is an integral ingredient in the Sazerac cocktail and can be used as a substitute for Angostura in many drinks, especially such cocktails as the Manhattan. The resultant cocktail will not duplicate the same drink made with Angostura, but Peychaud's will add its own nuances and complexities.

In 1795, Antoine Amedie Peychaud arrived in New Orleans after fleeing San Domingo (now Haiti) following the slave revolt there in 1791. His son, Antoine Amedie Peychaud Jr., was born in 1813. Twenty-five years later, Junior opened an apothecary at 123 Royal Street, in the French Quarter.

Using a secret family recipe brought to New Orleans by his father, Peychaud Jr. dispensed brandy mixed with bitters as a tonic; the same drink was served, circa 1850, at the Sazerac Coffee House in New Orleans. By the late 1860s, Peychaud had been hired by the coffeehouse, where the owner, Thomas H. Handy, marketed the product, which won a gold medal at the 1869 Grand Exhibition in Germany.

Peychaud's bitters can be obtained online or at most local liquor stores. Or visit www.sazerac.com for more details.

ORANGE BITTERS

Orange bitters used to be an integral ingredient in Dry Martinis, but started to fall from favor after Prohibition; now, they have made a comeback. These bitters work very well in Dry Gin Martinis, and they are called for in a number of different cocktail recipes.

My Regan's Orange Bitters No. 6 has been on the market for over a decade now, and it's proved to be very popular. Some people marry my orange bitters with the Fee Brothers' orange bitters at a 50:50 ratio, and this version, known in some circles as New York orange bitters, or Feegan's orange bitters, has become pretty well liked, too.

Angostura also makes a unique orange bitters that's a little pithy, and very interesting, and The Bitter Truth makes a great version, too. The fact is, there are now many bitters companies, and plenty of them offer orange bitters. You should sample and choose the bottling that works best for you, and remember that different versions work well in different cocktails, too.

DALE DEGROFF'S PIMENTO AROMATIC BITTERS

Made by renowned bartender Dale DeGroff and renowned absinthe distiller T.A. Breaux, Dale's bitters has a fabulous allspice foreground, backed up with hints of anise and many other herbs besides, providing a distinct new flavor that enhances many cocktails.

I prefer these bitters in my Manhattans; Dale also recommends using them in classic drinks such as Old-Fashioneds, Painkillers, and Sazeracs. Just try one Piña Colada with a few dashes of these bitters—you'll never go back.

OTHER BITTERS

There are now hundreds of different styles of bitters on the market—celery, dandelion and burdock; lemon bitters; chocolate bitters . . . search for it online and you're almost guaranteed to find it. The main players in this category are probably Bitter End, Bittermans, Bitter Truth, Dr. Adam Elmegirab, Fee Brothers, Hella, and Scrappys. And that's only scratching the surface.

REGAN'S ORANGE BITTERS NO. 5

I adapted this recipe from the guidelines set down in *The Gentleman's Companion*, volume 2: *Exotic Drink Book*, by Charles H. Baker Jr. Allow four weeks to prepare, and be warned: These bitters have a very high alcohol content and should not be consumed undiluted. They are for use in small quantities in cocktails and mixed drinks.

8 ounces dried orange peel, chopped very fine (see Note)
1 teaspoon cardamom seeds, taken out of their pods
½ teaspoon caraway seeds
1 teaspoon coriander seeds
1 teaspoon quassia chips
½ teaspoon powdered cinchona bark
¼ teaspoon gentian
2 cups grain alcohol
4½ cups water
1 cup granulated sugar

NOTE: You can purchase cinchona bark, dried orange peel, gentian, and quassia online.

Place the peel, cardamom seeds, caraway seeds, coriander seeds, quassia, cinchona bark, gentian, grain alcohol, and ½ cup water into a half-gallon mason jar and push the ingredients down so that they are covered by the alcohol and water. Seal the jar.

Shake the jar vigorously once a day for 14 days.

Strain the alcohol from the solids through a cheesecloth; set the jar aside. Gather the ends of the cheesecloth to form a pouch and squeeze tightly to extract as much alcohol as possible. Place the solids in a strong bowl or mortar; reserve the alcohol in a clean mason jar and seal tightly.

Muddle the dry ingredients with a pestle or strong spoon until the seeds are broken.

Place the solids in a nonreactive saucepan and cover with 3½ cups of water. Bring to a boil over a medium-high heat, cover, turn the heat down, and simmer for 10 minutes. Allow to cool, still covered (about 1 hour).

Return the solids and water to the original mason jar that contained the alcohol. Seal the jar and let the liquid infuse for seven days, shaking the jar vigorously once a day.

Strain the water from the solids through a cheesecloth. Discard the solids and add the water to the alcohol.

Put the sugar in a small nonstick saucepan and place over medium-high heat. Stir constantly until the sugar becomes liquid and turns dark brown. Remove from the heat and allow to cool for 2 minutes.

Pour the sugar into the alcohol mixture. At this point the sugar may solidify, but it will quickly dissolve.

Allow the mixture to stand for seven days. Skim off any bits that float to the surface and carefully decant the clear liquid to separate it from any sediment resting on the bottom.

Measure the bitters; there should be about 12 fluid ounces. Add the remaining ½ cup (or half the amount of bitters produced) of water, and shake thoroughly.

Pour the bitters into a bitters bottle (or a bottle with an eye dropper). Store for up to one year at room temperature.

SAVORY PRODUCTS

CLAM JUICE AND BEEF BOUILLON

These potables are used in a few savory drinks, such as the Bloody Caesar and the Bull Shot, and should be purchased in small bottles or cans to eliminate waste. Both of these products should be refrigerated after being opened.

TOMATO JUICE

Tomato juice is one of my big downfalls—I just hate the texture. Therefore, my Bloody Mary skills are somewhat lacking. However, people whose opinions I respect assure me that most reputable commercial brands of tomato juice are perfectly viable in drink preparation.

TOMATO WATER

Although I'm not enamored of tomato juice, I do like tomato water—it makes for a wonderful ingredient in cocktail preparation. To make tomato water, simply roughly cut flavorful tomatoes, place them in a double layer of dampened cheesecloth, and squeeze the liquid from the fruit. This ingredient can be successfully employed in many savory cocktails.

HORSERADISH

Prepared horseradish, used in savory drinks such as the Bloody Mary, should be purchased in small jars and refrigerated after being opened.

HOT SAUCES

Although the regular bottling of Tabasco sauce is the norm behind the bar, that brand is now available in different flavors, such as garlic and chipotle, and there are many other brands of hot sauce from which to choose. Think about using these flavorings to differentiate your own Bloody Marys or to create a drink that's tied to a specific cuisine, such as Mexican food.

WORCESTERSHIRE SAUCE

Bottles of Worcestershire sauce, which is used in savory drinks such as the Bloody Mary, should always be at hand behind the bar.

SWEETENING AGENTS

SIMPLE SYRUP AND VARIOUS OTHER SWEETENERS

There has been much debate among cocktailians about the correct ratio of sugar to water when making simple syrup; the truth is that it doesn't really matter. I make my syrup using a 50:50 ratio, and because I'm aware of the sweetness it delivers, I usually know how much to add to a drink to achieve a good balance between it and any sour components, such as lemon juice. You may choose to use more sugar, so that you're adding less water to a drink when using this ingredient. Then you will get used to using simple syrup made to your formula, and as long as you always make it the same way, you'll end up with nicely balanced drinks.

I recommend that you store simple syrup refrigerated, in a clean bottle that can be fitted with a speed pourer for easy service.

SIMPLE SYRUP

One-fourth ounce of this syrup is equal in sweetness to 1 teaspoon of granulated sugar.

MAKES 1½ CUPS

1 cup granulated sugar
1 cup water

Combine both ingredients in a saucepan and cook over medium heat, stirring frequently, until the sugar is dissolved. Allow the syrup to rest until it cools to room temperature, then transfer it to a clean bottle.

Although superfine sugar dissolves easily in cold liquids, I far prefer to use simple syrup, which distributes itself quickly in cocktails and mixed drinks. Since confectioners' sugar contains traces of cornstarch to prevent clumping, it's not a viable alternative. I do, however, recommend the use of granulated sugar in the preparation of certain drinks.

When making drinks such as the Caipirinha, lime wedges should be muddled with granulated sugar until the sugar is completely dissolved. During this process, the coarse sugar abrades the zest of the lime and introduces the lime's essential oils to the drink. This method can be employed when making all sorts of cocktails that contain lime or lemon juice, and it adds an extra dimension to drinks like the Tom Collins.

Confectioners' sugar, though not suitable for making simple syrup, can be successfully used as a garnish when sprinkled onto items such as mint sprigs in a Julep. Brown sugar, bearing somewhat richer molasses notes, can be a good choice for Irish Coffee and many other hot drinks.

Two other sweetening agents—honey and maple syrup—are sometimes called for as ingredients in mixed drinks, but I find them overly sweet, and their flavors can easily mask other nuances in a cocktail if extreme care isn't taken to introduce them in very small quantities.

SIMPLE SYRUP VARIATIONS

We learned about the following variations of simple syrup largely when Wondrich's first edition of *Imbibe!* was released in 2007, and these have led to some wonderful variations on a theme. They are all made using the same methodology as described for simple syrup, but each one brings different nuances into play.

RICH SIMPLE SYRUP: Two cups of granulated sugar dissolved in 1 cup of hot water.

TURBINADO/DEMERARA/BROWN SUGAR SIMPLE SYRUP: One cup of turbinado, demerara, or brown sugar dissolved in 1 cup of hot water.

RICH TURBINADO/DEMERARA/BROWN SUGAR SIMPLE SYRUP: Two cups of turbinado, demerara, or brown sugar dissolved in 1 cup of hot water.

HONEY SIMPLE SYRUP: One cup of honey dissolved in 1 cup of hot water.

AGAVE SIMPLE SYRUP: One cup of agave nectar dissolved in 1 cup of hot water.

HERBAL SIMPLE SYRUP: Simply add approximately 1 cup of fresh herbs to any of the syrups listed as soon as the sugar has dissolved in the water. Stir briefly, and allow the mixture to come to room temperature before straining the herbs through a double layer of dampened cheesecloth.

GRENADINE

True grenadine is a syrup made from pomegranate juice, so check the labels on commercial brands to make sure that the word *pomegranate* appears as an ingredient. The Angostura company produces a pomegranate-based nonalcoholic grenadine, and both Jacquin's and Boulaine sirop de grenadine liqueurs are very low in alcohol (2.5 percent and 2 percent alcohol by volume, respectively); they are also made from pomegranate.

Jeffrey Morgenthaler offers a very easy-to-make recipe for homemade grenadine in his *Bar Book*—an indispensable guide to bartending techniques—and the following recipe is based on Morgenthaler's instructions.

GRENADINE

MAKES 3 CUPS

2 cups fresh pomegranate juice, or POM Wonderful pomegranate juice
2 cups raw sugar
2 ounces pomegranate molasses
1 teaspoon orange flower water

Gently heat the pomegranate juice in a nonreactive saucepan, then add the sugar, molasses, and orange flower water, stirring frequently, to dissolve the sugar. Don't allow the mixture to boil. As soon as the sugar is dissolved, remove the pan from the heat, and allow it to cool to room temperature.

Transfer the grenadine to bottles and refrigerate. The grenadine will last for around one month.

LIME CORDIAL

In 1867, sweetened lime juice was first produced commercially in Edinburgh, Scotland, by Lauchlin Rose, who patented his method of preserving the juice without the addition of alcohol. That same year it was made mandatory for all ships in both the Royal Navy and British merchant fleet to include lime juice in the sailors' daily rations, and Rose's lime juice soon became known throughout the world.

Sweetened lime juice should never be used in cocktails calling for fresh lime juice, but it is an integral part of such drinks as the Gimlet and Lager and Lime. The cocktailian might experiment with lime cordial as a sweetening agent, using it instead of, say, grenadine or simple syrup when creating new drinks.

You might notice that some bottlings of lime juice change color, becoming golden brown after a time as a result of oxidization. This isn't of great concern to most bars, since sweetened lime juice is used too quickly for it to oxidize. For home use, though, the Angostura company once again comes to the rescue here—Angostura Reconstituted Lime Juice is a sweetened product that always retains its original color.

ELDERFLOWER SYRUP

This syrup can usually be found at specialty German food stores or can be ordered online from www.germandeli.com.

ORGEAT SYRUP

Flavored with almonds and orange flower water, this sweet, nutty, citrusy syrup is used primarily in tropical drinks; it can usually be found in specialty food stores.

VARIOUS FLAVORED SYRUPS

Various recipes—The Clover Club, Gun Metal Blue, The Zombie, for instance—call for a variety of flavored syrups, such as raspberry and cinnamon. These syrups are often available at specialty food stores and can be ordered online from Monin (www.monin.com), a fine company, in my experience.

COCONUT CREAM

Canned coconut cream, used in drinks such as the Piña Colada, is very thick and syrupy. The can should be shaken well before it is opened, and even then, it's often necessary to stir the cream until all the oils, which float to the top, are incorporated into the cream.

EGGS AND DAIRY PRODUTS

EGGS

Very few drinks call for the use of raw eggs, but you can't make a Pisco Sour, Ramos Gin Fizz, or Eggnog without raw egg white. Although salmonella contamination in raw eggs is rare, it is certainly a consideration; in some states, it is illegal to serve raw eggs, so you should check your local laws. Eggs that have been pasteurized in their shells are also available, and these are recommended by the FDA when consuming them raw or undercooked.

When incorporating egg whites, yolks, or whole eggs in a drink, you'll need to work a little harder to get the correct texture. In order to fully combine all the ingredients (commonly referred to as emulsification), you can use a few techniques and tools.

One method you can use for any recipe that calls for eggs is the dry shake, introduced to me by Chad Solomon of Cuff and Buttons in Brooklyn. Add the egg and the other ingredients to the shaker without ice and shake for 5 to 10 seconds. Put some effort into this if you want the right results. Add ice and shake for an additional 10 to 15 seconds. This works well simply because eggs emulsify more readily at room temperature than they do when chilled.

Some bartenders remove the stainless-steel coil from a Hawthorne strainer and drop it into the shaker when they're dry-shaking, and this seems to have the effect of whisking the eggs as well as shaking them, thus helping emulsify the eggs faster.

You can also use a milk frother—an electric or battery-operated hand-held device used to foam milk for cappuccinos and the like—to properly emulsify drinks containing eggs. Once again, you should froth the egg in the shaker before adding ice. This technique, we think, came originally from Jamie Boudreau, the Seattle-based Canadian who is well known for his creative genius.

I've seen bartenders use a whisk, too, to achieve the same results. The bartender who used this technique, a certain Frenchman by the name of Maxime Hoerth, did it with much style and looked oh-so-French as he whipped up the drink in a small mixing bowl during one of Diageo's World Class Bartender Finals. He then transferred the drink to a shaker to chill and strain.

Raw eggs, if you choose to use them, should be cracked into a receptacle other than the mixing glass and checked for freshness before being added to the drink. You can also test whole eggs for freshness before you crack them by adding them to a bowl of water—if they float, or even if they stand upright rather than lying flat on the bottom of the bowl, they're old.

SALMONELLA A 2008 article in the *San Francisco Chronicle*, by Cindy Lee, quotes George Chang, food microbiologist and professor emeritus at UC/Berkeley, as saying, "In studies of clean, intact eggs from modern egg factory facilities, less than 1 percent of the eggs contain detectable salmonella," and that the risk of salmonella poisoning from eggs is "perhaps even lower than the risk of eating raw salads." The piece goes on to say that the risk is even smaller with egg whites, and quotes Lawrence Pong, principal health inspector and manager of food-borne illness outbreak investigations for the Department of Public Health in San Francisco: "Egg whites are alkaline in nature, and salmonella colonies cannot survive there."

FLAVORING EGGS

Some folks can't stand the odor that sometimes accompanies raw eggs, and Jon Bonné, my editor when I wrote for the *San Francisco Chronicle*, once advised me that a drop or two of bitters can mask this unpleasantness quite handily. At the time of writing, I believe that he was experimenting with raw egg white and orange bitters to make a Margarita. Hannah Lanfear, a bartender friend of mine in London, told me that she uses citrus twists to mask any unpleasant odors in her sours.

And you can also combat egg stench by flavoring them prior to use. If you're planning on making Ramos Gin Fizzes, for instance, you might think about flavoring your eggs with orange zest. Robert Wood, bar manager at the Kenilworth Hotel in Warwickshire, England, and Adam Elmegirab, Aberdeen-based bartender and bitters producer, also advised me about flavoring eggs, which is a practice that Adam thinks might have originated from the Italians, who used truffles to flavor eggs. Because of their porous shells, eggs are easy to flavor in their shells simply by storing them in herbs or teas, or by covering them with lemon twists. You'll detect the flavors as soon as the next day. And as I learned from Fred Yarm of cocktailvirgin.blogspot.com, covering eggs with a cloth soaked in lemon oil can work well to boost flavor, also.

MILK, CREAM, AND BUTTER

Recipes calling for milk, cream, or half-and-half can be made with any one of these products, but the resultant drink, of course, will be thicker and have a more pleasing consistency if cream is used. You should always check dairy products for freshness before using them.

If you want whipped cream, heavy cream is the easiest to whisk to the right consistency. Although some people like to whip it until it forms stiff peaks, I prefer to stop when the cream thickens somewhat but is still pourable. This way the cream will float easily on top of the drink and become part of it, as opposed to a food item that's better eaten with a spoon.

Butter, called for in a Hot Buttered Rum, should be kept refrigerated at all times, and for drink service you must use unsalted butter unless the recipe specifies otherwise.

FRUIT JUICES

LIME JUICE AND LEMON JUICE

Whenever possible, fruit juices used in drink preparation should be fresh, especially in the case of lime and lemon juice. Many bars use commercial products known as "sweet and sour" instead of either of these juices, but I've yet to find one that isn't overly sweet—not to mention that no one product could possibly take the place of two different juices. Doubtless it won't be long before some company issues viable products that save the bartender time. Meanwhile, if you use so much juice that squeezing your own fruit simply isn't viable, it's worth seeking out companies that offer frozen fresh juices.

If you work in a busy bar, you might want to presweeten your fresh lemon and lime juices; a good ratio to start with is ¾ ounce of simple syrup to 1 ounce of fresh lime juice or lemon juice. You can experiment with these ratios until you find a recipe that works for you, but I strongly suggest that you don't add too much syrup, since this results in unbalanced drinks. It's easy to add a little more sweetener to individual cocktails in order to satisfy the tastes of individual customers.

ORANGE, TANGERINE, AND GRAPEFRUIT JUICES

With orange, tangerine, and grapefruit juices, once again, fresh is best and frozen fresh juice comes in second. Some commercial brands of juice in cartons have gotten far better recently than they were a mere five years ago, so if that's all you have at hand, I can't say that I object to their use in drink preparation.

CRANBERRY JUICE

If you look at the label on a bottle or can of cranberry juice, you'll notice that it's usually sold as "cranberry juice cocktail." This is because straight cranberry juice is far too bitter to drink, so it must be sweetened for use at home or behind the bar. Most commercial brands of cranberry juice cocktail are perfectly acceptable for drink preparation.

PINEAPPLE JUICE

As with cranberry juice, I find that most commercial brands of canned pineapple juice are perfectly acceptable behind the bar.

TAMARIND JUICE

This sweet-tart tropical fruit juice can be found in many specialty food stores, especially those with an Asian focus. It can easily overpower other flavors in a cocktail, so be sure to add it to a drink gradually.

OTHER FRUIT JUICES AND NECTARS

Various other juices and nectars—made from papayas, mangoes, guavas, apples, peaches, and all manner of exotic fruits—are on the market, and their number seems to grow daily. Although fresh is always best, most of these commercial products are quite acceptable for drink preparation. Make sure to shake the container of nectars well before opening, since some of these products tend to settle and separate even before they hit the shelves.

VARIOUS AND SUNDRY SUPPLEMENTAL INGREDIENTS

DRY INGREDIENTS

Granulated sugar, coarse salt, cocoa powder, Old Bay seasoning, and other dry ingredients are often used to coat the rims of glasses for drinks such as Sidecars, Margaritas, Chocolate Martinis, and Bloody Marys. These ingredients should be stored in airtight containers overnight, but during service it's advisable to have them in saucers behind the bar, ready for use.

ORANGE FLOWER WATER

Used in few drinks—the Ramos Gin Fizz is the only one that easily springs to mind—this delicately perfumed ingredient, made from orange blossoms, is readily available at specialty food stores.

GELATIN

Used in the Jelly Shots on pages 179, 243, and 290, unflavored gelatin, in my opinion, is the only way to go when making this type of "drink."

FOOD COLORING

Usually found in the baking department of most food stores, food colorings are seldom used behind the bar, but you'll need some if you intend to make any of the Jelly Shots on pages 179, 243, and 290. It's also possible to substitute triple sec and blue food coloring for blue curaçao, but be sure to add the coloring sparingly until you arrive at the correct hue.

TEA

Tea is becoming more and more popular these days as a cocktail ingredient, and when it's called for, there is simply no substitute. Since there are so many flavored teas on the market, the cocktailian bartender might look in this direction when composing new drinks. I have experimented a little with this ingredient and advise you to make a somewhat stronger brew than you would if you were going to drink it from a cup. You should also prepare it well in advance so that it has time to cool to room temperature.

SODAS

Soda from "guns" is, thank God, becoming less and less prevalent in today's bars, and you now have a great range of well-made bottled sodas from which to choose. Good bars stock the smallest bottles available of the best brands of lemon-lime soda, cola, ginger ale, ginger beer, club soda, and tonic water, as well as a selection of the various new and wonderful fanciful flavors that, as with fruit juices, appear on a regular basis. If you use these small bottles of soda, pour just a little soda into the glass, place the bottle on a cocktail napkin or coaster next to the drink, and allow the customer to use his judgment in adding more soda to the drink.

Root beer, sarsaparilla, birch beer, and various other spicy sodas are readily available, and these are wonderful additions to the basic line of sodas. Since the better brands are not overly sweet, they provide a viable alternative for adult customers who don't drink alcohol or who are driving. Most other sodas are too sweet for many adults to drink more than one.

An ingredient that can be very successfully used as a nonalcoholic cocktail ingredient and is also very refreshing when served over ice is San Pellegrino San Bitter, a soda that tastes very much like Campari. The company also makes sophisticated lemon and orange sodas, known respectively as limonata and aranciata, and all three of these bottlings can be found in many Italian specialty food stores. For professional use, wholesalers that stock San Pellegrino bottled water should be able to supply bars and restaurants with these products.

One more soda should be mentioned here. It's seldom seen in the United States, but it's a very good mixer when used with gin or vodka. Bitter lemon soda is merely tonic water with lemon flavoring, and it's easily made by adding fresh lemon juice to regular tonic, then adjusting the sweetness with a little simple syrup to suit individual tastes.

GARNISHES

Fruit garnishes are very important to the bartender, and it's imperative that they be as fresh as possible. There's nothing I enjoy better than seeing a bartender cut a lemon twist from the fruit immediately before using it, but this isn't always possible in busy bars. The vast majority of bartenders must prepare garnishes prior to service, endeavoring to cut only as much as he thinks he will need that day or evening.

Some garnishes, such as lemon twists, will keep overnight provided they are covered with a dampened paper napkin. It's up to the bartender to check these for freshness the following day and decide whether or not they are fit for use.

As the name suggests, garnishes are additional ingredients meant to make drinks more pleasing to the eye; some of them are also drink ingredients, so again, freshness comes into play. Citrus wedges, for example, will start to lose juice the moment they are cut, so it's essential that they be discarded as soon as it becomes apparent that they are no longer viable. This is easily accomplished by squeezing one wedge out of a batch and observing how much juice is left in it (one quarter of a lime, for example, should contain about a quarter ounce of juice).

LEMON AND LIME WEDGES

I like to use large wedges of both of these fruits. Although it depends on the size of the lemon or lime you are cutting, most limes won't yield much more than four wedges, or six at the very most; lemons will normally yield six to eight wedges.

To prepare lemon and lime wedges, first remove both ends with a sharp paring knife; then slice the fruit in half either vertically or horizontally, depending on the style of wedge you prefer. Because of size variances, I usually cut limes horizontally and lemons vertically. Now cut each half into equal-size wedges, remembering that size matters; you need to end up with a wedge large enough to yield about ¼ ounce of juice. A rule of thumb is that one quarter of one lime or one sixth of one lemon should contain this amount.

One half of a lemon that has been cut vertically will yield long slender wedges that are easy to squeeze. One half of a lime, cut horizontally, will give you shorter, squat wedges, but they, too, will be easy to handle during service.

LEMON, LIME, AND ORANGE TWISTS

Citrus twists can be cut in many different ways, but in my opinion, bigger is better. The twists give up their essential oils to the cocktail being garnished with them (see pages 96–97), so the larger the twist, the more oils will be added to the drink.

To prepare citrus twists, remove the stem end of the fruit in order to give it a base, stand it on that base, and carefully cut strips of the zest away from the fruit. The width of the twist will depend on the size and shape of the fruit you are using, but try for as wide as possible in each case. Some of the white inner pith must remain on the twist so that it will be sturdy enough to use properly, but you should make sure that you never cut into the inner pulp of the fruit. The length of each twist, once again, will depend on the size of the fruit, but long is preferable, short is not.

You can also produce twists in the form of spirals by cutting around the fruit in one continuous motion, but these twists can prove difficult to handle. If, however, you'd like to line the inside of a glass with a citrus spiral, you should prepare the glass prior to service and use a slim glass like a champagne flute.

FRUIT WHEELS

Oranges are the garnishes most commonly cut into the shape of a wheel, but limes and lemons are sometimes cut in this fashion, too. Orange wheels, however, can be eaten by the customer, while this is seldom the case with limes and lemons. Lime and lemon wheels are not good substitutes for wedges since they are almost impossible to squeeze successfully, and hence don't do the same job as wedges, but they can be visually pleasing.

Orange wheels are often cut in half, depending on the size of the fruit. It's the job of the bartender to assess the size of both the fruit and the glass before deciding whether a whole wheel or a half wheel would be more suitable for any specific drink.

To cut fruit wheels, first remove both ends of the fruit, cutting deep enough to expose the inner pulp. Then, holding the fruit steady, slice off ¼-inch wheels. If a whole wheel is called for, cut through the peel up to the center of the fruit, creating a slit that will fit over the rim of a glass. When using half wheels, you should cut a slit from the center of the fruit up to the white pith, so that the garnish can be hung over the side of the glass.

PINEAPPLE GARNISHES

Pineapples are delicious edible garnishes, but this fruit can be hard to handle, and the shape into which you cut it will largely depend on the ripeness of the fruit, which governs the sturdiness of the resultant garnishes. Sturdier pineapples can be cut into spears, whereas riper ones are usually best cut into chunks or cubes. You can also use cookie cutters to make all manner of shapes; if this is your desire, there's no need to remove the outer skin first. Simply cut the fruit into ½-inch wheels and use the cookie cutter to create the garnish, making sure to avoid the hard center core.

To make spears or cubes, slice off the top and bottom of the pineapple, then remove the outer skin by cutting downward, following the shape of the fruit. Any black spots remaining on the outside of the fruit should be cut out with a paring knife. Next, cut slices from the side of the fruit, about ½ inch wide, until you reach the hard center. You can now cut spears from these slices; pare them down, if need be, to fit the glass you intend to garnish. Otherwise, cut the fruit into ½-inch cubes and impale them with toothpicks or cocktail picks for easy handling.

MARASCHINO CHERRIES

The old-fashioned maraschino cherries that taste of almonds and are made in a process that involves calcium chloride, sugar, food coloring, pasteurization, and flavorings, are, thankfully, on their way out.

Far more common in cocktailian bars in the twenty-first century are homemade maraschino cherries, and the simplest way to make these is to buy frozen pitted black cherries, place them in a mason jar, and cover them with a high-quality maraschino liqueur; tighten the lid and allow the cherries to steep in the fridge for up to 1 month before using. Thanks to Louise Owens of The Windmill Lounge in Dallas, for teaching me this. And, of course, there's no need to make only maraschino-flavored cherries—you can marinate them in brandy, bourbon, or any other spirit or liqueur for specific cocktails.

CELERY

Stalks of celery, thoroughly washed, trimmed, and usually shortened to fit the glass, are a great way to garnish a Bloody Mary. You must make sure, though, that the celery is crisp and fresh; if you keep some on display, it's best to place them in a container with some iced water at the bottom.

FRESH HERBS

Herbs such as rosemary, thyme, cilantro, sage, basil, and mint can be used as very successful garnishes, but the bartender must be careful to match the scent of the herb with the appropriate cocktail. Rosemary and thyme, for instance, both go well with gin-based mixed drinks, cilantro works in Bloody Marys, and mint is commonly called for in the Mojito—a rum-based tall drink—and, of course, the Mint Julep. Fresh herbs are best stored in a container with iced water at the bottom.

OLIVES AND OTHER SAVORY GARNISHES

Olives can be found in a variety of sizes, and stuffed with any number of other ingredients, such as almonds, blue cheese, pimientos, and anchovies. Since these fruits are usually used as a Dry Gin Martini garnish and Martini drinkers tend to be very specific about their drinks, many customers are choosy when it comes to which type of olive they want. Using plain pitted olives in some sort of brine is the safest way to go, but you might want to keep some stuffed olives on hand in order to offer a selection.

If you would like to personalize your olives, you can make your own "brine" by adding fresh herbs such as basil, thyme, and/or rosemary to dry vermouth, simmering the liquid for about 5 minutes on the stovetop, covering the mixture, and allowing it to return to room temperature. Discard the brine from the bottle of olives, and replace it with the herbed vermouth.

Caper berries also make good Martini garnishes, and I've even seen regular capers added to the drink, but the most common "other" Martini garnish is the pearl onion, again packed in brine, which turns the Martini into a Gibson. The only real rule of thumb when using any of these berry-type garnishes is that an odd number of them must always be used: One olive is standard, three are acceptable, but two are verboten. This, I believe, comes from an old superstition, but I can't find a good reference to it. The same rule, incidentally, applies to coffee beans when added to a glass of sambuca.

I have also seen Martini recipes that call for dilly beans (pickled green beans), pickled okra, tiny pickled tomatoes, and even pickled mirliton (also known as chayote), a squash that should be cut into small cubes for use as a garnish. There are no rules here—simply pick something edible that suits your fancy.

CHOCOLATE SYRUPS, SHELLS, SPRINKLES, AND SHAVINGS

Most commercial brands of chocolate syrups and sprinkles are fine to use in drink preparation, and I've even seen one recipe that calls for Chocolate Magic Shell, a product made by Smuckers that hardens when chilled. Chocolate shavings, sometimes used as a garnish, are easily made by simply grating cold chocolate, but if you do this prior to service, keep the shavings refrigerated.

VARIOUS OTHER GARNISHES

Almost anything edible that looks good in or on a drink can be employed by the cocktailian bartender. Hershey's Hugs or Kisses dress up a clear Chocolate Martini, multicolored sprinkles can be used to adorn the lip of a glass with a chocolate-syrup-coated rim, and miniature candy canes look splendid in holiday-time cocktails.

Whole cloves are often used in hot drinks such as the Hot Toddy, and although they serve as a garnish, their primary purpose is to add flavor to the drink. Cinnamon sticks, candied ginger, and vanilla beans can also be used as garnishes, and kiwis, strawberries, bananas, and countless other fruits are perfectly acceptable, providing they are matched to the appropriate drink. Kiwis and bananas should be peeled and sliced, and strawberries hulled; "notches" should then be cut into these fruits to enable them to be placed on the lip of the glass.

One practice that faded from fashion about a hundred years ago is the custom of topping drinks, especially those made with crushed ice, with mounds of berries and small slices of other fruits, such as strawberries and bananas. In the days when these drinks were served at first-class bars, the customers were provided with short spoons with which to eat the fruit—it's a practice I'd love to see return to the barrooms of America.

TOOLS AND VESSELS

Liquor Pump, Mallet, Filtering Bag or Paper, Brace and Bit, Liquor Gauge, Gimlet, Bung Starter, Rubber Hose for drawing Liquor, Liquor Thieves, Thermometer, Hot Water Kettle, Lemon Squeezers, Liquor Gigger, Cork Press, Champagne Faucets, Molasses Jugs, Postal Cards, Demijohns, Spittoons, Shot for Cleaning Bottles, Railroad Guide.

—HARRY JOHNSON,
excerpted from "Complete List of Utensils, Etc., Used in a Bar Room," *New and Improved Bartender's Manual of How to Mix Drinks*, 1900

IT'S ESSENTIAL FOR THE BARTENDER to have the right tools on hand to mix every sort of drink, and it's also necessary to know how to use bar equipment properly. That said, there's nothing wrong with adding your own style when it comes to drink preparation. I once saw a bartender using two metal cones instead of one glass and one metal piece, the usual set that makes up the Boston shaker. Since the cones came from different manufacturers, one had a slightly larger mouth than the other, so the combination worked well, and the all-metal shaker looked very smart when in use. It turned out that the bar hadn't ordered the correct glassware for a Boston shaker, so this guy had just improvised. Even when the right glasses arrived, he decided to keep using the two metal pieces. Nothing wrong with that—it displays showmanship and imagination. Here's a list of equipment you'll need to properly set up a bar.

COCKTAIL AND MIXED-DRINK PREPARATION

Listed here are standard pieces of equipment that have been used behind bars for well over a hundred years. These days, bartenders also use all manner of chemistry beakers and fancifully designed mixing glasses produced by different companies all over the world. It's not a bad way to differentiate oneself behind the bar.

BOSTON SHAKER: This consists of two pieces: a mixing glass, usually 16-ounce capacity, and a slightly larger, flat-bottomed metal cone. The glass can be used on its own when drinks are stirred over ice; the two are used in tandem, with the metal part fitting over the glass, for shaking drinks.

BARSPOON: This long-handled spoon with a twisted shaft and shallow bowl is used for stirring drinks in order to chill and dilute them.

HAWTHORNE STRAINER: This flat-topped, perforated metal device with a continuous coil of wire around its perimeter, which helps keep the strainer snugly in place, has a short handle and either two or four "thumbs" that extend from the top and sides to keep it in place on the Boston shaker. The Hawthorne strainer is used when drinks are strained from the metal half of the Boston shaker.

JULEP STRAINER: A perforated metal soupspoon-shaped strainer used when drinks are strained from a mixing glass.

MARTINI PITCHER: Seldom used these days, glass Martini pitchers are usually tall and elegant, have a tightly pinched spout to prevent ice from falling into the drinks, and generally come with a glass rod for stirring cocktails.

COCKTAIL SHAKER: A metal cocktail shaker has a tight-fitting top, which covers a strainer, and the strainer fits into a metal cone. Cocktail shakers come in many elegant designs and are considered completely acceptable for use in the home or behind a professional bar.

SHORT SHAKER: This is a miniature version of the metal half of the Boston shaker. It is placed on top of a glass—usually an old-fashioned glass (see the following chapter)—in order to shake a drink that has already been poured into the glass. I find these devices more or less useless.

ELECTRIC BLENDER: Used to prepare frozen drinks, to crush ice, and to puree fruit. Commercial blenders with strong motors are essential for bar use, since crushing ice demands a great deal of force and strong blades. You'll need to use a barspoon (see page 141) in conjunction with the blender to make smooth frozen drinks.

GARNISH PREPARATION

CUTTING BOARD: Small wooden or plastic cutting boards are necessary for preparing fruit garnishes and are easily stored behind the bar.

PARING KNIVES: Small, sharp paring knives are needed to prepare fruit garnishes.

MUDDLER: A wooden pestle, used to crush and blend ingredients in the serving glass or a mixing glass. The flattened end is used for this procedure.

GRATER: A small metal grater is useful for grating items such as nutmeg onto the tops of cocktails.

BOTTLE AND CAN OPENERS AND STORAGE

BOTTLE OPENER: Most bars have professional bottle openers, complete with a receptacle to catch the tops, installed behind the bar. Otherwise, bartenders should keep a pocket-size bottle opener at hand.

CHURCH KEY: Metal church keys serve a dual purpose: one end punches holes in cans so the liquid contents can be poured out, and the other end opens bottles.

CORKSCREW: There are many different kinds of corkscrews from which to choose. The *winged corkscrew* fits easily onto the neck of the bottle; two arms extend when the cork is impaled, and pushing the arms downward removes the cork. The *screw-pull corkscrew* removes the cork by first impaling it; as the user keeps turning the wingnut-shaped handle clockwise, the device pulls the cork from the bottle. The *rabbit corkscrew* is simple to use and highly recommendable—it has easy-to-handle grips, and the cork can be swiftly ejected from the worm after being pulled from the bottle. The *Ah-So cork puller* works when the two thin blades are inserted between the cork and bottle—they grip the cork, and the user can pull it from the bottle; I find this style of cork remover unsatisfactory. *Waiter's corkscrews* are penknife-like tools that fit easily into the pocket. They have a blade for cutting the foil from the top of a bottle, a worm that screws into the cork, and a fitting that rests on the lip of the bottle so that when the user pulls the handle upward, the cork is removed. I highly recommend this style of corkscrew for professional bartenders.

CHAMPAGNE KEEPERS: These spring-loaded devices clamp onto the top of an opened bottle of champagne or sparkling wine and seal the bottle to prevent carbonation from escaping. A necessary tool for the bartender.

JUICE EXTRACTORS AND SERVICE

CITRUS REAMERS: Reamers come in two basic styles. One is the typical glass or plastic reamer with a pointed cone, onto which the fruit is pressed to extract the juice. The cone is surrounded by a well that collects the juice; nubbles in the well are meant to prevent seeds from falling into the juice, but they seldom do the job satisfactorily. Wooden reamers, consisting of a handle topped with a pointed cone, look very professional when wielded behind the bar. This tool should be used in conjunction with a strainer to catch the seeds.

LEVER-PULL JUICE EXTRACTORS: These professional-quality contraptions look wonderful on the bar and do a great job of extracting all the juice from the fruit. The fruit is placed on top of a perforated metal cone; when the lever is pulled downward, a metal cap pushes the fruit onto the cone, and the juice drips down into a glass or other container. If you want to prepare large quantities of juice for use during the day, this type of juicer is highly recommendable; I use it in tandem with a strainer to catch both seeds and the majority of the pulp from the fruit.

ELECTRIC JUICERS: Similar in design to glass reamers, the cones on these machines spin around to supposedly make juice extraction easier, but you still have to apply lots of pressure to release the juice. I find these machines unsatisfactory.

PITCHERS AND CARAFES: Glass pitchers and carafes can be used for fruit-juice storage and service.

JUICE BOTTLES: These liter-sized plastic juice bottles have detachable necks fitted with pourers for easy service. The pourer, as well as the lid that screws onto the bottle when the neck is removed, is available in many colors, thus making it possible to color-code your juices.

ICE STORAGE, PREPARATION, AND SERVICE

ICE BUCKETS: Metal ice buckets are needed for the service of chilled wine. For keeping ice cubes handy, look for a smaller plastic ice bucket fitted with a perforated interior, through which water can drip into the bottom of the container, keeping it separate from the ice. These are useful in a home-bar setting but seldom are needed in a professional bar, where ice is usually stored in sinks.

ICE CRUSHERS: Ice can be crushed in a lint-free tea towel using a rubber mallet, or even a rolling pin, but electric and hand-cranked machines are available. The hand-cranked machines can be hard to use, and many electric models are very noisy, so professional bartenders should crush ice prior to service.

ICE SCOOP AND TONGS: Metal ice scoops make it easy to fill glasses quickly, whereas only one ice cube at a time can be moved with tongs. Nevertheless, in small, tony bars and in home bars, the use of ice tongs is a tasteful touch.

MEASURING DEVICES

JIGGERS: Most metal jiggers have two cones, joined at the pointed end; one cone holds 1 ounce, and the other 1½ ounces. The use of jiggers is visually pleasing when precise measurements are needed.

MEASURING SPOONS: A set of metal or plastic measuring spoons is sometimes necessary for dry ingredients—for example, when ¼ teaspoon of salt is called for in a savory drink.

MEASURED POURER: Some pourers are fitted with measuring devices that make sure that the bartender cannot pour more than a certain amount—usually 1½ ounces—without returning the bottle to an upright position and pouring another shot. I hate these devices. They are an insult to the cocktailian.

BITTERS BOTTLES: Commercial brands of bitters are fitted with a device known as a dasher that ensures only small amounts can be released from the bottle. Antique bitters bottles are available from various sources and are very pleasing to the eye. Empty commercial bitters bottles, once they are thoroughly washed and their labels removed, can be used to dispense absinthe, Bénédictine, and other strongly flavored ingredients called for in small quantities. Antique bitters bottles, of course, can be used in this fashion, too, or you can use small bottles fitted with an eye-dropper, easily available online, if you like.

SPEED POURERS: Metal (preferred) or plastic (despised) pourers should fit snugly into the necks of bottles for fast, efficient service. Since bottles have varying neck sizes, pourers can be hard to work into some bottles, and can be a little loose in others. Pourers' spouts also vary in width—the larger ones, which pour liquor more quickly, are usually referred to as *California pourers*. Individual bars should select one specific size and brand of pourer so that bartenders know how quickly the liquor will pour. It will also be pleasing to the eye if every bottle is fitted with the same style of pourer. Pourers should also be affixed to bottles used for lime juice, lemon juice, and simple syrup—ingredients that are normally used in small quantities.

DRINK SERVICE

SIPSTICKS OR STIRRERS: These short, thin straws and stirrers (those with no hole through the center) are usually used in Highballs and drinks served on the rocks. They should be stored on or behind the bar, within easy reach of the bartender.

STRAWS: Various sizes and lengths of drinking straws should be readily available for frozen drinks, Juleps, and many other drinks.

COCKTAIL NAPKINS AND COASTERS: Paper cocktail napkins or sturdier cardboard coasters are placed underneath glasses to absorb condensation and spillage.

COCKTAIL PICKS: Short, pointed sticks, typically bamboo or plastic, are used to impale garnishes and are then usually placed on top of the serving glass.

GLASSWARE

The bartender's particular attention must be given to keeping the glassware in a clean, bright condition. The glasses he hands out to the customers for the purpose of allowing them to help themselves, as well as the glasses he uses for mixing drinks, should be without a speck on them.

—HARRY JOHNSON, *New and Improved Bartender's Manual of How to Mix Drinks,* 1900

EVERY BAR, whether commercial or in the home, needs a good stock of many styles and sizes of glasses if lots of different drinks are to be served. It's important to think about what drinks will be offered at any bar before investing in glassware. For simplicity and economy, consider using one style of glass for a variety of drinks. Hurricane glasses, for instance, won't be necessary unless you intend to offer Hurricanes, but if you do wish to serve that particular drink, consider using the glasses for all frozen drinks, and perhaps for other tropical-style drinks, such as the Planter's Punch.

It's also advisable to check the space available behind the bar for glass storage—some glasses can be quite tall and might not fit on your shelves. Also check the space between the beer spigots and the drainage tray so you won't buy beer glasses that don't fit between the two. I can tell you from personal experience that this situation can prove very frustrating. Here's a list of various styles of glassware, along with approximate capacities; be aware, however, that glasses are available in so many shapes and sizes that if you look hard enough, you'll probably be able to find almost any glass in any size.

LIQUOR AND FORTIFIED WINE SERVICE

BRANDY SNIFTER
5–8 ounces

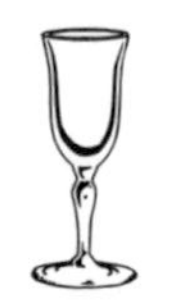

CORDIAL GLASS
2–3 ounces

SHERRY COPITA
3–4 ounces

SHOT GLASS
1–2 ounces

VODKA GLASS
1–3 ounces

WINE SERVICE

CHAMPAGNE FLUTE
6–8 ounces

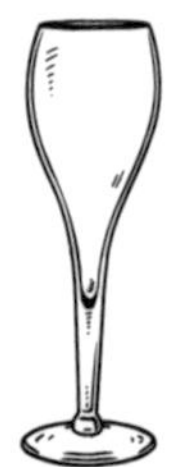

CHAMPAGNE TULIP
6–8 ounces

CHAMPAGNE COUPE OR SAUCER
6–8 ounces

RED WINE GLASS
8–12 ounces

WHITE WINE GLASS
8–12 ounces

BEER SERVICE

BEER MUG
10–16 ounces

BRITISH BEER MUG
20 ounces

MIXING GLASS
(also used for beer service) 16 ounces

PILSNER GLASS
10–14 ounces

COCKTAIL AND MIXED-DRINK SERVICE

COCKTAIL OR MARTINI GLASS
4–8 ounces

COLLINS GLASS
8–12 ounces

HIGHBALL GLASS
8–10 ounces

HURRICANE GLASS
14–20 ounces

IRISH COFFEE GLASS
8–10 ounces

OLD-FASHIONED, DOUBLE OLD-FASHIONED, OR ROCKS GLASS
4–8 ounces

POUSSE-CAFÉ GLASS
2–4 ounces

SOUR GLASS
3–6 ounces

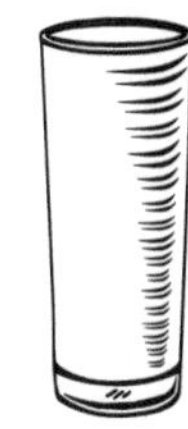
ZOMBIE GLASS
10–12 ounces

BIRDS OF A FEATHER:

COCKTAIL AND MIXED-DRINK FAMILIES

A family is a place where minds come in contact with one another. If these minds love one another, the home will be as beautiful as a flower garden. But if these minds get out of harmony with one another, it is like a storm that plays havoc with the garden. If discord arises within one's family, one should not blame others but should examine one's own mind and follow a right path.

—BUDDHA

MY JOURNEY TO DEFINE drink families began when I started to compile notes on how various other writers have described drinks in the past. Paying much attention to the works of Thomas, Johnson, Embury, and Grimes, and consulting with other cocktailians—Ted Haigh being my most frequently used source and mentor—I looked at definitions, then came to arbitrary decisions about which ingredients must be used in order for a drink to belong in a specific group.

It was Ted Haigh, again, who steered me toward creating new families, when he pointed out that the Margarita was nothing more, and certainly nothing less, than a variation on the Sidecar: Both call for a base spirit, a citrus juice, and an orange-flavored liqueur—tequila, lime juice, and triple sec in the first instance, and brandy, lemon juice, and triple sec in the second. There must be more drinks that follow this rule, I thought. And I was right.

The purpose of grouping these drinks together, though, is not merely for the sake of giving them somewhere to hang their hats.

In many cases, listing these drinks and their ingredients one under the other—as you will see in the various charts beginning on page 158—makes whole strings of drinks far easier to memorize. Once you know the formula for, say, New Orleans Sours, the family in which you'll find the Margarita and the Sidecar, you will understand that the Kamikaze is just a vodka-based Margarita and that the Cosmopolitan, using citrus vodka as a base, follows the same formula, with just a little cranberry juice thrown in for color. It is my hope that you will be able to use this, and other formulas, when creating drinks of your own.

Since the first edition of this book was released I've had much time to think about these categories, and I've also chatted about this subject with bartenders all over the world. This has resulted in my simplifying these categories and focusing on families of drinks that make sense when it comes to putting them into charts for easy reference, and for learning purposes. Here's hoping this works for you!

DUOS AND TRIOS

Duos call for two ingredients, usually a spirit and a liqueur; trios call for cream or a cream liqueur to be added to a Duo to make a whole new drink. Although two-ingredient drinks look simplistic, and some of them are, when one of the ingredients is a complex liqueur, such as Jägermeister, or perhaps a multilayered single-malt scotch, they can be quite intricate.

The drinks in this category, perhaps more than any other, are ideal for experimentation. If a recipe calls for two parts spirit and one part liqueur, for instance, you can easily make a drier, more sophisticated drink by altering the ratios and using far more liquor in relationship to the liqueur. With Trios, it's often possible to substitute a cream liqueur, such as Baileys, for the cream called for in drinks such as the Brandy Alexander, to make an interesting variation. The reason I chose to group these drinks together is far more obvious when you look at the chart on page 158.

Definition: Duos are composed of two ingredients, usually a base spirit and a liqueur, and are normally served in an old-fashioned glass.

Trios are duos to which cream or a cream liqueur has been added. Not all duos can be made into trios. Not all trios start out as duos.

FRENCH-ITALIAN DRINKS

Drinks included in the French-Italian family all contain vermouths, either sweet, dry, or both, or sometimes brand-named products, such as Lillet, an aperitif wine that's closely related to vermouth. The name of this family of drinks is derived from the fact that people used to call sweet vermouth "Italian" and dry vermouth "French," referring to their countries of origin (regardless of where specific bottlings were actually produced).

The French-Italian family is headed by the Manhattan and the Martini; you'll notice that many other classic cocktails—the Rob Roy and the Bronx Cocktail among them—belong here, too. As you look at the recipes, note the similarities as well as the differences between each one; also observe that when these drinks call for gin, genever, vodka, or tequila as a base, they *usually* employ dry vermouth as the secondary ingredient, whereas the cocktails with a base of whiskey or brandy *normally* call for sweet vermouth as a modifier.

You will find two sets of charts detailing French-Italian drinks on pages 159–61. One set features drinks based on gin, genever, vodka, and tequila, while the other details whiskey- and brandy-based cocktails; if you compare them, you will discover how similar many of these recipes can be. By soothing the soul of a distilled spirit, vermouth creates a great cornerstone for a cocktail, and can often be successfully used as a base for creative new drinks.

Bitters often come into play in French-Italian drinks, especially when whiskey or brandy is called for as a base, and the creative bartender should always bear that in mind when composing new formulas. By experimenting with Angostura, Peychaud's, orange, or any other flavor of bitters, you can change the character of the resultant cocktail quite dramatically.

Definition: French-Italian drinks contain a distilled spirit and sweet or dry vermouth, or sometimes both. They can be modified by other ingredients

SIMPLE SOURS

When Jerry Thomas detailed Sours in 1862, he was making them with a base spirit, sugar, water, a quarter of a lemon (the use of which he neglected to mention, but we'll presume he squeezed it), and another "small piece of lemon, the juice of which must be pressed in the glass." By 1887, he had revised his formula and was calling for sugar dissolved in carbonated water, lemon juice, and a spirit. Thomas's rival, Harry Johnson, also used carbonated water to make his sours, but in 1895 George J. Kappeler made an Apple Brandy Sour using gum (simple) syrup, lemon juice, and apple brandy, and that formula fits the one used today by cocktailian bartenders.

The Sours family can be broken down into many different categories, so here's how I've listed them in the charts on pages 163–67:

For instance, Sours that are sweetened by grenadine, rather than simple syrup, were once known as Daisies, and Fixes were Sours sweetened by pineapple juice. I have gathered most of these under the Simple Sours family umbrella, but I have broken the category down even more than I did for the first edition, mainly because twenty-first-century bartenders seem to have created a new style of Sours, Enhanced Sours, detailed next.

Definition: Simple Sours contain a base liquor, citrus juice, and a nonalcoholic sweetening agent, such as simple syrup, grenadine, or orgeat syrup.

ENHANCED SOURS

Over the past, say, ten years, enough Sours calling for vermouth have appeared in the bars of the world to justify this brand-new family.

Definition: Enhanced Sours call for a spirit, citrus juice, a sweetening agent of any kind, plus vermouth or any other aromatized or fortified wine.

NEW ORLEANS SOURS

Discovering this category of drinks was the most exciting thing that happened to me while writing the first edition of this book. I owe a debt of gratitude to Dr. Cocktail, a.k.a. Ted Haigh, for pointing out that the Sidecar is a variation on the Brandy Crusta, and that the Margarita is also built on the same formula.

The Brandy Crusta first appeared in New Orleans, probably in the first half of the nineteenth century. It was the creation of Joseph Santini, a restaurateur who once managed the City Exchange, a bar and restaurant where, reportedly, gumbo was created. The first recorded recipe for the Brandy Crusta appears in Jerry Thomas's 1862 book on mixology; it calls for brandy, curaçao (an orange-flavored liqueur), bitters, simple syrup, and lemon juice. The drink was served in a glass with a sugared rim and a spiral of lemon peel that covered the interior of the glass. Some later recipes for the Brandy Crusta substituted maraschino liqueur for the curaçao. The drink is now arcane, but the formula has spawned many classics, and New Orleans Sours are highly important to the cocktailian bartender.

You will notice that some of the world's greatest cocktails are members of this family—the Sidecar, the Margarita, and the Cosmopolitan among them. Study these drinks carefully, referring to the chart on page 165. Having a firm grasp of the formula that New Orleans Sours follow is imperative to the cocktailian bartender.

Definition: New Orleans Sours call for a base spirit, citrus juice, and an orange-flavored liqueur.

INTERNATIONAL SOURS

This category needs no real introduction, though I should probably mention that I descried these drinks as *international* because their sweetening agents include liqueurs from the four corners of the world rather than simple syrup, or products such as grenadine.

Definition: International Sours contain a spirit, citrus juice, and a liqueur as a sweetening agent.

SPARKLING SOURS

And this, our final member of the Sour family, covers drinks with a little fizz-water in them. And fizz-water, as you probably know, comes in many wild and wonderful styles from club soda, right through to the finest champagnes.

Definition: Sparkling Sours contain a spirit, some citrus juice, a sweetening agent of any style, and some bubbly to make the drink tickle your nose.

ADDITIONAL CATEGORIES

The families just defined are further explored in charts that follow this section. Recipes that fit into other categories also have been tagged, as follows:

BOTTLED COCKTAILS

Now more often referred to as "batched cocktails" in the industry, here you'll find recipes for bottled versions of the Cosmopolitan, the Jack Rose Royale, the Manhattan, the Margarita, and the Sidecar Deluxe.

CHAMPAGNE COCKTAILS

The original Champagne Cocktail from the mid-1800s, still going strong today, is detailed in the recipe chapter (page 197), as are these other bubbly classics: Kir Royale, Mimosa, Dale DeGroff's Ritz Cocktail, and the somewhat controversial Seelbach Cocktail.

DAIQUIRIS

All Daiquiris are Sours of one stripe or another, so the name doesn't encompass a family all its own, but the following drinks are labeled as Daiquiris and there's absolutely nothing you can do about it: the Daiquiri, the Hemingway Daiquiri, La Floridita Daiquiri, the Luau Daiquiri; and make sure you sample the awesome power of the late Gregor De Gruyther's Nuclear Daiquiri.

FROZEN DRINKS

There's just one frozen drink in this book: the Piña Colada. Recipe by Dean Callan, the undisputed King of Piña Coladas.

HIGHBALLS

I've let go of those hits from the 1980s such as Sex on the Beach, and the Woo-Woo in this edition, and I haven't included obvious Highballs such as Gin & Tonic or Scotch and Soda, either. The Highballs I did detail, though, are important to know when you step behind the bar. These are the Highballs you'll find in this book: Americano, Cuba Libra, Cuzco Cocktail, Dark and Stormy, Gin-Gin Mule, Greyhound, Harvey Wallbanger, Long Island Iced Tea, Mamie Taylor, Moscow Mule, Salty Dog, and the Tart Gin Cooler.

HOT DRINKS

I've included a few important winter warmers in the lineup, specifically Café Brûlot, Hot Buttered Rum, Hot Toddy, and the most delicious Irish Coffee recipe you ever did taste—straight from New York's Dead Rabbit, one of my alma maters

INFUSIONS

There are just two infusions included in the recipe section, and both of them are pretty stunning. You'll find Chef Bradley Ogden's Lark Creek Inn Tequila Infusion here, and a great Limoncello formula straight from the late George Germon and his wife, Johanne Killeen of Al Forno in Providence, Rhode Island.

JELLY SHOTS

I've included three Jelly Shot formulas—Banana Daiquiri, Margarita, and Whiskey Sour—in the recipe chapter, just so you have an idea of ratios to use should you wish to serve these babies, all of which are made with fresh juices and unflavored gelatin.

JULEPS

The Mint Julep in the recipe chapter is followed by two variations (one modern-day and one nineteenth-century formula) and the Old Cuban

Cocktail, the Mojito, the Southside Cocktail, and the Southside Fizz, all of which boast a minty profile to one degree or another.

OLD-FASHIONEDS

You'll find a formula for the original Old-Fashioned Whiskey Cocktail in the recipe chapter, and it's followed by a Fruit-Style Old-Fashioned that I highly recommend, despite protestations from my peers. David Wondrich's Old Bay Ridge, and the late Dick Bradsel's Treacle, both variations on the Old-Fashioned theme, are also included.

ORPHANS

Cocktails that don't fit into any of the drink families or categories above are labeled as "Orphans" in the recipes that follow. They have no easily defined formulas.

PUNCHES

I confess to not being enamored of punches, and I doubt that the two punch recipes I've included are technically considered to be punches by aficionados of the category. Nevertheless, I've included formulas for the Fishhouse Punch and a Planter's Punch.

SNAPPERS

All drinks containing tomato juice make up this small family: The Bloody Bull, Bloody Caesar, Bloody Mary, and the Red Snapper can all be found in the recipe section.

TIKI

I've a new respect for Tiki drinks, and I owe that to Jeff "Beachbum" Berry, who patiently introduced me to some bitters-laden tropical potions that really rocked my boat. The lineup includes the Fog Cutter, Luau Daiquiri, Mai Tai, Scorpion, U.S.S. Wondrich—one of my very favorites—and, of course, the Zombie

FAMILY CHARTS

I have not included every single drink in each family, but there are enough examples of each style of drink for the charts to be very useful in gaining an understanding of each family.

DUOS AND TRIOS			
Godfather	scotch	amaretto	
Godmother	vodka	amaretto	cream
Debonair	scotch	Domaine de Canton ginger liqueur	
Rusty Nail	scotch	Drambuie	
Stinger	cognac	white crème de menthe	
Tremblement de Terre	cognac	absinthe	
Black Russian	vodka	Kahlúa	
White Russian	vodka	Kahlúa	cream
Mudslide	vodka	Kahlúa	Baileys Irish Cream
Grasshopper	white crème de cacao	green crème de menthe	cream
Alexander	gin	white crème de cacao	cream
Brandy Alexander	cognac	dark crème de cacao	cream

FRENCH-ITALIAN: GIN, RUM, GENEVER, VODKA, AND TEQUILA

The similarities among the first four drinks here are obvious, but when you start adding liqueurs to the spirit/vermouth template, lo and behold, the Negroni appears, and with it come a series of sweeter cocktails that build their reputations on the backs of the Martini. Note also that both the Martinez and Satan's Whiskers fit neatly into this family.

Martini	gin or vodka	dry vermouth			orange bitters
Gibson	gin or vodka	dry vermouth			(onion garnish)
Dirty Martini	gin or vodka	dry vermouth			olive brine
Vesper Martini	gin and vodka	Lillet Blonde			
Goldfish Cocktail	gin	dry vermouth	Danziger Goldwasser		
Negroni	gin	sweet vermouth	Campari		
Negroni d'Or	gin	Dolin Blanc vermouth	Gran Classico bitter		
Hanky-Panky	gin	sweet vermouth	Fernet Branca		
Dutch Coupe	genever	Carpano Antica formula	Cynar	orange flower water	orange bitters
White Walker	tequila	Dolin Blanc vermouth	maraschino liqueur		lemon bitters
Martinez	Old Tom	sweet vermouth	maraschino liqueur		Boker's bitters
Martinez by Perrone	gin	Punt e Mes	maraschino liqueur	orange curaçao	Abbott's bitters
Bitter Stripper	gin	Dolin Blanc vermouth	Salers Gentiane	Cointreau	
Satan's Whiskers	gin	sweet and dry vermouths		orange curaçao or Grand Marnier	

FRENCH-ITALIAN: WHISKEY AND BRANDY

The top three cocktails in this chart form the backbone of this family, and they are followed closely by three more drinks that are worthy of note. Then come five formulas that all call for a bitter liqueur such as Cynar or Amaro CioCiaro as a modifier; after these I have listed half a dozen drinks that use Bénédictine as their liqueur of choice. These drinks—will we ever get to the end of this chart?—are rounded out by another six cocktails, each of which calls for a specific modifying liqueur.

Manhattan	rye or bourbon	sweet vermouth		Angostura bitters
Paddy Cocktail	Irish whiskey	sweet vermouth		Angostura bitters
Rob Roy	scotch	sweet vermouth		Peychaud's bitters
Blackthorn	Irish whiskey and absinthe	sweet vermouth		Angostura bitters
Phoebe Snow Cocktail	brandy and absinthe	Dubonnet		
Corpse Reviver No. 1	brandy and calvados	sweet vermouth		
Little Italy	rye whiskey	sweet vermouth	Cynar	
Perfect 10	rye whiskey	Punt e Mes	sloe gin and E**X**R** liqueur	
Bensonhurst	rye whiskey	sweet vermouth	maraschino liqueur and Cynar	
Bottom Line	scotch	sweet vermouth	Amaro CioCiaro and Bärenjäger liqueur	
Brooklyn Heights	rye whiskey	dry vermouth	Luxardo Amaro Abano and Campari	orange bitters

A Tale of Two Roberts	scotch and absinthe	sweet vermouth	Bénédictine	
Vieux Carré	rye whiskey and brandy	sweet vermouth	Bénédictine	Angostura and Peychaud's bitters
Preakness Cocktail	bourbon or rye whiskey	sweet vermouth	Bénédictine	Angostura bitters
King Louis the 4th	scotch	Lillet Rouge and tawny port	Bénédictine	mole bitters
Am I Blue	scotch	sweet vermouth	Bénédictine and maraschino liqueur	orange bitters
Bobby Burns	scotch	sweet vermouth	Bénédictine or absinthe	
Bedford	rye whiskey	Dubonnet	Cointreau	orange bitters
Remember the Maine	rye whiskey and absinthe	sweet vermouth	cherry brandy	
Leaving Manhattan	bourbon	Punt e Mes	dark crème de cacao	lapsang smoked tea syrup
Manhattan Perfecto	rye whiskey	sweet and dry vermouth	maraschino liqueur	Angostura bitters
The Williamsburg	bourbon	Punt e Mes and Dolin dry vermouth	Yellow Chartreuse liqueur	
Greenpoint	rye whiskey	sweet vermouth	Yellow Chartreuse liqueur	Angostura and orange bitters
The Slope	rye whiskey	Punt e Mes	apricot brandy	Angostura bitters

FRENCH-ITALIAN: THE MANHATTAN

Six new drinks named for various neighborhoods in New York have been created over the past decade or so, and they are all Manhattan variations of sorts. I've put them all together here so you'll have a quick and easy guide to the Manhattan and her many progeny!

Manhattan	rye whiskey or bourbon	sweet vermouth		Angostura bitters
Bensonhurst	rye whiskey	sweet vermouth	Cynar	maraschino liqueur
Brooklyn Heights	rye whiskey	dry vermouth	Luxardo Amaro Abano	Campari and orange bitters
Greenpoint	rye whiskey	sweet vermouth	Yellow Chartreuse liqueur	Angostura and orange bitters
Little Italy	rye whiskey	sweet vermouth	Cynar	
The Slope	rye whiskey	Punt e Mes	apricot brandy	Angostura bitters
The Williamsburg	rye whiskey	Punt e Mes	Yellow Chartreuse liqueur	

This chart contains drinks with a spirit, citrus, and a sweetening agent, and the first nine cocktails contain nothing more. The next four drinks treat themselves to double citrus, and the final group contains a little something extra such as egg white, bitters, and/or both.

Daiquiri	rum	lime juice	simple syrup	
Bacardi Cocktail	rum	lime juice	grenadine	
Jack Rose	applejack	lemon juice	grenadine	
Caipirinha	rum	lime juice	sugar	
Caipiroska	vodka	lime juice	sugar	
Whiskey Sour	bourbon or rye	lemon juice	simple syrup	
Penicillin	scotch	lemon juice	honey-ginger syrup	
Tommy's Margarita	tequila	lime juice	diluted agave fructose	
Hurricane	rum	lemon juice	passionfruit syrup	
Scorpion	rum and brandy	lemon and orange juice	orgeat syrup	
Luau Daiquiri	rum	lime and orange juice	vanilla syrup	
Zombie	rum	lime and grapefruit juice	cinnamon syrup	
Ward Eight	rye whiskey	lemon and orange juice	grenadine	
Trinidad Sour	rye	lemon juice	orgeat syrup	Angostura bitters
Earl Grey MarTEAni	gin	lemon juice	simple syrup	egg white
Pisco Sour	Pisco	lime juice	simple syrup	egg white and Angostura bitters
Southside Cocktail	gin	lemon juice	sugar	mint leaves

ENHANCED SOURS

The enhancement of these sours comes in the form of a little fortified wine, or our good friend Lady Vermouth.

Bronx Cocktail	gin	sweet and dry vermouth	orange juice	orange bitters
Income Tax Cocktail	gin	sweet and dry vermouth	orange juice	Angostura bitters
Clover Club Cocktail	gin	dry vermouth	lemon juice	raspberry syrup
Scofflaw Cocktail	rye or bourbon	dry vermouth	lemon juice	grenadine
Ruby Can't Fail	gin	ruby port	orange and lemon juices	simple syrup
Little Dragon	gin	dry sherry	lemon juice	mango puree, honey, and green tea powder
Leap-Year Cocktail*	gin	sweet vermouth	Grand Marnier	lemon juice
Oriental Cocktail*	rye whiskey	sweet vermouth	triple sec	lime juice
Gotham Cocktail†	cognac	dry vermouth	créme de cassis	lemon juice

* This is also a New Orleans Sour.

† This is also an International Sour.

NEW ORLEANS SOURS

Pay attention: This is probably the most important family of Sours, and you'll know why when you look at the first seven drinks listed here. I'm sure you'll agree that these cocktails are essential for any bartender worth his or her salt. It's interesting, too, that the four cocktails that follow these leaders all contain vermouth—food for thought when experimenting behind the bar.

Brandy Crusta	brandy		orange curaçao	lemon juice	Angostura or Boker's bitters
Cable Car	spiced rum		orange curaçao and simple syrup	lemon juice	
Cosmopolitan	citrus vodka		Cointreau	lime juice	cranberry juice
Kamikaze	vodka		triple sec	lime juice	
Lemon Drop	citrus vodka		triple sec	lemon juice	
Margarita	tequila		triple sec	lime juice	
Pegu Club Cocktail	gin		orange curaçao	lime juice	Angostura and orange bitters
Sidecar	brandy		Cointreau	lemon juice	Angostura bitters
Corpse Reviver No. 2	gin and absinthe	Lillet Blonde	triple sec	lemon juice	
James Joyce Cocktail	Irish whiskey	sweet vermouth	triple sec	lime juice	
Leap-Year Cocktail*	gin	sweet vermouth	Grand Marnier	lemon juice	
Oriental Cocktail*	rye whiskey	sweet vermouth	triple sec	lime juice	

*This is also an Enhanced Sour.

INTERNATIONAL SOURS

International Sours must include liqueurs other than triple sec, or other orange-flavored liqueurs, in order to live within this family, and it's interesting to note how often both maraschino liqueur and Green Chartreuse get called for here. The Final Ward is the only twenty-first-century cocktail that calls for these ingredients; all the other drinks with these two liqueurs are pre-1950s formulas.

Hemingway Daiquiri	rum	maraschino liqueur		lime juice and grapefruit juice	
La Floridita Daiquiri	rum	maraschino liqueur		lime juice	simple syrup
Mary Pickford	rum	maraschino liqueur		pineapple juice	grenadine
Aviation	gin	maraschino liqueur	crème de violette	lemon juice	
Aviation World Class Style	gin	maraschino liqueur	Parfait Amour	lemon juice	
Last Word	gin	maraschino liqueur	Green Chartreuse	lime juice	
Nuclear Daiquiri	rum	velvet falernum	Green Chartreuse	lime juice	simple syrup
Final Ward	rye whiskey	maraschino liqueur	Green Chartreuse	lemon juice	
RBS Special	rye whiskey	kümmel liqueur		lemon juice	grenadine
Gun Metal Blue	mezcal	blue curaçao	peach brandy	lime juice	
Monkey Gland Cocktail	gin	absinthe or Bénédictine		orange juice	bitter cinnamon and simple syrup
Cuzco Cocktail	Pisco with a kirschwasser rinse	Aperol		lemon juice and grapefruit juice	simple syrup
Twentieth-Century Cocktail	gin	white crème de cacao		lemon juice	
Gotham*	cognac	dry vermouth	crème de cassis	lemon juice	

SPARKLING SOURS

Here are the remaining Sours, each one with a spot of fizz in one of its various forms.

French 75	gin		champagne	lemon juice	simple syrup
Ramos Gin Fizz	gin		club soda	lemon and lime juices	orange flower water, cream, and egg white
Southside Fizz	gin		club soda	lemon juice	sugar and mint leaves
Gin-Gin Mule	gin		ginger beer	lime juice	simple syrup
Tom Collins	gin		club soda	lemon juice	simple syrup
John Collins	bourbon or genever		club soda	lemon juice	simple syrup
Old Cuban Cocktail	rum		champagne	lime juice	simple syrup, Angostura bitters, and mint leaves
Singapore Sling	gin	Bénédictine and Cherry Heering	club soda	lime juice	Angostura bitters
Singapore Sling as the Straights Sling	gin	Bénédictine and kirschwasser	club soda	lemon juice	Angostura and orange bitters
Floss 75	gin	Camorra Fairy Floss liqueur	prosecco	ruby red grape-fruit juice	
Bellini			prosecco	white peach puree	

THE RECIPES

It is only fitting that the subject of cocktails should be approached with levity slightly tinctured with contempt because, for every good compound, arrangement, or synthesis of liquors, wines, and their adjacent or opposite fruits and flavors chilled and served in a variety of glasses, there are approximately a million foul, terrifying, and horrendous similar excitements to stupefaction, cuspidor hurling, and nausea.

—Lucius Beebe, 1945

FOR THIS EDITION I have kept the classic drink recipes that were in the original *Joy of Mixology*, and in some instances I've revised and updated them to be as close as possible to their original formulas while also maintaining our modern standards for taste. I discarded any recipes that are no longer in use in cocktail bars today. Best of all, I've added many new drinks that have been created since my original edition was published.

I've tried to include many of the drinks that seem to have caught the attention of the global bartender community, such as the Gin-Gin Mule, Penicillin, and the Chartreuse Swizzle, all cocktails that you might find in craft cocktail bars almost anywhere in the world, and I've also included some drinks that are a little less well known but that deserve mention for all sorts of reasons.

It's inevitable that I've overlooked some wonderful potions in this chapter, and for that I apologize. I do think that this time around at least I've assembled a great collection of really good quaffs.

Dates: Wherever possible, I have included the birthdates of individual cocktails, but although some of these dates are absolutely verifiable, in other cases, as I have noted, they refer only to the first printed mention I have been able to find. My library of vintage cocktail books is extensive but by no means complete; I welcome any information that challenges the dates used here.

Ingredients and ratios: It's important to note that even though I might refer to a certain book as having detailed specific drinks, the recipes that follow are not necessarily the exact formulas as in the original drinks. For the most part, ratios have been altered to suit today's tastes, and at times I have substituted certain ingredients—usually because the original spirit or liqueur is no longer available or is very hard to find.

Names and creators: Ingredients for almost every cocktail can vary from bar to bar, and drinks calling for the same formulas can masquerade under different names in different places. The recipes in this chapter detail the ingredients that I believe to be correct, or at least each recipe is the best of the various versions I have tested; and wherever possible, I have credited the person whom I believe created the drink.

THE MOST IMPORTANT LESSON FOR THE COCKTAILIAN BARTENDER

I strongly believe that bartenders should rarely follow recipes precisely. They should learn to be able to feel their way around a drink by developing a keen taste memory for ingredients, or should actually taste all the ingredients in a drink before putting them together. I have worked with students who had no prior cocktailian experience, and I have observed them successfully utilizing this method of making drinks after as little as two days' training.

That said, the fact is that recipes must have measurements; but in the vast majority of cases, I hope that you will regard them as mere guidelines. You must learn to alter proportions when making drinks such as the Rob Roy, since the ratios depend on which particular bottling of scotch you use, and you should learn to vary proportions in order to satisfy individual tastes. Again, never forget: *Nothing is written in stone.*

METHODOLOGY

Instead of repeating specific instructions over and over on how to make each drink included in this chapter, I have elected to provide one set of instructions here. The key words in each recipe indicate which instructions to follow. For instance, if you see "STIR AND STRAIN into a chilled cocktail glass," simply follow the directions given here under the heading "Stir and Strain." For discussions of all methods of mixing drinks, refer to the chapter titled "The Craft of the Mixologist."

BUILD

Fill the glass with ice, if called for, and add the ingredients in the order given. Add any garnish called for, stir briefly, and serve.

DRY SHAKE

Add all the ingredients to an empty shaker and shake for around 20 seconds to emulsify the egg white with the other ingredients. Add ice to the shaker, shake for approximately 15 seconds, and strain the drink into the appropriate glass.

FLOAT

After making the drink, float the last ingredient on top by pouring it slowly over the back of a barspoon.

LAYER

Pour the first ingredient into the glass. Then slowly pour each of the other ingredients, in the order given, over the back of a barspoon, so that each successive ingredient floats on top of the previous ingredient.

MIX AND CHILL

Combine the ingredients in a large container, stir thoroughly, and store the container in a refrigerator until well chilled.

MUDDLE

Put the ingredients into an empty glass and grind them with a muddler until all the juices have been extracted from the fruit and any sugar in the recipe is completely dissolved.

RINSE

Pour the ingredient called for into the glass and, by tilting the glass and rotating it at the same time, coat the entire interior of the glass. Discard any excess.

SHAKE AND STRAIN

Fill a shaker two-thirds full of ice and add the ingredients in the order given. Shake for approximately 15 seconds and strain the drink into the appropriate glass.

STIR AND STRAIN

Fill a mixing glass two-thirds full of ice and add the ingredients in the order given. Stir for approximately 30 seconds, then strain the drink into the appropriate glass.

YIELD

Unless otherwise noted, each recipe makes one drink.

ALASKA

FAMILY: **DUOS AND TRIOS** || Experiment with ratios when preparing this drink. Chartreuse can easily overpower other ingredients, and it's vital to consider which brand of gin you are using. Tanqueray, for example, will stand up to more Chartreuse than, say, Bombay will.

1½ ounces gin
½ ounce Yellow Chartreuse

STIR AND STRAIN into a chilled cocktail glass.

ALEXANDER

FAMILY: **DUOS AND TRIOS** || According to historian Barry Popik, in 1929 a New York columnist explained the birth of the Alexander cocktail by recounting a tale about Rector's, New York's premier lobster palace prior to Prohibition. George Rector is said to have referred to his place as "a cathedral of froth."

The bartender at Rector's was a certain Troy Alexander, and it was he who created his eponymous cocktail in order to serve a white drink at a dinner that was held to celebrate "Phoebe Snow," a fictitious character who was used in an advertising campaign for the Delaware, Lackawanna and Western Railroad. This company powered its trains with anthracite, a clean-burning form of coal, and they emphasized this by showing Phoebe Snow traveling on their locomotives wearing a snow-white dress. The earliest known printed recipe for the Alexander can be seen in the 1915 book *Recipes for Mixed Drinks*, by Hugo Ensslin. (See more on Phoebe Snow on page 263.)

2 ounces dry gin
1 ounce white crème de cacao
1 ounce cream

SHAKE AND STRAIN into a chilled cocktail glass.

A rehearsal of "Red, Hot and Blue!" was in progress. The star of the show, Jimmy Durante, sat on a shaky chair tilted against the bare bricks in the back wall of the stage. He looked as if he were trying to get as far away from other humans as possible. His face was haggard. When he took his cigar out of his big, ragged mouth his hands shook.

"I can't drink," he said, shivering. "Only my great sense of responsibility forced me to show up at the pickle works today. I can't drink. It's alright if I take a glass of vermoot, or some red wine. Yeh, that's all right. But last night I'm feeling thirsty, so I go to this joint across the street and I say to the bartender, 'recommend me something.' So he give me what he called an Alexander. I had about six of these Alexanders, and I get dizzy. When I go home I hit the bed and it whirls around like an electric fan. I am seasick. I'm in an awful fix. I want to die."

—JOSEPH MITCHELL, *My Ears Are Bent*

ALMOST BLOW MY SKULL OFF

FAMILY: ORPHANS || Blow My Skull Off was a cocktail devised in Australia during the 1850s. A gold rush was occurring at the time, and according to "Spiers & Pond: A Memorable Australian Partnership," a short story by Phillip Andrew, prospectors were more than fond of this concoction that contained opium, cayenne pepper, rum, and "spirits of wine." According to Andrew, "A couple of good swigs and the mounted police would turn out. [They had to] hit everyone they could see before the brawl reached the proportions of a riot." Inspired by this story, I created Almost Blow My Skull Off, and I've recently updated the drink—this version, I believe, tastes a little more like the original. Though we'll never really know . . .

¼ ounce Ancho Reyes Verde liqueur
2 ounces cognac
½ ounce Jägermeister

RINSE a chilled cocktail glass with the Ancho Reyes Verde liqueur. STIR AND STRAIN the cognac and Jägermeister into the glass.

AMARO CRUSTA

FAMILY: ORPHANS || Adapted from a recipe by Max La Rocca and Giuseppe Santamaria, Barcelona, Spain. When this recipe came to me Max La Rocca wrote that the drink is "an Italian twist on a very old classic showcasing nice herbal notes, a slightly thick mouthfeel from using marmalade, and a pleasant bitter and orange aftertaste. [It's] an excellent after-dinner drink with loads of herbs that will help your digestion and your soul!"

1 full barspoon bitter orange marmalade
2 teaspoons fresh lemon juice
2 teaspoons fresh lime juice
⅔ ounce Amaro Montenegro
2 teaspoons Rabarbaro Zucca
2 teaspoons Amer Picon orange bitters
Vanilla sugar, for rimming the glass (see Note)
1 orange twist, for garnish

Dissolve the marmalade into the citrus juices in a shaker. Add ice and the remaining ingredients, shake and finely strain into a chilled shaker; shake the hell out of it. Double-strain into a small, chilled wine glass rimmed with vanilla sugar. Add the garnish.

NOTE: To make vanilla sugar, take 1 vanilla bean, slice it down the center, and scrape the seeds from the inside of the bean into a jar containing 2 cups granulated sugar. Add the bean to the jar and stir well. Let sit for 24 hours before using.

AMERICANO

FAMILY: HIGHBALLS || I think this drink fares well when made with equal parts Campari and vermouth, but this is purely a matter of personal preference—experiment with ratios until you find your own perfect Americano.

1½ ounces Campari
1½ ounces sweet vermouth
2 ounces club soda
1 orange twist, for garnish

BUILD in the order given in an ice-filled highball glass. Add the garnish.

AM I BLUE

|| FAMILY: FRENCH-ITALIAN: WHISKEY AND BRANDY ||

"Apparently, asking questions without question marks was another characteristic of [Fuka-Eri's] speech."

— HARUKI MURAKAMI, *1Q84*, 2011

This Rob Roy variation that I created uses a very special scotch and a scant ¼ ounce of maraschino to differentiate it from a traditional Rob Roy. I also topped it off with champagne, a twist that works well with many standard drinks. Sidecars, for instance, can be splendid with a little bubbly in them.

1½ ounces Johnnie Walker Blue Label scotch
½ ounce Noilly Prat sweet vermouth
¼ ounce Luxardo maraschino liqueur
1 dash Regan's Orange Bitters No. 6
Chilled champagne
1 flamed orange twist, for garnish

STIR AND STRAIN all ingredients except for the champagne into a chilled champagne flute. Top with chilled champagne and add the garnish.

ANGEL'S SHARE

FAMILY: ORPHANS || Adapted from a recipe by Jacques Bezuidenhout, Harry Denton's Starlight Room, San Francisco. I featured this great drink in the *San Francisco Chronicle* in 2005—it's an early example of a drink using very expensive ingredients, and back then it sold for $200 at the Starlight Room.

2 to 3 dashes Chartreuse V.E.P. liqueur
1¼ ounces Remy Martin Louis XIII cognac
1¼ ounces Nostalgie Black Walnut liqueur
½ ounce Porto Rocha 20-year tawny port

RINSE a brandy snifter with the Chartreuse and, using a match, ignite the liqueur, allowing it to burn for a few seconds before extinguishing the flame by placing a saucer on top of the glass. STIR AND STRAIN the remaining ingredients into the prepared glass.

APEROL SPRITZ

FAMILY: **ORPHANS** || Aperol, sometimes known as "Campari Light," forms the base of this refreshing quaff. I usually don't bother with the club soda, preferring to add another splash of prosecco instead.

2 ounces Aperol
3 ounces prosecco
1 splash club soda
1 orange wheel, for garnish

BUILD in the order given in an ice-filled collins glass, or a double old-fashioned glass, and stir briefly. Add the garnish.

ATOM LIMO

FAMILY: **ORPHANS** || Adapted from a recipe by Stephan Hinz, Shepheard American Bar, Cologne, Germany.

1 ounce plus 1 teaspoon Wild Turkey bourbon
1 ounce plus 1 teaspoon Lustau Pedro Ximenez sherry
½ ounce fresh lemon juice
1 ounce plus 2 teaspoons fresh apple juice
2 pieces fresh ginger
Ginger ale
1 mint sprig, for garnish
1 apple slice, for garnish
1 fresh cherry, for garnish

BUILD in the order given in an ice-filled double old-fashioned glass, stir briefly, and add the garnishes.

AUTUMN WINDS

FAMILY: **ORPHANS** || Adapted from a recipe by Matt Seiter, Trattoria Marcella, St. Louis, Missouri. In Missouri, Matt Seiter has a hard time getting lots of new products, so when he can't get his hands on an ingredient he simply makes his own. "I love going to the farmers' markets and getting inspiration and fresh ingredients for house-made items. You could say, then, that my mentality is if you can make it in-house with fresh ingredients, then do it," says Matt. One of Matt's most unusual creations is his Brown Butter Sage liqueur, and it's displayed at its best in his Autumn Winds cocktail. Matt incorporates fat-washing into this creation, and he says that a small amount of butter solids will remain in the mixture, so it's best to shake the bottle before using it in cocktails.

2 ounces Aviation gin
½ ounce Bénédictine
½ ounce Brown Butter Sage liqueur (recipe follows)
1 dash Angostura bitters
1 spanked sage leaf, for garnish

SHAKE AND STRAIN into a chilled cocktail glass, and add the garnish.

BROWN BUTTER SAGE LIQUEUR

12 to 15 fresh sage leaves
5 ounces (10 tablespoons) unsalted butter
¾ ounce fresh lemon juice
Pinch of kosher salt
1 cup simple syrup made at 1:1 ratio (page 124)
12 ounces vodka (Matt prefers Sobieski, a rye-based vodka)

Stack the sage leaves, roll them tightly, and slice thinly, making a chiffonade of sage leaves.

Make brown butter by cutting the butter into small pieces and melting it in a medium nonreactive saucepan. Stir constantly until the butter starts to take on a light brown color, then remove from the heat.

Add the lemon juice and sage leaves and allow the mixture to rest for 10 minutes. Add the simple syrup and vodka, and allow the mixture to stand for 4 to 6 hours at room temperature.

Transfer the mixture to a sealable container and allow it to rest in the refrigerator overnight. Skim any solids from the top of the mixture, strain it through a double layer of dampened cheesecloth, and transfer the infusion to a bottle.

AVIATION COCKTAIL

FAMILY: INTERNATIONAL SOURS || The first printed mention of this drink appeared in *Recipes for Mixed Drinks* by Hugo Ensslin, in 1916, during the First World War, when aviators began being lauded for their heroic deeds. When this drink first captured the attention of twenty-first-century cocktailians, it was impossible to recreate it, but now that the once unavailable crème de violette is back on the scene in the United States, we can again taste the drink as it was once enjoyed.

I use the Rothman and Winter bottling of crème de violette. Maraschino-wise, I'm a fan of the highly scented Luxardo brand, which marries very well to a good gin. I like a straightforward, gutsy gin for Aviations. There's actually a gin called Aviation, which works well here; otherwise, go with Beefeater, Junipero, Plymouth, G'Vine Nouaison, or Tanqueray.

This is a great drink to serve to people who are fond of saying, "I don't like gin." It tends to go down far better than a slap upside their head as you yell, "Well, it's about time you learned to like it!"

2 ounces gin
½ ounce crème de violette
¼ ounce maraschino liqueur
½ ounce fresh lemon juice

SHAKE AND STRAIN into a chilled cocktail glass.

AVIATION: WORLD CLASS STYLE

FAMILY: INTERNATIONAL SOURS || In 2010, I tasted the very best Aviation cocktail I've ever encountered. I was in Athens, Greece, helping to judge Diageo's World Class Bartender Competition, and the bartender who prepared the cocktail was Takumi Watanabe. In 2017, I contacted him about his recipe, and had a light-bulb moment when he mentioned that, since there was no crème de violette available to him at the time, he had used Marie Brizard's Parfait Amour, a liqueur that's similar in color but boasts orange and vanilla notes rather than floral ones. Here, then, is the recipe—and the methodology—for what I believe to have been Takumi's Aviation Cocktail.

1½ ounces Tanqueray No. Ten gin
½ ounce Giffard Marasquin maraschino liqueur
⅛ ounce Marie Brizard Parfait Amour liqueur
⅓ ounce fresh lemon juice
1 lemon twist, for garnish

Pour the gin into a shaker without ice and stir it to release the aromas. Add ice and the remaining ingredients. Shake and finely strain into a chilled cocktail glass. Add the garnish.

AZTEC'S MARK

AMILY: ORPHANS || Adapted from a recipe by Neyah White when e worked at Nopa, San Francisco. This is a great example of a recipe ıat looks like it won't work, but when constructed properly, it's a gem. nd it comes from a very important bartender who, in keeping with Eric lapton's notoriety, was once called "God" in a San Francisco blog postıg. He's just that good.

1¼ ounces Maker's Mark bourbon
¼ ounce Bénédictine
½ ounce dark crème de cacao
2 drops Tabasco sauce
1 orange twist, for garnish

HAKE AND STRAIN into a chilled cocktail glass. Add the garnish.

BACARDI COCKTAIL

AMILY: SIMPLE SOURS || In 1936 this drink had become so popuır that the Bacardi family took a bar owner to court for using a rum other ıan Bacardi in his Bacardi Cocktails, and an injunction was granted. et that be a lesson to you. The Bacardi Cocktail is nothing more than a aiquiri made with grenadine.

1½ ounces Bacardi light rum
¾ ounce grenadine
½ ounce fresh lime juice

HAKE AND STRAIN into a chilled cocktail glass.

BANANA DAIQUIRI JELLY SHOT

|| FAMILY: JELLY SHOTS ||

1 ounce fresh lime juice
1 ounce simple syrup
1 ounce water
1 package unflavored gelatin (¼ ounce)
3 ounces rum
3 ounces crème de banane
Food coloring (optional)

PLACE the lime juice, simple syrup, and water in a small glass measuring cup, and add the gelatin. Allow this to sit for 1 minute, then microwave the mixture on high for 30 seconds. Stir thoroughly to make sure that all the gelatin has dissolved, then add the rum, banana liqueur, and food coloring (if desired). Stir thoroughly again and pour the mixture into a mold. Refrigerate for at least 1 hour or, preferably, overnight.

THE BEDFORD

FAMILY: FRENCH-ITALIAN DRINKS: WHISKEY AND BRANDY ||

Adapted from a recipe by Del Pedro, of Grange Hall/Pegu Club, New York. Grange Hall, the joint where this baby was born, was one of the very first places in New York to take their cocktails seriously. We owe much to Del Pedro, creator of this drink. Note that Del uses Dubonnet Rouge here, rather than sweet vermouth; other aromatized wines such as Byrrh or other quinquinas, as well as Amari like Amaro Ramazzotti, can also be employed instead of vermouth in variations on the Manhattan.

2 ounces straight rye whiskey
¾ ounce Dubonnet Rouge
1 teaspoon Cointreau
2 dashes orange bitters
1 orange twist, for garnish

SHAKE AND STRAIN into a chilled cocktail glass. Add the garnish.

BELLINI

|| FAMILY: SPARKLING SOURS* ||

Adapted from a recipe by Giovanni Venturini, Venice.

*I'm allowing peaches into the citrus family—it's debatable, but it works in this instance.

According to *Harry's Bar*, by Arrigio Cipriani, the Bellini—perhaps the most sophisticated Italian drink—was created in 1948 by Harry Cipriani at Harry's Bar in Venice. It was named for the fifteenth-century Italian artist Jacopo Bellini, most of whose works apparently included a "pink glow," which is reproduced in the resultant drink. In 1990, Arrigio licensed the drink to an entrepreneur, who promptly added raspberry juice to the recipe. This angered Arrigio so much that in 1995 he took the entrepreneur to arbitration and regained ownership of the name.

Classically made with white peaches, this is a beautiful drink, but it can be somewhat hard to pour since the fruit puree makes the wine effervesce more than usual. The drink should be made with prosecco, an Italian sparkling wine that's sweeter than most champagnes used in this type of cocktail; if you use champagne instead, go with a sec or demi-sec bottling. And if white peaches aren't available, use any fresh peach.

You can also experiment with this drink by substituting purees of fruits other than peaches, such as raspberries, strawberries, or apricots, but take into consideration the relative sweetness of the fruit, and alter the amount of lemon juice accordingly.

I was given a recipe for this drink by Giovanni Venturini, a bartender at the private palace of the Ciprianis in Venice. It contained a little too much peach puree for my liking, so although I've used Venturini's recipe for the puree itself, I've altered his proportions for what I think is a better-balanced drink.

2 ounces white peach puree (recipe follows)
3½ ounces chilled prosecco

Add the peach puree to a champagne flute, then slowly add the chilled prosecco, stirring constantly to incorporate the ingredients.

WHITE PEACH PUREE

In a blender, puree the flesh, including the skin, of 1 white peach with 2 or 3 ice cubes and ½ teaspoon of fresh lemon juice.

THE BENSONHURST

FAMILY: FRENCH-ITALIAN: WHISKEY AND BRANDY || Adapted from a recipe by Chad Solomon of Cuffs and Buttons, this is one of a bunch of drinks named for various neighborhoods in and around New York City. The dry vermouth and the maraschino waltz well with the whiskey here, but it's that barspoon of Cynar that brings this drink to the finish line.

2 ounces rye whiskey
1 ounce dry vermouth
⅓ ounce maraschino liqueur
1 barspoon Cynar

SHAKE AND STRAIN into a chilled cocktail glass.

BETSY ROSS

FAMILY: FRENCH-ITALIAN: WHISKEY AND BRANDY || I enjoy the combination of brandy and port, so this recipe from the 1950s caught my eye. It's a little too sweet without the bitters—I recommend at least three dashes. Orange bitters can also be successfully substituted for the Angostura.

1½ ounces brandy
1½ ounces ruby port
½ ounce orange curaçao
2 to 3 dashes Angostura bitters

STIR AND STRAIN into a chilled cocktail glass.

BITTER STRIPPER

FAMILY: FRENCH-ITALIAN: GIN, RUM, GENEVER, VODKA, AND TEQUILA || Adapted from a recipe by Dee Allen in Perth, Australia. Dee Allen's intention with this drink was to "replicate the flavours of a Negroni without using Campari or a sweet vermouth, to create a clear drink." This isn't the only white Negroni in the world, but the marriage of Salers Gentiane and Cointreau as a substitute for Campari is a thing of great beauty.

1 ounce plus 2 teaspoons Plymouth gin
½ ounce Dolin Blanc vermouth
½ ounce Cointreau
2 teaspoons Salers Gentiane
1 orange twist, for garnish

STIR AND STRAIN into a chilled martini glass. Add the garnish.

BLACK CAT

FAMILY: ORPHANS || Dedicated to the late Quentin Crisp, a writer/actor/celebrity I knew, just a little. This cocktail I created is based on the Dog's Nose—porter, sugar, gin, and nutmeg, served hot. The drink is named for a café that Quentin frequented in London when he was a young man, and it's made with Guinness because Quentin loved Guinness.

1½ ounces G'Vine Nouaison gin
1½ ounces Guinness
½ ounce Monin Gingerbread syrup (and not one drop more)
1 lemon twist, for garnish

STIR AND STRAIN into a chilled coupe, then add the garnish.

BLACK FEATHER COCKTAIL

FAMILY: FRENCH-ITALIAN: WHISKEY AND BRANDY || Adapted from a recipe created in 2000 by Robert Hess (a.k.a. DrinkBoy) in Seattle, this is a clear case of a classically styled cocktail formulated in a modern era.

2 ounces brandy
1 ounce dry vermouth
½ ounce triple sec
Angostura bitters to taste
1 orange twist, for garnish

STIR AND STRAIN into a chilled cocktail glass. Add the garnish.

BLACK RUSSIAN

FAMILY: DUOS AND TRIOS || In the late 1940s, Perle Mesta, the American Ambassador to Luxemburg at the time, was hanging out in the bar at the Hotel Metropole in Brussels, and Gustav Tops, the bartender there, decided to create a drink for her. The cold war with Russia was just about getting off the ground at the time, so by taking some Russian vodka and making it black by adding Kahlúa, Tops came up with the Black Russian, a very appropriate drink for the time.

2 ounces vodka
1 ounce Kahlúa

STIR AND STRAIN into an ice-filled old-fashioned glass.

BLACKTHORN

FAMILY: FRENCH-ITALIAN: WHISKEY AND BRANDY || Adapted from a recipe in Harry Craddock's *The Savoy Cocktail Book* (1930), this variation on the Manhattan originally called for dry vermouth and no garnish at all. I, personally, prefer the drink with sweet vermouth. Likewise, in 1930, a 50:50 ratio of whiskey to vermouth was considered to be delightful. I like more whiskey. And be very careful not to overpower this drink with too much absinthe.

2 ounces Irish whiskey
1 ounce dry or sweet vermouth
3 dashes Angostura bitters
1 to 2 dashes absinthe
1 lemon twist, for garnish

STIR AND STRAIN into a chilled cocktail glass. Add the garnish.

BLOOD AND SAND

FAMILY: ORPHANS || This drink calls for an unusual bunch of ingredients, but it works very well indeed. Introduced to me by Dale DeGroff, the recipe here is adapted from *The Savoy Cocktail Book* (1930); the drink was probably named for Rudolph Valentino's 1922 silent movie about bullfighting and, of course, love, which was based on the 1908 book by Vicente Blasco Ibáñez. I'm fond of making this drink in a highball glass, using considerably more orange juice, and serving it at brunch.

¾ ounce scotch
¾ ounce sweet vermouth
¾ ounce cherry brandy
¾ ounce fresh orange juice

SHAKE AND STRAIN into a chilled cocktail glass.

BLOODY BULL

FAMILY: SNAPPERS || The bouillon in this drink makes it more palatable for me than a Bloody Mary. Use different spices for variations.

2 ounces vodka
2 ounces tomato juice
2 ounces beef bouillon
Fresh lemon juice to taste
Salt or celery salt to taste
Black pepper to taste
Prepared horseradish to taste
Worcestershire sauce to taste
Hot sauce to taste
1 lemon wedge, for garnish
1 celery stalk, for garnish

SHAKE AND STRAIN into an ice-filled collins glass. Add the garnishes.

BLOODY CAESAR

FAMILY: SNAPPERS || The Bloody Caesar was created in 1969 by Walter Chell, the head bartender at the Owl's Nest Lounge in what is now the Westin Hotel, Calgary, Canada, and was formerly the Calgary Inn. It's said that he based the drink on the sauce used to make Spaghetti con Vongole, though traditionally there are no tomatoes in that clam-based dish. Chell came up with the Bloody Caesar—sometimes called the Caesar Cocktail—as a signature drink for Marco's the Italian restaurant in the Calgary Inn that opened in 1969.

2 ounces vodka
2 ounces tomato juice
2 ounces clam juice
Fresh lemon juice to taste
Black pepper to taste
Salt or celery salt to taste
Prepared horseradish to taste
Worcestershire sauce to taste
Hot sauce to taste
1 lemon wedge, for garnish
1 celery stalk, for garnish

SHAKE AND STRAIN into an ice-filled collins glass. Add the garnishes.

B

BLOODY MARY

FAMILY: **SNAPPERS** || One story about the birth of the Bloody Mary has it that the owner of a New York speakeasy created it, as the Bloody Meyer, during Prohibition. But the more popular, and almost certainly true, tale is that it was first concocted at Harry's New York Bar in Paris, circa 1924, by bartender Fernand "Pete" Petiot.

In 1934, Petiot was hired by John Astor, then owner of New York's St. Regis Hotel, and there he presided over the King Cole Room, introducing New Yorkers to his creation. At some point the Bloody Mary was known as the Red Snapper; one story has it that Astor objected to the Bloody Mary name and insisted it be changed. A recipe for the Red Snapper is detailed in the 1945 book *Crosby Gaige's Cocktail Guide and Ladies Companion*. It was donated to the author by Gaston Lauryssen, manager of the St. Regis at the time, and it's a far cry from the drink we know today as the Bloody Mary. The main differences between today's and yesteryear's versions is that the latter contained as much vodka as tomato juice and was served straight up as a cocktail, as opposed to being presented on the rocks in a highball glass.

When did the Red Snapper regain its original name? Probably sometime during the late 1940s. The first printed recipe for a Bloody Mary I can find is in *The Bartender's Book* (1951), and the authors, Jack Townsend and Tom Moore McBride, didn't much care for the drink, calling it "a savage combination of tomato juice and vodka." The following year, David Embury, in the second edition of *The Fine Art of Mixing Drinks*, described the Bloody Mary as being "strictly vile."

BLOODY MARY TIPS FOR THE PROFESSIONAL BARTENDER

1. If you prepare a batch of Bloody Mary mix in quantity rather than mixing drinks individually, base your recipe on the amount of tomato juice in a standard no. 5 can (46 fluid ounces).
2. Never add the vodka to the mix until the drink is ordered. Many customers want Virgin Marys.
3. To make enough mix to last a week—and still be able to serve freshly made drinks, combine all the spices, seasonings, and sauces (without the lemon juice) in a small jar and shake well. Prepare as many of these jars as you will need in the course of a week, and refrigerate them. When you need a batch of Bloody Marys, mix

one jar of spices with one can of tomato juice and the lemon juice.

In the mid-1950s comedian George Jessel was featured in a Smirnoff vodka advertising campaign for the Bloody Mary, in which he claimed to have invented the drink at "five in the morning" when the bartender was asleep. The tale, of course, isn't true, but the campaign served to popularize the drink throughout the United States.

Personally, I don't like Bloody Marys—I'd even go so far as to put myself in Embury's camp and call it strictly vile—but my dislike for this potion doesn't have anything to do with the flavor; it's the texture of tomato juice that I can't stand. I love tomatoes, and I enjoy tomato water in some cocktails (see page 123), but in general, savory drinks are not to my liking. One tip I can offer, though, is that lemon juice marries with tomato juice far better than does lime juice.

This is a generic recipe—feel free to use different spices and/or spirits for variations.

2 ounces vodka
4 ounces tomato juice
Fresh lemon juice to taste
Black pepper to taste
Salt or celery salt to taste
Prepared horseradish to taste
Worcestershire sauce to taste
Hot sauce to taste
1 lemon wedge, for garnish
1 celery stalk, for garnish

SHAKE AND STRAIN into an ice-filled collins glass. Add the garnishes.

THE BLUE BLAZER

FAMILY: ORPHANS || Herbert Asbury, in the introduction to the 1928 edition of Jerry Thomas's book *How to Mix Drinks, or The Bon Vivant's Companion*, states that this drink was created by Thomas in San Francisco, circa 1850. The recipe is detailed in Thomas's 1862 edition. According to Asbury, the drink was a result of a gold prospector's demanding, "Fix me up some hell-fire that'll shake me right down to my gizzard!"

This is a somewhat simple drink, and its main attribute is pyrotechnical, since when it is properly prepared, a stream of flaming whiskey is poured back and forth between two mugs. (Thomas recommended silver-plated receptacles.) The problem with this recipe is that if you follow Thomas's formula, combining equal amounts of scotch and boiling water, the mixture will be hard to ignite.

It's highly probable that Thomas used a high-proof whiskey to make this drink, since to save on shipping charges, spirits were often shipped at high proof, then diluted by saloon keepers upon arrival. This practice was fairly common right up to the early years of the twentieth century. I have seen Dale DeGroff make this drink when he was at the Rainbow Room, and he tells me that he heats the whiskey, ignites it, then pours it into the second mug, which contains the hot water. He assures me that the mixture stays lit if you use this method. With the addition of a little sugar and lemon, as Thomas prescribed, the Blue Blazer is a heartwarming drink. This is a legitimate opportunity for accomplished bartenders to display their dexterity, but when you get right down to brass tacks, this is a showman's drink, not a cocktailian masterpiece. Here's Thomas's original formula:

(Use two silver-plated mugs, with handles.)

1 wine-glass Scotch whiskey
1 wine-glass boiling water

Put the whiskey and the boiling water in one mug, ignite the liquid with fire, and while blazing, mix both ingredients by pouring them four or five times from one mug to the other. . . . If well done this will have the appearance of a continued stream of liquid fire.

Sweeten with one teaspoonful of pulverized white sugar, and serve in a small bar tumbler, with a piece of lemon peel.

The "blue blazer" does not have a euphonious or classic name, but it tastes better to the palate than it sounds to the ear. A beholder gazing for the first time upon an experienced artist, compounding this beverage, would naturally come to the conclusion that it was a nectar for Pluto rather than Bacchus. The novice in mixing this beverage should be careful not to scald himself. To become proficient in throwing the liquid from one mug to the other, it will be necessary to practise [sic] for some time with cold water.

BLUE DEVIL

FAMILY: **ORPHANS** || Adapted from a recipe in Dale DeGroff's *The Essential Cocktail* (2008). Dale DeGroff created this one as a result of a challenge of sorts from me to Dale. During a session of Cocktails in the Country, I gave Dale three ingredients and asked him if he could come up with a decent drink using all of them. He showed me that he knew how to mix a drink! Dale did get his revenge on me for my nefarious actions. See DAM, a cocktail detailed on page 204, for details.

1½ ounces Hpnotiq liqueur
1½ ounces dry vermouth
½ ounce Laphroaig 10-year-old single-malt scotch

Pour the Hpnotiq and dry vermouth into an ice-filled old-fashioned glass and stir briefly. FLOAT the Laphroaig on top of the drink.

BOBBY BURNS

FAMILY: **FRENCH-ITALIAN: WHISKEY AND BRANDY** || Albert Stevens Crockett, author of *The Old Waldorf-Astoria Bar Book*, noted that this drink, then called the Robert Burns, was created prior to Prohibition. He intimated that it was born at the Waldorf Astoria: "It may have been named after the celebrated Scotsman. Chances are, however, that it was christened in honor of a cigar salesman, who 'bought' in the Old Bar." And, indeed, a brand of cigars named Robt. Burns was available back then, and continued to sell in the United States up to the 1960s, so it's possible they were buttering up a well-heeled punter when they named the drink.

The Waldorf recipe includes a dash of absinthe, whereas the Savoy recipe (1930) calls for three dashes of Bénédictine instead. In the 1950s, David Embury suggested that Drambuie could be used in this drink instead of either absinthe or Bénédictine. My preference for a Bobby Burns is to use Bénédictine, but it is interesting to try these variations.

2 ounces scotch
1 ounce sweet vermouth
2 to 3 dashes absinthe, Bénédictine, or Drambuie
1 lemon twist, for garnish

STIR AND STRAIN into a chilled cocktail glass. Add the garnish.

BOTTOM LINE

FAMILY: FRENCH-ITALIAN: WHISKEY AND BRANDY || Adapted from a recipe by Kevin Diedrich, Clover Club, Brooklyn. This recipe won Kevin the Bärenjäger Cocktail Competition, which was held in September 2009 in New York.

1½ ounces Highland Park 18-year-old single-malt scotch
1 ounce manzanilla sherry
¾ ounce Bärenjäger honey liqueur
¼ ounce Amaro CioCiaro
1 dash orange bitters
1 dash Angostura bitters

STIR AND STRAIN into a chilled cocktail glass.

BRANDY ALEXANDER

FAMILY: DUOS AND TRIOS || Created before 1930, this drink was once known as the Panama. It had received the name Brandy Alexander by 1936, but it was often still referred to as the Panama until well into the 1940s. And just by the way, I can tell you that Brandy Alexanders were very popular in Manhattan in the 1970s, and since we had poor glass-washing machines back then—such as a few spinning brushes in a sink full of lukewarm water—we bartenders hated this cocktail since we had to change the water every time we washed a Brandy Alexander glass.

2 ounces brandy
1 ounce dark crème de cacao
1 ounce cream
Freshly grated nutmeg, for garnish

SHAKE AND STRAIN into a chilled cocktail glass. Add the garnish.

BRANDY CRUSTA

FAMILY: NEW ORLEANS SOURS || This, the drink that launched a thousand classics—I'm given to exaggeration—was created in the mid-1800s by Joseph Santini, an Italian bar owner in New Orleans. His recipe became the template for a string of cocktails we know as New Orleans Sours, and this drink was also the first cocktail that included citrus juice, an aspect of the Crusta that didn't occur to me until Dave Wondrich set me straight.

The formula here is based on the recipe found in Jerry Thomas's 1862 book *How to Mix Drinks, or The Bon Vivant's Companion*, and although the drink is not well balanced, the marriage of spirit, orange liqueur, and fresh citrus juice, seen in cocktails such as the Margarita and the Sidecar, was consummated in this drink. Let no man put them asunder.

2 ounces brandy
1 teaspoon simple syrup
1 teaspoon fresh lemon juice
½ teaspoon orange curaçao
2 dashes aromatic bitters such as Angostura or Boker's
1 continuous spiral of lemon peel taken from 1 whole lemon, for garnish

SHAKE AND STRAIN into a small, chilled wine glass with a sugared rim into which the lemon spiral has been arranged to line the whole glass.

THE BREAKFAST MARTINI

FAMILY: INTERNATIONAL SOURS || Adapted from a recipe by Salvatore Calabrese, Bound by Salvatore, at the Cromwell Hotel, Las Vegas; Salvatore at Maison Eight, Kowloon, Hong Kong; and at Mixology 101, Los Angeles. Salvatore Calabrese, known as "The Maestro," is one of the world's most celebrated bartenders, and rightly so. He is based in London, and at the time of this writing he doesn't have a bar there, but through his various cocktail bars, he makes his presence known all over the world. And I defy anyone to show me a bar where the service is better than at one of Salvatore's joints. He's second to none when it comes to service. The Breakfast Martini, his signature cocktail, was created at London's Lanesborough Hotel.

1¾ ounces Bombay gin
½ ounce Cointreau
½ ounce lemon juice
1½ teaspoons orange marmalade
Shredded orange peel, for garnish

SHAKE vigorously and STRAIN into a chilled cocktail glass. Add the garnish.

B

BRONX COCKTAIL

FAMILY: **ENHANCED SOURS** || The story of the creation of this drink is detailed in Albert Stevens Crockett's *The Old Waldorf-Astoria Bar Book*, and although the book claims that it was created prior to 1917, no clue is given as to the precise year of its birth. According to the book, the bartender who first made the Bronx was a certain Johnnie Solon (or Solan), and he made the drink as a response to a challenge from a waiter by the name of Traverson. The Bronx was a variation of a popular drink of the time known as the Duplex (sweet and dry vermouth with orange bitters), and it became so popular that the bar was soon using more than a case of oranges per day. The book quotes Solon as saying, "I had been at the Bronx Zoo a day or two before, and I saw, of course, a lot of beasts I had never known. Customers used to tell me of the strange animals they saw after a lot of mixed drinks. So when Traverson said to me, as he started to take the drink in to the customer, 'What'll I tell him is the name of this drink?' I thought of those animals, and said, 'Oh, you can tell him it is a Bronx.'"

The chances that the story above is true are remote, and David Wondrich, in *Imbibe!*, offers a few other people who might have created this drink, but we have no definite proof who first put the Bronx Cocktail together. I do so love the Solon story, though . . .

This formula is loosely based on the recipe seen on Esquire.com, formulated by Dave Wondrich. I added orange bitters, and the garnish.

2 ounces gin
¼ ounce sweet vermouth
¼ ounce dry vermouth
1 ounce fresh orange juice
1 dash orange bitters
1 orange twist, for garnish

SHAKE AND STRAIN into a chilled cocktail glass. Add the garnish.

BRONX COCKTAIL À LA *IMBIBE!*

FAMILY: **ENHANCED SOURS** || Recipe derived from David Wondrich's findings in the first edition of his wonderful book, *Imbibe!* Wondrich nails the date of this variation to approximately 1900, and although he notes that he enjoys a fair amount of orange juice in his Bronx, he then does us the favor of finding a recipe that calls for very little. This recipe was printed in *World Drinks and How to Mix Them* by William

T. Boothby, a book published in 1908, and it is labeled "à la Billy Malloy, Pittsburgh, PA."

1 ounce Plymouth gin
1 ounce dry vermouth
1 ounce sweet vermouth
1 teaspoon fresh orange juice
2 dashes orange bitters

SHAKE AND STRAIN into a chilled cocktail glass.

BROOKLYN HEIGHTS

FAMILY: FRENCH-ITALIAN: WHISKEY AND BRANDY || Adapted from a recipe by Maxwell Britten, New York. This drink's all over the darned place, shooting arrows into every last taste bud on your tongue, but everything comes together neatly by the time it glides down your throat. Maxwell either knows the craft very thoroughly, or God gave him a break and made this one work!

½ ounce Campari, as a rinse
1½ ounces Rittenhouse 100-proof rye
¼ ounce Luxardo Amaro Abano
½ ounce Luxardo maraschino liqueur
½ ounce Noilly Prat dry vermouth
2 dashes Regan's Orange Bitters No. 6

RINSE a chilled cocktail glass with the Campari. STIR AND STRAIN into the prepared glass.

BUTTER LEMON SMOKE

FAMILY: ORPHANS || Adapted from a recipe by T. J. Vytlacil, Blood and Sand, St. Louis, Missouri.

T. J. Vytlacil made this drink for a customer who told him that he liked spice, smoke, citrus, and softness. After his first sip the guest said that it tasted like butter, lemon, and smoke, hence the name. The drink is a great example of twenty-first-century bartender creativity.

1½ ounces Peat Monster scotch
1 ounce Germain-Robin's Fine Alambic brandy
¾ ounce Green Chartreuse
¾ ounce Bénédictine
1 lemon twist, for garnish.

STIR AND STRAIN into a chilled cocktail glass. Add the garnish.

CABLE CAR

FAMILY: NEW ORLEANS SOURS || Adapted from a recipe by Tony Abou-Ganim. Known as "The Modern Mixologist," Tony Abou-Ganim created this drink in the late 1990s while he was working at Harry Denton's Starlight Room in San Francisco. It was an instant success.

1½ ounces Captain Morgan Spiced Rum
¾ ounce orange curaçao
1 ounce fresh lemon juice
½ ounce simple syrup
Cinnamon and sugar, for rimming the glass
1 orange twist, for garnish

SHAKE AND STRAIN into a chilled cocktail glass rimmed with cinnamon and sugar. Add the garnish.

CAFÉ BRÛLOT

FAMILY: HOT DRINKS || Adapted from a recipe from Commander's Palace, New Orleans.

MAKES 2 DRINKS

1 lemon
1 orange
1 ounce triple sec
1 ounce brandy
1 cinnamon stick
4 whole cloves
1½ cups hot, strong coffee

Using a paring knife, remove the lemon and orange peels in one continuous strip so that they form a spiral. As you peel the fruit, hold it over a brûlot bowl (or fondue pot) so that any juices drop into the bowl. Set the flesh aside. Place the lemon peel in the brûlot bowl and set it over a Sterno heater. Add the triple sec, brandy, and cinnamon stick. Stud the orange peel with the cloves and hold it with a fork over the brûlot bowl.

Carefully ignite the brandy mixture and use a spoon to ladle the flaming liquid over the orange peel. Slowly pour the coffee into the bowl to extinguish the flames. Ladle the coffee into demitasse cups and sweeten to taste with fresh-squeezed juice from the peeled orange.

CAIPIRINHA

FAMILY: SIMPLE SOURS || This Brazilian drink has been in vogue in the United States, and around the world, for a couple of decades, and justifiably so. The name (pronounced K-EYE-PIR-EEN-YA) translates roughly to "country bumpkin," and the drink calls for cachaça, a Brazilian style of rum. It's difficult to note how many wedges of lime to use when making this drink because limes can differ quite drastically in size; my rule of thumb is to add enough wedges to fill the glass to the halfway mark.

4 to 6 lime wedges
1 tablespoon granulated sugar
3 ounces cachaça

MUDDLE the limes and sugar in an old-fashioned glass. Add crushed ice and cachaça, and stir thoroughly.

CAIPIROSKA

FAMILY: SIMPLE SOURS || The vodka-based cousin to the Caipirinha, for those who aren't enamored of cachaça.

4 to 6 lime wedges
1 tablespoon granulated sugar
3 ounces vodka

MUDDLE the limes and sugar in an old-fashioned glass. Add crushed ice and vodka, and stir thoroughly.

C

CALVADOS COCKTAIL

FAMILY: NEW ORLEANS SOURS || Adapted from a recipe in *Jones' Complete Barguide.*

1½ ounces calvados
¾ ounce triple sec
1 ounce fresh orange juice
2 dashes orange bitters

SHAKE AND STRAIN into a chilled cocktail glass.

CARICATURE COCKTAIL

FAMILY: NEW ORLEANS SOURS || I created this in 2001 for graphic artist Jill DeGroff, Dale's wife, but it's nothing more than a variation on Dale DeGroff's Old Flame cocktail.

1½ ounces gin
½ ounce sweet vermouth
¾ ounce triple sec
½ ounce Campari
½ ounce fresh grapefruit juice
1 orange twist, for garnish

SHAKE AND STRAIN into a chilled cocktail glass. Add the garnish.

CASANOVA COBBLER

FAMILY: ORPHANS || Adapted from a recipe for Valentine's Day by Erick Castro, California.

This cocktail takes its inspiration from the eighteenth-century Venetian Casanova, who was one of the most famous lovers in history. San Francisco cocktail bar Rickhouse's menu from February 2010 notes, "This frosty, yet sublime creation is chillingly reminiscent of a doomed but enchanting love affair that can only be described as bittersweet."

½ ounce fresh lemon juice
2 dashes simple syrup
1 orange wheel
1½ ounces Punt e Mes
¾ ounce Wild Turkey rye whiskey
½ ounce Cointreau
1 brandied cherry and 1 orange wheel, for garnishes

MUDDLE the lemon juice, simple syrup, and orange wheel in a collins glass. Add crushed ice and BUILD the remaining ingredients in the glass. Add the garnishes.

CHAMPAGNE COCKTAIL

FAMILY: CHAMPAGNE COCKTAILS || The original Champagne Cocktail is detailed in Jerry Thomas's 1862 book *How to Mix Drinks, or The Bon Vivant's Companion*, but his methodology is a little strange: "Fill tumbler one-third full of broken ice, and fill balance with wine. Shake well and serve." The ingredients are listed as champagne, ½ teaspoon of sugar, one or two dashes of bitters, and one piece of lemon peel, and that's pretty much what we use to make a Champagne Cocktail today; but the idea of shaking the drink is somewhat mystifying—the shaker would explode when opened.

We know that our forefathers were sipping Champagne Cocktails in the mid-nineteenth century, but what else do we know about the history of this drink? In 1906, bartender Louis Muckensturm recommended rubbing the sugar cube onto lemon peel before adding it to the glass—not a bad idea at all—and in 1927 a book titled *Here's How*, by Judge Jr., proclaimed that the drink had been created at the Ritz Hotel in Paris and was considered "very high hat." By the 1930s, the Champagne Sour, using lemon juice instead of bitters, had been introduced into the mix, and W.J. Tarling's *Café Royal Cocktail Book* prescribed "a dash of brandy as required" in 1937. Variations were springing up.

A couple of years later, Charles H. Baker Jr. detailed quite a few deviations from the norm in his book *The Gentleman's Companion*. They included the Maharajah's Burra-Peg: "And we would sip various things, including—on Washington's birthday, of course—a quartet of champagne Burra Pegs, and he [their host] would recount to us certain toothsome bits of 'under the punkah' tales about maharajahs and people; and how, actually, the young new one we'd just met preferred one wife to the regiment of 400 or so that his dad had thoughtfully left to him." Baker suggested that the Burra Peg was best made in a sixteen-ounce glass, into which he poured three ounces of brandy, which was topped off with champagne. He also dropped a bitters-soaked sugar cube into the glass, along with a spiral of lime peel.

In 1945, recipes for eight Champagne Cocktails with names such as She Couldn't Say No, Her Sarong Slipped, and Widow's Might appeared in *Crosby Gaige's Cocktail Guide and Ladies' Companion.* Crosby also noted, "Maidens wed without champagne . . . are bound to become husband beaters."

More variations on this drink have appeared every decade—perhaps even every month or every week—since the forties. We now have such a wide array of ingredients suitable to add to champagne that I dare say there are thousands of recipes out there, and thousands more, made using the methodology detailed below, some strictly, some loosely, are on their way.

1 sugar cube soaked in Angostura bitters
5½ ounces chilled champagne
1 lemon twist, for garnish

BUILD in the order given in a champagne flute. Add the garnish.

CHARTREUSE SWIZZLE

FAMILY: ORPHANS || Adapted from a 2003 recipe by Marcovaldo Dionysos, San Francisco. This is one of those fabulous twenty-first-century drinks that became a fairly common sight on craft-bar menus all over the world. Nice one, Sir!

1½ ounces Green Chartreuse
½ ounce velvet falernum
1 ounce pineapple juice
¾ ounce fresh lime juice
1 mint sprig, for garnish
Grated nutmeg, for garnish

BUILD in a collins glass filled with crushed ice. Stir briefly and add the garnishes.

CLOVER CLUB COCKTAIL

FAMILY: **ENHANCED SOURS** || According to Albert Stevens Crockett, author of *The Old Waldorf-Astoria Bar Book*, this drink originated at the "old Belleview-Stratford, where the Clover Club, composed of literary, legal, financial and business lights of the Quaker City, often dined and wined, and wined again." And therein lies a tale, since George Charles Boldt, the first manager of the old Waldorf Astoria, hailed from Philadelphia.

Born on the Isle of Rügen, in the Baltic Sea, Boldt came to the United States in 1864, at age thirteen. By 1888, he owned two hotels in Philadelphia—the Bellevue and the Stratford. It was a dark and stormy night, circa 1890, when a couple entered the lobby of one of these hotels looking for a room; but since there were three conventions being held in the city, all the rooms were booked. Boldt, though, let the couple sleep in his own room. Before they left the following morning, the man told Boldt that he ought to be operating a better hotel, and that one day he might build one for him. The stranger turned out to be William Waldorf Astor, and that's how Boldt ended up at the Waldorf Astoria.

Boldt eventually returned to Philadelphia, where in 1904 he opened the Bellevue-Stratford, the hotel to which Crockett refers as being host to the Clover Club, but it's possible that the drink could actually predate this grand hotel: In 1881, Boldt's Bellevue Hotel had been host to Philadelphia's Clover Club, and the society obviously had quite an impact on his life. He married in 1877, and he and his wife, Louise, had two children, George Jr., and Louise Clover.

This formula is adapted from the recipe used at Brooklyn's Clover Club cocktail bar. It's one of bartender/owner Julie Reiner's joints, and it's also a bar where you get the finest of welcomes on any day of the week.

1½ ounces dry gin (Clover Club uses either Plymouth or Bombay Dry)
½ ounce Dolin dry vermouth
½ ounce lemon juice
½ ounce Clover Club raspberry syrup (recipe follows)
¼ ounce egg white
2 fresh raspberries on a skewer, for garnish

DRY SHAKE, add ice, shake again, and strain the drink into a chilled coupe. Add the garnish.

CLOVER CLUB RASPBERRY SYRUP

C

1 cup fresh raspberries
2 cups sugar
1 cup water

In a saucepan, smash the berries into the sugar. Add the water and heat on very low until sugar is dissolved, about 10 minutes max. Do not bring to a boil. Let sit for 30 minutes, and then fine strain the ingredients into a jar.

COMPASS BOX COCKTAIL

FAMILY: ORPHANS || Adapted from a recipe by beer writer and author Stephen Beaumont. The Compass Box Cocktail is a fabulous creation, and Stephen Beaumont was, as far as I know, the first guy to figure out how to use beer properly in a cocktail. Prior to this drink we basically had Lager and Lime, Shandies, and Black & Tans as beer-based mixed drinks.

1 ounce Compass Box Peat Monster blended malt scotch
3 ounces imperial stout
3 dashes Angostura bitters
1 maraschino cherry, for garnish

STIR AND STRAIN into a chilled cocktail glass, and add the garnish.

CORPSE REVIVER NO. 1

FAMILY: FRENCH-ITALIAN: WHISKEY AND BRANDY || Corpse Revivers were a category of drinks we might call eye-openers or hair of the dog. Craddock detailed two of these in *The Savoy Cocktail Book*, and for this one he instructed the reader that the drink should be "taken before 11 a.m., or whenever steam and energy are needed."

1½ ounces cognac
¾ ounce calvados
¾ ounce sweet vermouth

STIR AND STRAIN into a chilled cocktail glass.

CORPSE REVIVER NO. 2

FAMILY: NEW ORLEANS SOURS || Based on Craddock's 1930 recipe, about which he noted, "Four of these taken in swift succession will unrevive the corpse again."

¾ ounce gin
¾ ounce triple sec
¾ ounce Lillet Blonde
¾ ounce fresh lemon juice
1 dash absinthe

SHAKE AND STRAIN into a chilled cocktail glass.

COSMOPOLITAN

FAMILY: NEW ORLEANS SOURS || Boy, oh boy, has this drink caused some upsets. When the first edition of this book came out in 2003, no one was quite sure where the recipe came from, but much has transpired since then. The good folk at Cointreau told me that a Miami bartender by the name of Cheryl Cook had first created the drink, but I couldn't find this woman to save my life. Then, on Sunday, September 25, 2005, I received the following email from a certain someone in Florida: "I was recently made aware of various articles written about me and the Cosmopolitan." Cook went on to say that she had, indeed, created the Cosmopolitan when she worked at The Strand in South Beach, Miami. Her original recipe called for "Absolut Citron, a splash of triple sec a drop of Rose's lime juice and just enough cranberry to make it 'Oh so pretty in pink' and topped with a curled lemon twist."

The two bartenders who are often credited with this creation, Dale DeGroff and Toby Cecchini, both say that their versions were riffs on a simpler recipe. Cheryl's formula fits this description to a T and no one else lays claim to the drink. That said, it's true to say that we tend toward Dale's and Toby's recipes when we make this drink today, using fresh lime juice and a high-quality triple sec such as Cointreau. This recipe is adapted from Dale's formula, detailed in his wonderful book, *The Craft of the Cocktail.*

C

1½ ounces citrus vodka
½ ounce Cointreau
½ ounce fresh lime juice
1 ounce cranberry juice
1 flamed orange twist, for garnish

SHAKE AND STRAIN into a chilled cocktail glass. Add the garnish.

COSMOPOLITAN (BOTTLED)

MAKES 22 OUNCES

10 ounces citrus vodka
4 ounces triple sec
2 ounces fresh lime juice
1 ounce cranberry juice
5 ounces bottled water

MIX AND CHILL for a minimum of 6 hours. Serve in chilled cocktail glasses.

CUBA LIBRE

FAMILY: HIGHBALLS || In the late 1930s, when Charles H. Baker Jr. wrote *The Gentleman's Companion*, this drink was just coming into vogue. According to his book, the best way to make it is to squeeze the juice from a small lime into a collins glass, drop the lime into the glass, and muddle it so that the oils coat the interior of the glass; then add the rum, lots of ice, and cola. These days it seems that most bartenders merely make a rum and cola with a wedge of lime—a very unsatisfactory drink.

Although it isn't necessary to muddle the lime—with no sugar to abrade the zest, few of the essential oils are released, and with sugar the drink becomes unbearably sweet—it is necessary to add at least one ounce of lime juice to balance out the sweetness of the cola. This drink is seldom held in high regard, but when made properly it can be a heavenly potion.

2 ounces light rum
1 ounce fresh lime juice
3 ounces cola
1 lime wedge, for garnish

BUILD in the order given in an ice-filled highball glass. Add the garnish.

D

CUZCO COCKTAIL

FAMILY: INTERNATIONAL SOURS || Adapted from a recipe by Julie Reiner, Clover Club, Brooklyn, and Flatiron Lounge, New York, 2006. Julie Reiner created this drink after a trip to Peru in 2006 with a bunch of other mixologists, and me, who visited quite a few pisco distilleries, Machu Picchu, and the Urubamba Valley, a.k.a. the Sacred Valley of the Incas.

½ ounce kirschwasser, as a rinse
2 ounces Mendiola Pisco Select Peruvian Italia grape brandy
¾ ounce Aperol
½ ounce fresh lemon juice
½ ounce fresh grapefruit juice
¾ ounce simple syrup
1 grapefruit twist, for garnish

RINSE a highball glass with the kirschwasser, discard the excess, and fill the glass with ice. SHAKE AND STRAIN into the prepared glass, and add the garnish.

DAIQUIRI

FAMILY: SIMPLE SOURS || Most sources claim that the Daiquiri was created in 1898, by a couple of Americans working in Cuba just after the Spanish-American War. It's said that the drink was made as a cure for or a medicine to ward off malaria. Whatever the truth, this Sour calls for lime juice instead of lemon juice; and of course the base spirit is rum.

The first printed mention of the Daiquiri I can find appears in Frank Shay's 1929 book *Drawn from the Wood*, and the authors insist that Bacardi rum be used if the drink is to be properly constructed. Of course, any white rum will suffice in the making of this drink, but the same is not true of the Bacardi Cocktail (page 179).

2 ounces light rum
1 ounce fresh lime juice
½ ounce simple syrup
1 lime wedge, for garnish

SHAKE AND STRAIN into an ice-filled wine glass. Add the garnish.

D

DAM

FAMILY: **ORPHANS** || Created by gaz regan for the Museum of the American Cocktail's World Cocktail Day, 2007, New York. Dale DeGroff, president of the museum, asked me to create a new drink for the celebration, and he mandated that Laphroaig single-malt scotch, a very smoky dram that can be hard to work with when creating cocktails, must be one of the ingredients. It took me the best part of a very frustrating afternoon to find the right ingredients to marry to the Laphroaig, and although I admit that I was pleased with the resultant drink, I'll never forget cursing Dale for a few hours while I worked. It won't be everyone's cup of tea, but it went nicely with the barbecued ribs with which it was paired at the celebratory dinner. The name, DAM, is an acronym, standing for *Dale's a Mutha . . .*

1¼ ounces Dubonnet Rouge
½ ounce Pallini Limoncello
¼ ounce Laphroaig 10-year-old single-malt scotch
1 lemon twist, for garnish

SHAKE AND STRAIN into a chilled wine goblet. Add the garnish.

DARK AND STORMY

FAMILY: **HIGHBALLS** || A Bermudan drink made with dark Bermudan rum and cloudy, if not quite stormy, ginger beer.

2 ounces Gosling's Black Seal rum
3 ounces ginger beer
1 lime wedge, for garnish

BUILD in an ice-filled highball glass. Add the garnish.

DEBONAIR

FAMILY: **DUOS AND TRIOS** || I came up with this one in the early nineties. It's based on the Whisky Mac, a somewhat popular drink in the United Kingdom that calls for scotch and green ginger wine. I suggest two bottlings of single malt here, chosen for their briny characteristics, which play well off the ginger liqueur. Remember that if you use any bottling other than the ones suggested here, you'll have to fool around with ratios to get the right balance.

2½ ounces Oban or Springbank single-malt scotch
1 ounce Domaine de Canton ginger liqueur
1 lemon twist, for garnish

STIR AND STRAIN into a chilled cocktail glass. Add the garnish.

DIRTY MARTINI

FAMILY: FRENCH-ITALIAN: GIN, RUM, GENEVER, VODKA, AND TEQUILA || This is probably one of the world's worst drinks when made incorrectly, but when properly prepared, with not too much olive brine added, it can be a sterling potion. And if you strive for consistency, you might want to think about investing in a bottle of bottled olive brine from the Dirty Sue company—it's bartender owned.

2½ ounces gin or vodka
½ ounce dry vermouth
Olive brine to taste
1 olive, for garnish

STIR AND STRAIN into a chilled cocktail glass. Add the garnish.

DOG'S NOSE

FAMILY: ORPHANS || The Dog's Nose is mentioned in Dickens's *Pickwick Papers,* and his great-grandson, Cedric Dickens, claimed in his book *Drinking with Dickens* that a certain Mr. Walker thought that tasting a Dog's Nose twice a week for twenty years had lost him the use of his right hand. Mr. Walker had since joined a temperance society. This is a strange mixture, indeed, but it works very well.

12 ounces porter or stout
2 teaspoons brown sugar
2 ounces gin
Freshly grated nutmeg, for garnish

Pour the porter or stout into a large sturdy glass and heat it in a microwave for about 1 minute. Add the brown sugar and gin and stir lightly. Add the garnish.

THE DUBLINER

D

FAMILY: FRENCH-ITALIAN: WHISKEY AND BRANDY || Created by gaz regan for St. Patrick's Day, 1999.

This is an easy recipe to break down and analyze. Without the Grand Marnier, the formula is a Manhattan-style drink that calls for Irish whiskey instead of bourbon or rye. Add the Grand Marnier, supplement the orange flavors with some orange bitters, and voilà, it's a new drink.

2 ounces Irish whiskey
½ ounce sweet vermouth
½ ounce Grand Marnier
Orange bitters to taste
1 maraschino cherry (green, if possible), for garnish

STIR AND STRAIN into a chilled cocktail glass. Add the garnish.

DREAMY DORINI SMOKING MARTINI

FAMILY: ORPHANS || Adapted from a recipe by Audrey Saunders, New York City's Libation Goddess, this drink displays the height of the cocktailian craft. If you know the Laphroaig single-malt scotch at all, you'll be aware that the ten-year-old bottling is unforgiving in terms of peat and smoke, and Pernod can easily take over a drink if it's not used with caution. Here, Audrey thought it all out. One thing that Pernod can't easily quell is Laphroaig, and adding the vodka brings both the scotch and the Pernod to their knees. The whole drink comes together in harmony, and a masterpiece is born. I've also used Ardbeg ten-year-old single-malt scotch to make this one, and I've been delighted with the results.

2 ounces Grey Goose vodka
½ ounce Laphroaig 10-year-old single-malt scotch
2 to 3 drops Pernod
1 lemon twist, for garnish

STIR AND STRAIN into a chilled cocktail glass. Add the garnish.

DUBONNET COCKTAIL

FAMILY: **FRENCH-ITALIAN: GIN, RUM, GENEVER, VODKA, AND TEQUILA** || The original Dubonnet Cocktail, from the 1930s, had no garnish, but I find that a lemon twist works well here. If you alter the ratios, using twice as much gin as Dubonnet, and add a couple dashes each of curaçao and Angostura bitters, plus one dash of absinthe, you have yourself a Dubonnet Royal, as detailed in W. J. Tarling's *Café Royal Cocktail Book* (1937).

1½ ounces Dubonnet Rouge
1½ ounces gin
1 lemon twist, for garnish

STIR AND STRAIN into a chilled cocktail glass. Add the garnish.

DUTCH COUPE

FAMILY: **FRENCH-ITALIAN: GIN, RUM, GENEVER, VODKA, AND TEQUILA** || Adapted from a recipe by Tess Posthumus, Door 74, Amsterdam, The Netherlands. Tess, who has become a friend over the years, told me she created this drink to commemorate the abdication of Queen Beatrix of the Netherlands in 2013. Using a typical Dutch spirit as her base and both orange bitters and orange flower water to represent the royal house of Orange-Nassau, Tess noted that "the addition of some bitterness is part of a tradition. The Dutch royals used to drink a bitter orange liqueur called 'Oranjebitter' whenever there was a festive event. After zesting the orange, place it as a garnish on the rim and make it look like a feathered hat, which is Queen Beatrix' signature."

2 ounces Bols 6-year-old Corenwyn Jenever
½ ounce Carpano Antica Formula
2 teaspoons Cynar
1 dash orange flower water
1 dash orange bitters
1 orange twist, for garnish

STIR AND STRAIN into a chilled coupe. Add the garnish.

EARL GREY MAR*TEA*NI

FAMILY: SIMPLE SOURS || Adapted from a recipe by Audrey Saunders, Pegu Club, New York.

1¾ ounces Earl Grey–Infused Tanqueray gin (recipe follows)
¾ ounce fresh lemon juice
1 ounce simple syrup
1 egg white
1 lemon twist, for garnish

SHAKE AND STRAIN into a chilled, sugar-rimmed champagne coupe glass. Add the garnish.

EARL GREY–INFUSED TANQUERAY GIN

1 tablespoon high-quality loose Earl Grey tea
1 cup Tanqueray gin

Combine the tea and gin in a small bowl. Let sit at room temperature for 2 hours. Strain and discard the tea solids, but do not press down on solids when straining as this will release additional tannins, which is undesirable. Chill before serving.

EL PRESIDENTE

FAMILY: FRENCH-ITALIAN: GIN, RUM, GENEVER, VODKA, AND TEQUILA || The drink recipe I featured in the first edition of this book bears no resemblance to this formula—it was based on a recipe I found in an *Old Mr. Boston* book from 1949, and it's better off being forgotten, in my opinion. This recipe is my adaptation of the formula I found in *Imbibe* magazine, then considering Dave Wondrich's musings on the drink in the publication. It's a far better quaff.

1½ ounces good white rum
1½ ounces Dolin Blanc vermouth
1 teaspoon orange curaçao
½ teaspoon grenadine
1 orange twist, for garnish

SHAKE AND STRAIN into a chilled cocktail glass. Add the garnish.

FINAL WARD

FAMILY: **INTERNATIONAL SOURS** || Adapted from a recipe by Philip Ward, Mayahuel, New York. In this variation on the classic Last Word (page 232), rye whiskey replaces the gin, and Ward changed the citrus from lime to lemon. These simple switches result in a very different drink.

¾ ounce Rittenhouse rye whiskey
¾ ounce Luxardo maraschino liqueur
¾ ounce Green Chartreuse
¾ ounce fresh lemon juice

SHAKE AND STRAIN into a chilled cocktail glass.

FISH HOUSE PUNCH

FAMILY: **PUNCHES** || The Fish House Club in Philadelphia was founded in 1732 when a group of fishermen formed a society dedicated to gastronomy, as well as angling. Although the club is officially known as the "State" in Schuylkill, it's often referred to as the "Schuylkill Fishing Company" or the "Fish House Club." George Washington dined at this club, and some historians say that three blank pages in his diary reflect the effects of the Fish House Punch that he indulged in during his visit.

MAKES 10 TO 12 FIVE-OUNCE SERVINGS

1 bottle (750 ml) dark rum
9 ounces brandy
4 ounces peach brandy
4 ounces simple syrup
5 ounces fresh lime juice
5 ounces fresh lemon juice
1 large block of ice, for serving

Pour all the ingredients into a large nonreactive pan or bowl; stir well. Cover and refrigerate until chilled, at least 4 hours. Place the large block of ice in the center of a large punch bowl. Add the punch.

FLAME OF LOVE

FAMILY: ORPHANS || Adapted from a recipe created for Dean Martin by Pepe, the longtime bartender at Chasen's in West Hollywood. The drink has been served to Frank Sinatra, Gregory Peck, Tommy Lasorda, and (then presidential hopeful) George H. W. Bush.

½ ounce dry sherry
2 orange twists
3 ounces gin or vodka

RINSE a chilled cocktail glass with the sherry and discard the excess. Flame one of the orange twists into the glass. STIR AND STRAIN the gin or vodka into the glass, then flame the remaining orange twist over the drink.

FLOSS 75

FAMILY: SPARKLING SOURS || Recipe by Gorge Camorra, 18th Amendment Bar, Geelong, Australia. Full disclosure: I've never tasted this drink. Mainly because I don't have any of Gorge Camorra's Fairy Floss liqueur, but I must admit that this product really fascinates me. It tastes, I'm told, like cotton candy, a.k.a. candy floss, so it sounds very sweet. Gorge Camorra, though, is one of the most extraordinary characters in the bar business, and he's the real reason I'm featuring his drink here. That, plus the fact that he had the chutzpah to call one of his liqueur creations Fairy Floss . . .

⅔ ounce gin
⅔ ounce Camorra Fairy Floss liqueur
1 ounce ruby red grapefruit juice
2 dashes Regan's Orange Bitters No. 6
Prosecco
1 grapefruit twist, for garnish

SHAKE AND STRAIN into a chilled coupe, and top with prosecco. Add the garnish.

FOG CUTTER

FAMILY: TIKI || Adapted from a recipe in *Beachbum Berry's Grog Log*, the world's finest guide to Tiki drinks.

2 ounces light rum
1 ounce brandy
½ ounce gin
1 ounce fresh orange juice
2 ounces fresh lemon juice
½ ounce orgeat syrup
½ ounce sweet sherry, as a float

SHAKE AND STRAIN everything except the sherry into an ice-filled collins glass. FLOAT the sherry.

FRENCH 75

FAMILY: SPARKLING SOURS || The French 75 is one of those wonderful cocktails that is bound to stir up controversy: Should it be prepared with gin or cognac, lemon juice or lime juice? The oldest recipe that I've seen is in *The Savoy Cocktail Book* (1930); Harry Craddock prescribes gin and lemon juice and remarks, "Hits with remarkable precision."

To my knowledge, it wasn't until David Embury stated that the drink should be made with cognac that the brandy version reared its head, and according to my dear friend David Wondrich, the French 75 "has the distinction of being the only classic born in America during the dry period [Prohibition]."

½ teaspoon simple syrup
½ ounce fresh lemon juice
2 ounces gin
4 ounces chilled champagne

BUILD in the order given in a collins glass filled with crushed ice. Stir briefly.

FROZEN PIÑA COLADA

FAMILY: **FROZEN DRINKS** || There are a couple of stories about the birth of this drink, but the most plausible is that it was created in 1954 by bartender Ramón (Monchito) Marrero at the Caribe Hilton Hotel, in Puerto Rico. It is one of the very few sweet drinks I love. I like to use fresh pineapple to make Piña Coladas, but canned pineapple chunks will suffice, and the sweetness of the canned variety is more dependable.

2 ounces dark rum
½ cup pineapple cubes or 2 ounces pineapple juice
1½ ounces coconut cream
1 maraschino cherry, for garnish
1 pineapple cube, for garnish

Add the ingredients to a blender. Blend with enough ice to almost fill a 12-ounce collins glass. Add the garnishes.

GIBSON

FAMILY: **FRENCH-ITALIAN: GIN, RUM, GENEVER, VODKA, AND TEQUILA** || The Gibson was reportedly created in the 1930s at New York's Players Club by bartender Charlie Connolly. It was named for famed magazine illustrator Charles Dana Gibson, who requested "something different" from Connolly. This is merely a Martini with a different garnish, but the cocktail onions work well as a foil for either gin or vodka, so perhaps it does deserve a name all its own.

2½ ounces gin or vodka
½ ounce dry vermouth
1 or 3 cocktail onions, for garnish

STIR AND STRAIN into a chilled cocktail glass. Add the garnish.

GIMLET

FAMILY: **DUOS AND TRIOS** || The Royal Navy notes on its website that the name of this drink was inspired by the naval surgeon Sir Thomas D. Gimlette, KCB, "who introduced this drink as a means of inducing his messmates to take lime juice as an anti-scorbutic." He joined the navy as surgeon in 1879 and retired as surgeon general in 1913.

Legendary bartender Jim Meehan, in his new book *Meehan's Bartender Manual* (2017), states that he's not fond of Rose's lime juice, and I do understand why, but for me, this drink just isn't right if you use a homemade lime cordial instead. No doubt this is because of my many wonderful memories of Gimlets in the 1970s—it's certainly not good taste on my part!

2½ ounces gin
¾ ounce lime juice cordial, such as Rose's
1 lime wedge, for garnish

STIR AND STRAIN into an ice-filled old-fashioned glass. Add the garnish.

GIN-GIN MULE

FAMILY: SPARKLING SOURS AND HIGHBALLS || Adapted from a recipe by Audrey Saunders, Pegu Club, New York. Here's one of the first cocktails created in the modern era that spread its wings and can now be found in craft cocktail bars all over the world. Taste it once and you'll understand why. And Audrey notes that her Homemade Ginger Beer is an excellent non-alcoholic mixer for health tonics and teas, or a vibrant addition to your scotch toddy.

¾ ounce fresh lime juice
1 ounce simple syrup
2 mint sprigs (one for muddling and one for garnish)
1¾ ounces Tanqueray gin
1 ounce homemade ginger beer (recipes follow for small and large quantities)
1 lime wheel, for garnish
1 piece candied ginger, for garnish

MUDDLE lime juice, simple syrup, and a mint sprig in a mixing glass. Add the gin, ginger beer, and ice. SHAKE AND STRAIN into an ice-filled highball glass, and add garnishes and straws.

HOMEMADE GINGER BEER (LARGE BATCH)

MAKES 1 GALLON

1 gallon water
1 pound fresh ginger, minced
2 ounces fresh lime juice
4 ounces light brown sugar

Heat 1 cup of the water and pour into a food processor with the ginger. Process until almost mulch-like. Add this to the rest of the water in a large pan and bring it to a boil. Cover, remove from the heat, and allow it to stand for 1 hour.

Strain through a fine-mesh strainer and discard the pulp, add the lime juice and light brown sugar to the flavored water, stir well to dissolve, and allow the ginger mixture to come to room temperature before serving. To store, transfer to pint or quart glass jars, cover, and keep in the refrigerator for up to a week.

NOTE: When you are straining the ginger water, use a spoon or ladle to firmly press down on the ginger to extract the flavor. The strongest part of the ginger essence is still in the pulp and needs to be pressed out manually. The water will be cloudy; this is natural.

HOMEMADE GINGER BEER (SMALL BATCH)

MAKES 1 CUP

1 cup water
2 tablespoons finely grated fresh ginger
½ teaspoon fresh lime juice
1 teaspoon light brown sugar

Place the water and ginger in a saucepan, and bring to a boil. Cover, remove from the heat, and allow to stand for 1 hour. Strain through a fine-mesh strainer and discard the ginger pulp. Add the lime juice and light brown sugar to the ginger water, stir well to dissolve the sugar, and allow the mixture to come to room temperature before serving. To store, transfer to a small glass container, cover, and keep in the refrigerator for up to a week.

NOTE: When straining the ginger water, use a spoon or ladle to firmly press down on the ginger to extract the most flavor.

GODFATHER

|| FAMILY: DUOS AND TRIOS ||

2 ounces scotch
1 ounce amaretto

STIR AND STRAIN into an ice-filled old-fashioned glass.

GODMOTHER

|| FAMILY: DUOS AND TRIOS ||

2 ounces vodka
1 ounce amaretto

STIR AND STRAIN into an ice-filled old-fashioned glass.

GOLDEN CADILLAC

FAMILY: DUOS AND TRIOS || This drink, which appeared in the sixties or seventies, was reputedly created at Poor Red's, a barbecue joint in El Dorado, California. This place is now the nation's leading "consumer" of Galliano liqueur, reportedly going through as many as 40,000 bottles in 2016 and 2017.

The formula here is generally accepted as being the ratios used at Poor Red's, though I've seen one recipe that called for coconut cream rather than heavy cream, and I must admit that sounds interesting—provided you have a very sweet tooth, of course.

1 ounce white crème de cacao
1 ounce Galliano liqueur
1 ounce cream

SHAKE AND STRAIN into a chilled cocktail glass.

GOLDFISH COCKTAIL

FAMILY: FRENCH-ITALIAN: GIN, RUM, GENEVER, VODKA, AND TEQUILA || Served at the Aquarium Speakeasy in Manhattan during Prohibition, the original recipe, detailed in *On the Town in New York* by Michael and Ariane Batterberry, called for equal amounts of each ingredient. The proportions in my recipe result in the gin not being so overpowered by the goldwasser; the vermouth forms a subtle backdrop.

2 ounces gin
1 ounce dry vermouth
½ ounce Danziger goldwasser

STIR AND STRAIN into a chilled cocktail glass.

GOTHAM COCKTAIL

FAMILY: INTERNATIONAL SOURS AND ENHANCED SOURS || Adapted from a recipe created by David Wondrich in 2001 for the debut issue of New York's *Gotham* magazine.

2 ounces cognac
1 ounce Noilly Prat dry vermouth
½ ounce crème de cassis
2 dashes fresh lemon juice
1 lemon twist, for garnish

STIR AND STRAIN (using cracked ice) into a chilled cocktail glass and garnish with the lemon twist.

GRASSHOPPER

FAMILY: DUOS AND TRIOS || Here's a simple formula for a classic Grasshopper—just the way we made them in the 1970s. It works well, though the variation that follows is the real masterpiece.

1½ ounces green crème de menthe
1½ ounces white crème de cacao
1 ounce half-and-half
Grated nutmeg, for garnish

SHAKE AND STRAIN into a chilled coupe. Add the garnish.

GRASSHOPPER: MORGENTHALER STYLE

FAMILY: ORPHANS || Although the classic Grasshopper isn't a bad quaff at all, this reformulated version, created by Jeffrey Morgenthaler of Clyde Common, Portland, Oregon, is a masterpiece. When I featured this drink as one of my 101 Best New Cocktails in 2014, Morgenthaler noted, "We wanted to pay homage to the classic Midwestern style of ice cream drink, so we toyed around with the recipe until we got it right. The Fernet Branca added a whole lot more complexity, but brought unwanted bitterness to the party, so that's how we ended up with a pinch of sea salt."

1½ ounces green crème de menthe
1½ ounces white crème de cacao
1 ounce half-and-half
1 teaspoon Fernet Branca
Pinch of sea salt
4 ounces (½ cup) vanilla ice cream
8 ounces (1 cup) crushed ice
Mint sprig, for garnish

Add the ingredients to a blender. Blend until smooth, and serve in a chilled collins glass. Add the garnish.

GRASSHOPPER, GRASSHOPPER, GO TO HELL!

The legend of Saint Urho—a fictitious saint—originated in northern Minnesota in the 1950s when a group of Minnesotans of Finnish descent grew tired of their Irish-American friends taking over their town every March 17 to celebrate Saint Patrick's Day. Saint Patrick, as you probably know, is credited with driving all the snakes from Ireland. Saint Urho is said to have chased all the grasshoppers out of Finland, thus saving the grape crop and the jobs of Finnish vineyard workers. He did this by uttering the phrase *"Heinäsirkka, heinäsirkka, mene täältä hiiteen,"* which roughly translates to "Grasshopper, grasshopper, go to hell!"

And what does everyone drink during the Saint Urho's Day celebrations? That's right: Grasshoppers. Mark your calendars, then, for March 16, and raise a glass of chocolate-mint-fabulosity to the man who drove the grasshoppers out of Finland.

GREENPOINT

FAMILY: FRENCH-ITALIAN: WHISKEY AND BRANDY || Adapted from a recipe by Michael McIlroy, Attaboy, New York. See how Michael slipped some Yellow Chartreuse into his Manhattan here? It's a wise bartender who knows that, quite often, a little twist can go a very long way.

2 ounces straight rye whiskey
½ ounce Yellow Chartreuse
½ ounce sweet vermouth
1 dash Angostura bitters
1 dash orange bitters
1 lemon twist, for garnish

STIR AND STRAIN into a cocktail glass. Garnish with the lemon twist.

GREYHOUND

|| FAMILY: HIGHBALLS ||

2 ounces vodka
3 ounces fresh grapefruit juice

BUILD in an ice-filled highball glass.

GUN METAL BLUE

FAMILY: INTERNATIONAL SOURS || Adapted from a recipe by Nick Bennett, Porchlight, New York.

1½ ounces Del Maguey Vida mezcal
½ ounce blue curaçao
¼ ounce peach brandy
¾ ounce fresh lime juice
¼ ounce Bitter Cinnamon Simple Syrup (recipe follows)
1 orange twist, for garnish

SHAKE AND STRAIN into a chilled coupe. Carefully hold a lit match to the orange twist, which will lightly caramelize the oil (see page 97). Garnish the drink with the twist.

BITTER CINNAMON SIMPLE SYRUP

4 cinnamon sticks, broken into small pieces
2 ounces dried gentian root
4 cups granulated sugar
2 cups water

Heat the cinnamon sticks in a dry saucepan over low heat until aromatic. Add the gentian root, sugar, and water, and heat until the sugar has dissolved, stirring frequently. Remove from heat and allow to cool. Strain and refrigerate.

HANKY-PANKY

FAMILY: FRENCH-ITALIAN: GIN, RUM, GENEVER, VODKA, AND TEQUILA || Created by Ada Coleman, head bartender at London's Savoy Hotel from 1903 until 1926. Ada "Coley" Coleman was very popular when she worked at the Savoy, and she served drinks to all manner of celebrities, one of whom was Edwardian actor Charles Hawtrey. Hawtrey, Coley reported, once asked her for "something with a bit of punch in it." She created this cocktail for him, and after his first sip he declared, "By Jove! That is the real hanky-panky!"

1½ ounces gin
1½ ounces sweet vermouth
2 dashes Fernet Branca
1 orange twist, for garnish

STIR AND STRAIN into a chilled cocktail glass. Add the garnish.

HARVEY WALLBANGER

FAMILY: HIGHBALLS || According to an article by Brooks Clark in *Bartender* magazine, the Harvey Wallbanger was created at a party in the mid-1960s in Newport Beach, California. The host of the party was a certain Bill Doner, then a sports editor for a small newspaper, who, finding that the only potables he had on hand were vodka, frozen orange juice, and a bottle of Galliano, simply mixed them all together. In the early hours of the morning a guest by the name of Harvey was found banging his head against the wall and blaming Doner's concoction for his misery. A drink was born.

2 ounces vodka
3 ounces fresh orange juice
¼ to ½ ounce Galliano

BUILD the vodka and orange juice in an ice-filled highball glass. Stir briefly, then FLOAT the Galliano on top of the drink.

HEMINGWAY DAIQUIRI

FAMILY: INTERNATIONAL SOURS || These two recipes came straight from *To Have and Have Another: A Hemingway Cocktail Companion*, Philip Green's wildly entertaining and incredibly informative book that centers on the drinking habits of Papa Hemingway, as he was often affectionately known. Philip, an old friend of mine, generously agreed to let me use these formulas in this book. You can read more about this book on his blog, tohaveandhaveanother.wordpress.com.

H

E. HEMINGWAY SPECIAL (CA. 1937)

This first recipe came from a 1937 booklet from La Florida, a famous bar in Havana. La Florida, by the way, was usually known as Floridita—the Spanish diminutive for Florida.

2 ounces white rum
1 teaspoon maraschino liqueur
1 teaspoon grapefruit juice
½ ounce fresh lime juice

SHAKE AND STRAIN (using cracked ice) into a chilled cocktail glass.

PAPA DOBLE, A.K.A. THE WILD DAIQUIRI (CA. 1947)

This second recipe was found by Philip Greene within the pages of *Papa Hemingway* by A. E. Hotchner. Philip translated the formula from this passage: "Requested by most tourists, a Papa Doble was compounded of two and a half jiggers of Bacardi White Label Rum, the juice of two limes and half a grapefruit, and six drops of maraschino, all placed in an electric mixer over shaved ice, whirled vigorously and served foaming in large goblets."

3¾ ounces white rum
2 ounces fresh lime juice
2 ounces fresh grapefruit juice
6 drops maraschino liqueur

Add the ingredients to a blender. Blend well with ice and pour into a large chilled goblet.

> *"This frozen daiquiri, so well beaten as it is, looks like the sea where the wave falls away from the bow of a ship when she is doing thirty knots."*
>
> —Ernest Hemingway, *Islands in the Stream*

HOT BUTTERED RUM

FAMILY: HOT DRINKS || A recipe for Buttered Toddy, calling for rum, water, honey, nutmeg, lemon juice, and "a piece of fresh butter about the size of a walnut," appeared in the 1860 book *Practical Housewife.* But the best Hot Buttered Rum I ever tasted was a fairly simple affair made with spiced rum, and hot apple cider instead of hot water. It was created by bartender Nick Hydos at Painter's Tavern, in Cornwall on Hudson, New York.

1 teaspoon honey
1 whole clove
4 ounces hot water or hot apple cider
2 ounces dark rum or spiced rum
½ teaspoon unsalted butter
Ground cinnamon to taste
1 cinnamon stick, about 4 inches long

PLACE the honey, clove, and hot water or apple cider in an Irish coffee glass, and stir well to dissolve the honey. Add the rum, butter, and cinnamon. Stir briefly with the cinnamon stick, and serve with the cinnamon stick in the glass.

HOT TODDY

FAMILY: **HOT DRINKS** || The name may derive from the Hindu *tári tádi,* which refers to fermented coconut milk or the fermented sap from various trees. When the drink arrived in Europe, Toddies were made with a base spirit, various spices, sometimes a twist of lemon or orange, and water. *The American Herbal,* published in 1801, called the Toddy a "salutary liquor," and Dickens mentions a Whisky Toddy in *The Pickwick Papers:* "I don't quite recollect how many tumblers of whisky toddy each man drank after supper."

Although Toddies were, at least in the 1700s, made with either cold or hot water, today all Toddies are hot. You can prepare them with hot tea instead of plain hot water, and the abundance of flavored teas currently on the market makes this drink ideal for experimentation. You can also experiment with different herbs and spices with which to flavor your Toddies, although most recipes call for the usual bunch of what I refer to as "Christmas spices"—cinnamon, cloves, nutmeg, allspice, and the like.

A Hot Toddy is one of the few drinks I can think of for which I recommend honey as a sweetening agent, and this works very well indeed when using a very peaty scotch as your base liquor. Other sweetening agents can be introduced in the form of liqueurs, of course, but many aren't suited to this drink, since they can detract from the subtle spiciness of the Toddy and overwhelm the drink. Nutty liqueurs such as amaretto or hazelnut work well here.

On the liquor front, I recommend that you stick with brown goods—whiskey, brandy, and dark rum all work well as a base. White goods such as gin, vodka, tequila, and light rum aren't the best vehicles here, as far as I'm concerned, though it's hard to beat an aged genever Toddy if it's well balanced.

3 whole cloves
1 cinnamon stick, about 4 inches long
1 teaspoon honey
4 to 5 ounces boiling water
2 ounces bourbon, scotch, rye, brandy, or dark rum
Freshly grated nutmeg or allspice
1 lemon twist, for garnish

Place the cloves, cinnamon stick, and honey in a preheated Irish coffee glass and add the boiling water. Stir briefly to dissolve the honey, and allow the mixture to stand for 3 to 4 minutes. Add the liquor, stir briefly, then dust the top of the drink with the nutmeg or allspice. Add the garnish.

"'The nectar of the gods pales into nothingness when compared with a toddy such as I make,' said he. 'Ambrosia may have been alright for the degenerates of old Grecian and Roman days, but an American gentleman demands a toddy—a hot toddy.'"

—*The Windsor Magazine*, vol. 17, 1903

HUMO DE COMAL

FAMILY: SIMPLE SOURS || I sampled this baby while visiting its creator, Osvaldo "Ossy" Vazquez, who is the beverage manager and so much more at the Chileno Bay Resort in Cabo San Lucas, Mexico. Making this takes a little preparation, but it's well worth the effort. Trust me.

2 ounces Espadín mezcal
3 ounces Peruvian Chicha Punch (recipe follows)
½ ounce fresh lime juice
½ ounce simple syrup
1 lime wheel, dusted with brown sugar, for garnish

SHAKE AND STRAIN into a tumbler containing one large ice cube. Float the garnish on top of the ice cube.

PERUVIAN CHICHA PUNCH

1 apple, cored and sliced
1 pear, cored and sliced
4 ounces fresh pineapple juice
1 cinnamon stick
1 teaspoon ground cardamom
5 pieces star anise
4 cups (1 pound) brown sugar

Add the apple and the pear slices to a nonreactive saucepan and stir in the other ingredients with 2 liters of water. Simmer over medium heat, stirring frequently, for 30 to 40 minutes, until the fruits are thoroughly cooked and the sugar is dissolved.

Remove the punch from the heat, allow it to cool to room temperature, and strain it through a double layer of dampened cheesecloth. Discard the solids and refrigerate the punch, covered, for up to 1 week.

HURRICANE

FAMILY: SIMPLE SOURS || This drink was created at Pat O'Brien's in New Orleans, and Jeff Berry dates it to the 1960s. This formula is from *Beachbum Berry's Grog Log* by Jeff Berry and Annene Kaye, 1998.

4 ounces dark Jamaican rum
2 ounces passionfruit syrup
2 ounces fresh lemon juice

BUILD in a large crushed-ice-filled hurricane glass or large tiki mug.

INCOME TAX COCKTAIL

I

FAMILY: ENHANCED SOURS || Note that this is merely a Bronx (page 192) with Angostura bitters—it's an ideal drink to offer when April 15 rolls around.

2 ounces gin
¼ ounce sweet vermouth
¼ ounce dry vermouth
1 ounce fresh orange juice
2 dashes Angostura bitters
1 orange twist, for garnish

SHAKE AND STRAIN into a chilled cocktail glass. Add the garnish.

IRISH COFFEE

FAMILY: HOT DRINKS || Irish Coffee was created in the 1940s by Joe Sheridan, a bartender at Shannon Airport in Ireland, who wanted to fix a drink that would appeal to American tourists. Stanton Delaplane, a reporter for the *San Francisco Chronicle,* sampled one of Sheridan's coffees and took the recipe to his local hangout, the Buena Vista, in San Francisco, which now claims to sell up to two thousand hundred Irish Coffees per day. The plaque on the wall outside the Buena Vista claims that it sold its first one in 1952.

Irish Coffee is a fairly simple affair, but it can be an appealing drink provided fresh cream is used. The drink should be sweetened according to the customer's liking—always ask before you make the drink, as once the cream is floated on top there's no turning back.

It's far easier to use whipped cream when making an Irish Coffee, since it can be spooned on top of the drink, where it will float with no problem whatsoever. It's better, though, to whip chilled fresh light cream in a cold bowl until it thickens, but not enough to achieve stiff peaks. Depending on the consistency of the cream at this point, you might be able to pour it slowly onto the top of the drink, where if it's thick enough it will float; or pour it over the back of a teaspoon as though you were making a Pousse-Café.

I prefer to use simple syrup rather than sugar to sweeten this drink, since the sugar is already dissolved and distributes itself quickly in the coffee. You might want to try making simple syrup with brown sugar for this one, too (page 125); it works very well. You can also think about using a liqueur to sweeten your Irish Coffee; of course, Irish Mist would be the natural choice, but other liqueurs, such as Bénédictine, can work quite well here, too—just be sure to let the customer know of your intentions.

And, of course, you can make this drink using a different spirit, a liqueur, or both, then change the name to, say, Highland Coffee if you used scotch, or Italian Coffee if you chose to pour amaretto instead of the Irish whiskey. Just remember to omit the sugar if you use a liqueur.

This specific recipe comes from The Dead Rabbit, the New York joint that raised the bar in the cocktail world, and a place where for a couple of years I pulled the occasional (short) shift. Dead Rabbit is frequently thought of as the bar that serves the perfect Irish Coffee.

1½ ounces Clontarf Irish whiskey
½ ounce Rich Demerara Syrup (recipe follows)
3½ ounces piping-hot medium blend hot coffee
1 ounce freshly whipped heavy cream (see Note)

BUILD in an Irish coffee glass, floating the whipped cream on top.

NOTE: Jillian Vose, the bar manager and beverage director at the Dead Rabbit, prefers a heavy cream with 33–35% fat content. This allows the cream to float on top of the drink.

RICH DEMERARA SYRUP

1 cup demerara sugar
½ cup boiling water

Dissolve the sugar in the water, and allow to cool to room temperature. Transfer to a clean jar, cover, and store in the fridge.

JACK ROSE

FAMILY: **SIMPLE SOURS** || In *The Old Waldorf-Astoria Bar Book*, Albert Stevens Crockett states that when properly concocted, the drink should be the exact shade of a Jacqueminot rose, and he suggests that the true name could have been Jacque Rose.

Imbibe!, David Wondrich's magnificent tome, suggests that the drink was probably created by Frank J. May, a bartender better known as Jack Rose, who worked in Jersey City, and he also points out that applejack is New Jersey's state spirit. He goes on to say that the recipe for this drink was seen in print in 1899, and as such it was the first drink containing citrus and no bitters that was accepted as a cocktail nonetheless.

2 ounces applejack
1 ounce fresh lemon or lime juice
¼ to ½ ounce grenadine
1 lemon twist, for garnish

SHAKE AND STRAIN into a chilled cocktail glass. Add the garnish.

> *"In the morning all the ashtrays would be full of butts and the wastebaskets would hold piles of crumpled copy paper and empty applejack bottles. Whenever I see a bottle of applejack I think of the Hauptmann trial."*
>
> —JOSEPH MITCHELL, *My Ears Are Bent*

JACK ROSE ROYALE (BOTTLED)

MAKES 22 OUNCES

12 ounces applejack
2½ ounces Chambord black raspberry liqueur
2½ ounces fresh lemon juice
5 ounces bottled water
Maraschino cherries, for garnish

MIX AND CHILL for a minimum of 6 hours. Serve in chilled cocktail glasses garnished with maraschino cherries.

JAMAICAN TEN-SPEED

FAMILY: **ORPHANS** || Created by Roger Gobler of Café Terra Cotta in Scottsdale, Arizona. This is one of those drinks that makes you think the bartender simply threw some ingredients together and it happened to work, but nothing could be further from the truth. Roger explained to me, in great detail, his methodology for creating the Jamaican Ten-Speed, and it involved much experimentation. This is also the type of drink I would shy away from after perusing the list of ingredients—it looks too sweet for my palate—but the formula has perfect balance and is well worth recreating.

1 ounce vodka
¾ ounce Midori melon liqueur
¼ ounce crème de banane
¼ ounce Malibu liqueur
½ ounce half-and-half

SHAKE AND STRAIN into a chilled cocktail glass.

JAMES JOYCE COCKTAIL

FAMILY: **NEW ORLEANS SOURS** || I created this one in 2001 while conducting bartender-training seminars. It's a simple variation on the Oriental Cocktail recipe found in 1930's *Savoy Cocktail Book*. Rye whiskey and white curaçao were employed in the Oriental Cocktail, so it didn't take a mastermind to twist that drink to create this one.

1½ ounces Irish whiskey
¾ ounce sweet vermouth
¾ ounce triple sec
½ ounce fresh lime juice

SHAKE AND STRAIN into a chilled cocktail glass.

JODY BUCHAN'S ROB ROY

FAMILY: **FRENCH-ITALIAN: WHISKEY AND BRANDY** || Jody Buchan, head bartender at The Voyage of Buck in Edinburgh, Scotland, sent me this variation, and aside from his great picks of spirits and vermouth, his maraschino rinse brings a whole new dimension to the drink.

½ ounce maraschino liqueur, as a rinse
1 ounce Lagavulin 16-year-old single-malt scotch
1 ounce The Balvenie Caribbean Cask 14-year-old single-malt scotch
1 ounce Cocchi Vermouth di Torino
1 maraschino cherry, for garnish (optional)

RINSE a chilled coupe with maraschino liqueur. STIR AND STRAIN into the glass, and add the garnish, if using.

JOHN COLLINS

FAMILY: SPARKLING SOURS || This drink was originally made with genever as a base, but these days bourbon is often the spirit of choice.

2½ ounces genever or bourbon
1 ounce fresh lemon juice
¾ ounce simple syrup
Club soda
1 maraschino cherry, for garnish
½ orange wheel, for garnish

SHAKE everything except for the club soda, and strain into an ice-filled collins glass. Top with club soda. Add the garnishes.

KAMIKAZE

FAMILY: NEW ORLEANS SOURS || When I first met this drink on the Upper East Side of Manhattan in the early seventies, it was a Shooter, made with only Stolichnaya vodka and just two or three drops of Rose's lime juice. It did much damage. When asked what the difference was between a Kamikaze and a Dry Vodka Gimlet, bartender Scott Lamb, sadly deceased, said, "You don't want to commit suicide after a Dry Vodka Gimlet." Today's formula is far more sophisticated, and it now falls into the New Orleans Sours family.

1½ ounces vodka
1 ounce triple sec
½ ounce fresh lime juice

SHAKE AND STRAIN into a chilled cocktail glass.

KENTUCKY LONGSHOT

FAMILY: ORPHANS || Adapted from a recipe by the late Max Allen Jr. of the Seelbach Hilton Hotel in Louisville, Kentucky. He created the drink as a signature cocktail for the 1998 Breeders' Cup. The three garnishes represent win, place, and show.

2 ounces bourbon
½ ounce Domaine de Canton ginger liqueur
½ ounce peach brandy
1 dash Angostura bitters
1 dash Peychaud's bitters
3 pieces candied ginger, for garnish

STIR AND STRAIN into a chilled cocktail glass. Add the garnishes—if you are using long strips of candied ginger, hang them over the lip of the glass; smaller pieces can be dropped into the drink.

KING LOUIE THE 4TH

K

FAMILY: FRENCH-ITALIAN: WHISKEY AND BRANDY || Adapted from a recipe by Anthony DeSerio, Connecticut. Anthony more or less spells out his thinking on this variation of the Vieux Carré—it's a good example of how far a bartender can stray from a formula that inspires him or her and still retain the integrity of the cocktail. As he explains: "I wanted to put a hefty twist on a Vieux Carré and the honey flavors of Monkey Shoulder were on my mind. I thought of honey and ginger. So instead of American whiskey, cognac and sweet vermouth, I subbed these all out for a lovely gateway blended scotch, ginger cognac, and port cut with Lillet. The chocolate bitters pull all the flavors together. This silky tannic twist gets its name from my friend's favorite monkey, King Louie [from Disney's 1967 adaptation of *The Jungle Book*], and the French Quarter of NOLA where the origins of this cocktail spun off from."

1 ounce Monkey Shoulder scotch
¾ ounce Domaine de Canton ginger liqueur
½ ounce Taylor Fladgate 10-year-old tawny port
½ ounce Lillet Rouge
1 teaspoon Bénédictine
4 to 5 drops chocolate mole bitters
1 skewered maraschino cherry, for garnish

STIR AND STRAIN into a chilled coupe. Add the garnish.

KIR

FAMILY: ORPHANS || This drink was originally called Vin Blanc Cassis in France, and it was a favorite of the mayor of Dijon, Canon Felix Kir, who was revered for his work in the French resistance during World War II. He served what came to be known as the Kir at official functions during his twenty-year service to Dijon, from 1945 until 1965. The drinks comprise two products made in the Burgundy region, a white wine made from aligoté grapes and crème de cassis, a black-currant liqueur. The crème de cassis sweetens the wine; usually ¼ to ½ ounce works well with 5 ounces of wine, but you should experiment until you achieve the ratios right for your taste.

5 ounces chilled dry white wine
Crème de cassis to taste
1 lemon twist, for garnish

BUILD in the order given in a wine glass. Add the garnish.

KIR ROYALE

|| FAMILY: CHAMPAGNE COCKTAILS ||

5 ounces chilled champagne
½ ounce crème de cassis
1 lemon twist, for garnish

BUILD in the order given in a champagne flute. Add the garnish.

LA FLORIDITA DAIQUIRI

FAMILY: INTERNATIONAL SOURS || The La Floridita Daiquiri recipe was found by Ted "Dr. Cocktail" Haigh in a 1934 recipe book from La Florida bar (nicknamed "La Floridita" by locals) in Havana, where Hemingway sipped these delicious drinks. The original recipe called for less maraschino. It's your call as to how much to use in your version.

2 ounces light rum
¼ ounce maraschino liqueur
¾ ounce fresh lime juice
½ ounce simple syrup

SHAKE AND STRAIN into a chilled cocktail glass.

LAISSEZ LES BONS TEMPS ROULER!

FAMILY: **ORPHANS** || Adapted from a recipe by Bob Brunner, Paragon Restaurant & Bar, Portland, Oregon. Easy-peasy and oh, so yummy. Take a Sazerac, hold the simple syrup, and in its place add a little cherry brandy and a few drops of ginger liqueur. Bob's your uncle!

½ ounce absinthe, as rinse
2 ounces Russell's Reserve 6-year-old rye whiskey
½ ounce Cherry Heering liqueur
½ ounce Domaine de Canton ginger liqueur
2 dashes Regan's Orange Bitters No. 6
1 orange twist, for garnish

RINSE a chilled cocktail glass with the absinthe; set aside. STIR AND STRAIN the remaining ingredients into the glass. Add the garnish.

LARK CREEK INN TEQUILA INFUSION

FAMILY: **INFUSIONS** || Created by Bradley Ogden of the Lark Creek Inn in Larkspur, California, in 1995. This is one of my all-time favorite infusions, but beware: It's important to taste this as soon as the initial forty-eight hours are over, and to strain the ingredients from the tequila as soon as you get a hint that the chile might be taking charge of the drink—it can soon overpower the rest of the ingredients. I usually serve this drink in small portions—1 to 2 ounces—straight from the freezer. It makes a great Shooter or Sipper, but don't let it get too warm.

MAKES 24 TO 30 OUNCES

1 serrano chile
1 pineapple, peeled, cored, and cut into 1-inch chunks
1 sprig tarragon
1 bottle (750 ml) reposado tequila

Cut the tip and top from the chile and discard them. Slice the chile lengthwise down the center, remove the seeds, and place the halves in a large glass container with the pineapple chunks and the tarragon.

Pour in the tequila and allow it to rest for 48 to 60 hours in a cool, dark place, tasting the infusion frequently to make sure that the chile doesn't overpower the liquid.

Strain the tequila mix through a double layer of dampened cheesecloth and discard the pineapple, chile, and tarragon. Return the tequila to the glass container and chill in the refrigerator or freezer for at least 12 hours.

LAST WORD

FAMILY: INTERNATIONAL SOURS || Adapted from a recipe found in Ted Saucier's *Bottoms Up*, 1951: "Courtesy Detroit Athletic Club, Detroit. This cocktail was introduced around here about thirty years ago by Frank Fogarty, who was very well known in vaudeville. He was called the 'Dublin Minstrel,' and was a very fine monologue artist."

In 1912, according to the *New York Morning Telegraph*, Frank Fogarty was considered to be the most popular entertainer in vaudeville. "The single thing I work to attain in any gag is brevity," said Fogarty when asked the secret of his success. "You can kill the whole point of a gag by merely [using one] unnecessary word."

Murray Stenson, a Seattle man considered to be one of the world's very best bartenders, brought this drink back to life in 2009 after he found the recipe in Saucier's book. "The drink became a cult hit around Seattle, then Portland and was eventually picked up at cocktail dens in New York City, where many bartending trends are set. The Last Word then started to appear on drink menus in Chicago and San Francisco and spread to several cities in Europe—especially around London and Amsterdam—and beyond," said Stenson in an article by Tan Vinh published in *The Seattle Times* on March 11, 2009.

L

¾ ounce dry gin
¾ ounce maraschino liqueur
¾ ounce Green Chartreuse
¾ ounce fresh lime juice

SHAKE AND STRAIN into a chilled cocktail glass.

LEAP-YEAR COCKTAIL

FAMILY: NEW ORLEANS SOURS AND ENHANCED SOURS || "This Cocktail was created by Harry Craddock, for the Leap Year celebrations at the Savoy Hotel, London, on February 29th, 1928. It is said to have been responsible for more proposals than any other cocktail that has ever been mixed" (*The Savoy Cocktail Book*, 1930).

This recipe is adapted from Craddock's original, and the drink is one that bartenders should keep in mind to serve as a specialty when February 29 rolls around.

2 ounces gin
½ ounce Grand Marnier
½ ounce sweet vermouth
¼ ounce fresh lemon juice
1 lemon twist, for garnish

SHAKE AND STRAIN into a chilled cocktail glass. Add the garnish.

LEAVING MANHATTAN

FAMILY: FRENCH-ITALIAN: WHISKEY AND BRANDY || Adapted from a recipe by Joann Spiegel, New York City. Leaving Manhattan won first place in the final for the Woodford Reserve Manhattan Experience competition, and I was one of the judges there, alongside my old pal, David Wondrich, and Leo Robitschek, bar director at New York's Nomad Hotel, and a man who I never seem to be able to recognize no matter how many times we meet. All three of us were duly impressed by Joann's creation, and if you make one for your own self, you'll no doubt see why.

2 ounces Woodford Reserve bourbon
½ ounce Punt e Mes
¼ ounce dark crème de cacao
¼ ounce Lapsang Smoked Tea Syrup (recipe follows)
2 dashes orange bitters
1 chocolate or orange-flavored stir stick wrapped with orange spiral (see Note)

STIR AND STRAIN into a chilled coupe. Add the garnish.

NOTE: When preparing the garnish, peel the orange spiral next to the glass so the essential oils spray over the glass and cocktail. Wrap the spiral around the chocolate stick and rest the garnish on the lip of the glass off to one side.

LAPSANG SMOKED TEA SYRUP

4 ounces hot strong lapsang souchong tea
½ cup granulated sugar

Combine the tea and sugar; stir to dissolve the sugar. Let cool to room temperature before using. Store in the refrigerator.

LEMON DROP

FAMILY: NEW ORLEANS SOURS || In memory of Steve Wilmot, who introduced me to this drink, and who drank far too many of them one Christmas Day. I believe the Lemon Drop was created shortly after citrus vodkas gained popularity in the late 1980s and early 1990s.

1½ ounces citrus-flavored vodka
1 ounce triple sec
½ ounce fresh lemon juice
1 lemon twist, for garnish

SHAKE AND STRAIN into a chilled, sugar-rimmed cocktail glass. Add the garnish.

LIMONCELLO

FAMILY: INFUSIONS || Adapted from a recipe by George Germon and Johanne Killeen of Al Forno in Providence, Rhode Island, where I was introduced to the drink in the 1990s. And I'm sorry to have to report that we lost George Germon, age seventy, in 2015. Limoncello is a traditional Sicilian after-dinner drink and should be served neat, straight from the freezer.

MAKES APPROXIMATELY 60 OUNCES

12 medium lemons
1 liter grain alcohol
2 cups granulated sugar
2 cups water

Carefully pare the zest from the lemons, taking care not to take any of the white pith along with the zest. Place the zest in a large glass container with a close-fitting lid, reserving the pulp and juice for another use. Pour in the grain alcohol and close the container. Leave the mixture in a dark place for 1 week, to mellow.

Combine the sugar and the water in a small saucepan. Bring to a boil over medium heat, stirring frequently, until the sugar has dissolved. Allow the syrup to cool to room temperature, then add it to the lemon-zest mixture. Close the container again and allow the limoncello to mellow for 1 more week.

Strain the mixture through a double layer of dampened cheesecloth into bottles, and store the bottles in the freezer.

LITTLE DRAGON

FAMILY: ENHANCED SOURS || Adapted from a recipe by Humberto Marques, Curfew, Copenhagen, Denmark. Marques, described in *Forbes* magazine in November 2017 as "A Portuguese Bartender [who] Shakes Up Copenhagen's Cocktail Scene," is a man for whom I have great respect as a cocktailian—we've been in touch for quite a few years now. When he sent me this recipe, it came with the following description: "A cocktail created for the summer menu, but this cocktail could be sipped all year. A perfect pairing between mango, green tea, and dry sherry makes a perfect match with Tanqueray gin along with tarragon to temper the coolness between all of the ingredients. As [the seventeenth-century English writer] John Evelyn says of tarragon: "'Tis highly cordial and friend to the head, heart and liver. A little dragon it is!"

1½ ounces Tanqueray gin
1½ ounces mango puree
⅔ ounce dry sherry
⅔ ounce fresh lemon juice
½ ounce honey
1 pinch matcha green tea powder
1 tarragon sprig, for garnish

SHAKE AND STRAIN into an ice-filled goblet. Add the garnish.

LITTLE ITALY

FAMILY: FRENCH-ITALIAN: WHISKEY AND BRANDY || Adapted from a recipe created in 2006 by Audrey Saunders, Pegu Club, New York.

Cynar pops up again in this Manhattan variation, and with good reason—let's just say that it helps build character in a drink. And if anyone knows how to build drinks with character, it has to be Audrey Saunders.

2 ounces Rittenhouse Bottled-in-Bond straight rye whiskey
¾ ounce Martini & Rossi sweet vermouth
½ ounce Cynar
3 Luxardo maraschino cherries, for garnish (optional)

STIR AND STRAIN into a chilled cocktail glass. Add the maraschino cherries, if using.

LONG ISLAND ICED TEA

FAMILY: **HIGHBALLS** || Robert Butt, a bartender at the Oak Beach Inn in Babylon, Long Island, lays claim to this drink's creation, and here's what he says about it, according to his website: "The world famous Long Island Iced Tea was first invented in 1972 by me, Robert Butt, while I was tending bar at the infamous Oak Beach Inn. Nicknamed 'Rosebud' by OBI owner Bob Matherson, I participated in a Cocktail creating contest. Triple Sec had to be included, and the bottles started flying. My concoction was an immediate hit and quickly became the house drink at the OBI. By the mid-1970's, every bar on LI was serving up this innocent looking cocktail, and by the 1980's it was known the world over. Though it looks like the Iced Tea your Mom serves on a summer day, it is actually a combination of 5 different alcohols, with a splash of Coke. Mention Long Island Iced Tea at a party, and almost everyone has a story to tell. . . ."

This might not be a cocktailian masterpiece, but it's undeniable that the Long Island Iced Tea works. It's pleasant, refreshing, and somewhat lethal.

L

1 ounce vodka
1 ounce gin
1 ounce light rum
1 ounce white tequila
1 ounce triple sec
1 ounce fresh lemon juice (see Note)
¾ ounce simple syrup
Cola
1 lemon wedge, for garnish

SHAKE AND STRAIN everything except the cola into an ice-filled collins glass. Top with the cola. Add the garnish.

NOTE: For the record, Butt uses sweet and sour mix instead of fresh lemon juice and simple syrup.

LUAU DAIQUIRI

FAMILY: **SIMPLE SOURS AND TIKI** || Created by Jeff "Beachbum" Berry for the Luau Restaurant in Beverly Hills, 2008. Jeff currently owns Latitude 29, a first-class Tiki bar in New Orleans. A little orange juice and vanilla syrup can make a huge difference in a Daiquiri.

2 ounces white Virgin Islands rum
¾ ounce fresh lime juice
¾ ounce fresh orange juice
½ ounce Fee Brothers or Sonoma Syrup Co. vanilla syrup
1 small edible purple orchid, for garnish

SHAKE AND STRAIN into a chilled cocktail glass. Add the garnish.

MAI TAI

FAMILY: TIKI || It's generally agreed that the Mai Tai was created by "Trader Vic" Bergeron, so I went to tradervics.com for the scoop. According to that site, in 1970 Bergeron wrote the following: "I originated the Mai Tai and have put together a bit of the background on the evolution of this drink. . . . In 1944, after success with several exotic rum drinks, I felt a new drink was needed. I thought about all the really successful drinks: martinis, manhattans, daiquiris. . . . All basically simple drinks. . . . I took down a bottle of 17-year-old rum. It was J. Wray Nephew from Jamaica; surprisingly golden in color, medium bodied, but with the rich pungent flavor particular to the Jamaican blends. . . . I took a fresh lime, added some orange curaçao from Holland, a dash of Rock Candy Syrup, and a dollop of French orgeat syrup, for its subtle almond flavor. A generous amount of shaved ice and vigorous shaking by hand produced the marriage I was after. Half the lime shell went in for color. . . . I stuck in a branch of fresh mint and gave two of them to Ham and Carrie Guild, friends from Tahiti, who were there that night. Carrie took one sip and said, 'Mai Tai—Roa Ae.' In Tahitian this means 'Out of This World—The Best.' Well, that was that. I named the drink 'Mai Tai.' . . . In fairness to myself and to a truly great drink, I hope you will agree when I say, 'Let's get the record straight on the Mai Tai.'"

This recipe is adapted from the formula found on Jeff "Beachbum" Berry's website, beachbumberry.com.

1 ounce fresh lime juice
1 ounce dark Jamaican rum (Appleton, Myers's)
1 ounce aged Martinique rum (Rhum Clément, Rhum JM)
½ ounce orange curaçao
½ ounce orgeat syrup
¼ ounce simple syrup
1 mint sprig, for garnish

Squeeze the juice from the lime and reserve the lime shell.

Shake all the ingredients with 2 cups crushed ice, and pour, unstrained, into a double old-fashioned glass. Sink the lime shell into the drink, and add the garnish.

MAMIE TAYLOR

FAMILY: HIGHBALLS || This is a drink with a little history. It used to belong in a category of drinks known as Bucks, but aside from the Gin Buck, the Mamie Taylor is more or less the last surviving member of the family.

To make a Buck, one always squeezes the citrus wedge into an empty highball glass before the ice is added, and the drink is then built in the glass. I'd like to hold on to this tradition and keep the Mamie Taylor intact, so that this distinct methodology will live on in at least one drink. The recipe for this drink that appears in Craddock's 1930 edition of *The Savoy Cocktail Book* calls for it to be made with a wedge of lime, but I prefer a lemon wedge.

1 lemon wedge
2 ounces scotch
3 ounces ginger ale

Squeeze the juice from the lemon wedge into a highball glass, and add the wedge to the glass. Add ice, the scotch, and ginger ale, and stir briefly.

MANHATTAN

FAMILY: FRENCH-ITALIAN: WHISKEY AND BRANDY || The drink that changed the face of cocktails. The Manhattan, as far as I can ascertain, is the first drink that called for vermouth as a modifier, and it is still going strong today. It is the father of the Martinez, the grandpop of the Martini, and the founder of all French-Italian cocktails. Quite simply, when properly constructed, it is the finest cocktail on the face of the earth.

2 ounces bourbon or straight rye whiskey
1 ounce sweet vermouth
2 to 3 dashes Angostura bitters
1 maraschino cherry, for garnish

STIR AND STRAIN into a chilled cocktail glass. Add the garnish.

MANHATTAN (BOTTLED)

MAKES 22 OUNCES

12 ounces bourbon
4 ounces sweet vermouth
5 ounces bottled water
1 teaspoon Angostura bitters
Maraschino cherries, for garnish

MIX AND CHILL for a minimum of 6 hours. Serve in chilled cocktail glasses garnished with maraschino cherries.

The history of the Manhattan is lost to us, but we do have some clues as to its origin, mostly uncovered by the ardent efforts of cocktail historian William Grimes, who detailed a few theories in his 2001 edition of *Straight Up or On the Rocks: The Story of the American Cocktail.* Dismissing as unsubstantiated the theory that the drink was created for a banquet thrown at the Manhattan Club in 1874 to celebrate an electoral success for Governor Samuel Tilden, Grimes says that the club's records indicate that the drink was, in fact, invented there, but no dates were noted.

In the 1923 *Valentine's Manual of Old New* York, William F. Mulhall, a bartender who plied his trade at New York's Hoffman House in the 1880s, wrote "The Manhattan cocktail was invented by a man named Black who kept a place ten doors below Houston Street on Broadway in the [eighteen] sixties—probably the most famous drink in the world in its time." No other evidence that substantiates this claim has been uncovered thus far, but I do think that this claim carries weight. It was written by a bartender, right? I think that it's safe to say, though, that this cocktail, with its simple formula and complex delivery, was a direct result of vermouth's increasing popularity with bartenders in the late 1800s.

The recipe that appears in Jerry Thomas's *The Bar-Tender's Guide, or How to Mix All Kinds of Plain and Fancy Drinks* (1887) calls for one pony—1 ounce—of rye whiskey, a wine glass—2 ounces—of vermouth, two dashes of curaçao or maraschino, and three dashes of Boker's bitters; the Manhattan Club's recipe indicates that its bartenders used equal amounts of whiskey and vermouth, with some orange bitters. By 1906, though, Louis Muckensturm, author of *Louis' Mixed Drinks with Hints for the Care and Service of Wines*, was calling for twice as much whiskey as vermouth, as well as dashes of curaçao, and Angostura and orange bitters—a drink that's not too far removed from the Manhattan we serve today.

The "drying" of the Martini that occurred in the 1940s almost happened to the Manhattan in the 1990s, and some untrained bartenders out there still think that the drink should be made with just a dash or two of vermouth. But to a large extent, cocktail drinkers know that the vermouth should make up at least one-fourth of the drink, and it usually takes Muckensturm's base proportion to properly balance this cocktail. However, as with all drinks made with a whiskey base, it's imperative to alter the ratios according to the whiskey you use to construct the Manhattan.

As for bitters, Angostura is the standard way to go here, even though Peychaud's and orange bitters both work well in this drink. If you go the Peychaud's route, you will notice a marked difference in your Manhattan—it works for some people, though not everybody. Most important, however, is that there *must* be bitters of some kind in a Manhattan. Unless, of course, a customer requests that you leave it out.

I hope, after digesting all the variables discussed here, you have some idea of why I think the Manhattan is the best cocktail on earth. It's so simple, but it's so darned complicated. You should take the construction of this drink as a challenge. For the record, the best Manhattans in Manhattan, according to an unscientific survey I conducted some years ago, are made by Norman Bukofzer at the Ritz-Carlton Hotel, on Central Park South. For more information on the Manhattan and its history, see Philip Greene's wonderful book on the subject, *The Manhattan: The Story of the First Modern Cocktail with Recipes*.

In 1998, on *Homicide*, the NBC police drama, Detective John Munch was seen ordering a Manhattan from Billie Lou, a forty-something bartender in a very seductive mood:

BILLIE LOU: Cherry?
DETECTIVE MUNCH: Always. Why do you think they call it a Manhattan?
BILLIE LOU: It's beautiful, seductive, intoxicating, and really bad for you.
DETECTIVE MUNCH: Thoughts on a maraschino cherry.
BILLIE LOU: Forbidden fruit?
DETECTIVE MUNCH: An allegory in a glass.

MANHATTAN PERFECTO

FAMILY: FRENCH-ITALIAN: WHISKEY AND BRANDY || Adapted from a recipe by Ted Kilgore, Planter's House, St. Louis, Missouri. Known in certain circles as "That Crazy Bastard," Ted Kilgore has a fabulous habit of combining seemingly odd ingredients to create decidedly fabulous drinks. This is one of his more conventional cocktails, and his use of a maraschino rinse is inspired, but it's the liberal dose of Angostura bitters in this drink that gives it the Kilgore signature.

½ ounce Luxardo maraschino liqueur, as a rinse
2 ounces straight rye whiskey
¾ ounce Noilly Prat dry vermouth
¾ ounce Noilly Prat sweet vermouth
4 dashes Angostura bitters
1 lemon twist, for garnish
1 maraschino cherry, for garnish

RINSE a chilled cocktail glass with the maraschino liqueur, and discard the excess. STIR AND STRAIN the remaining ingredients into the prepared glass. Add the garnishes.

MARGARITA

FAMILY: NEW ORLEANS SOURS || One of America's most popular cocktails, the Margarita has almost as many histories as rabbits have bunnies. Which is true? Let's take a look at these oft-told tales:

1. DANIEL (DANNY) NEGRETE created the drink for his girlfriend, Margarita, when he was the manager of the Garci Crespo Hotel in Puebla, Mexico, in 1936. Apparently Margarita liked to eat salt with whatever she drank, so the salted rim on the glass made it unnecessary for her to keep reaching into the salt bowl.
2. VERN UNDERWOOD, a tequila distributor for Jose Cuervo, named Johnnie Durlesser, a bartender at the Los Angeles restaurant the Tail of the Cock in the 1950s, as being the man who recreated a drink he'd had in Mexico, dubbing it the Margarita. Underwood took out full-page advertisements in various magazines that depicted himself wearing white tie and tails and red shoes, of all things, saluting a goddess, and declaring, "Margarita, more than a girl's name."

3. **JAZZ MUSICIAN TEDDY STAUFFER**, among others, attributed the drink to Margarita Sames of San Antonio, Texas. This claim was backed up by Helen Thompson, who wrote, in *Texas Monthly* magazine in 1991, that socialite Sames, who didn't like weak drinks or weak men, claimed to have created the drink for Nicky Hilton—one of the Hotel Hiltons, of course, and coincidentally, the owner of the Tail of the Cock at the time.
4. **SARA MORALES**, an expert on Mexican folklore, claimed that it was created, circa 1930, by Doña Bertha, the owner of Bertha's Bar in Taxco, Mexico. Morales added that the first drink created by this woman was called the Bertha; the Margarita was her second creation. This is partially substantiated by Charles H. Baker Jr. in *The Gentleman's Companion* (1946): "Tequila Special à la Bertita, Garnered, among other Things, in Lovely Taxco, in February of 1937. This is a shocker from the place of Bertita, across from the cathedral steps in Taxco. . . . It is a cooler as well and Americans find it very unusual. Take 2 ponies of good tequila, the juice of 1 lime, 1 tsp sugar, and 2 dashes of orange bitters. Stir in a collins glass with lots of small ice, then fill with club soda. No garnish except crushed halves of the lime." If Baker's account is true, then it's not much of a stretch to imagine Bertha, or Bertita, substituting triple sec for the orange bitters, and coming up with a Margarita.
5. **CARLOS "DANNY" HERRERA** is also said to have invented this drink in 1948, when he was running Rancho La Gloria, a hotel and restaurant close to Tijuana. Herrera supposedly named the drink for starlet Marjorie King, who, when in Mexico, took the name Margarita.
6. **DAVID WONDRICH**, cocktail historian and author of *Imbibe!*, reckons that, circa 1929, Americans who ventured south of the border to visit the racetrack just outside of Tijuana sipped tequila-based cocktails that fell under the now defunct category of drinks known as Daisies—spirit, citrus, and sweetening agent, and were delighted with them. The Spanish word for "daisy," of course, is *margarita*. And thus the drink was born.

As to who is right about the creation of this fabulous drink, I'll never truly know. But to my dying day I'll swear blind that Wondrich is right. Again.

And it's also worth noting that the Margarita formula follows the same path as other classics such as the Sidecar, the Kamikaze, and the Cable Car: It's a base spirit made sour by the addition of citrus juice and balanced for sweetness with triple sec.

1½ ounces white 100% agave tequila
1 ounce triple sec
½ ounce fresh lime juice
Salt, for glass (optional)

SHAKE AND STRAIN into a salt-rimmed (if using), chilled cocktail glass.

MARGARITA (BOTTLED)

MAKES 22 OUNCES

8 ounces white 100% agave tequila
6 ounces triple sec
3 ounces fresh lime juice
5 ounces bottled water
Salt, for glass (optional)
Lime wedges, for garnish

MIX AND CHILL for a minimum of 6 hours. Serve in salt-rimmed (if using), chilled cocktail glasses, and garnish with lime wedges.

MARGARITA JELLY SHOT

|| FAMILY: JELLY SHOTS ||

1 ounce fresh lime juice
1 ounce simple syrup
1 ounce water
1 package unflavored gelatin (¼ ounce)
3 ounces white tequila
2 ounces triple sec
Food coloring (optional)

Place the lime juice, simple syrup, and water in a small glass measuring cup, and add the gelatin. Allow this to sit for 1 minute, then microwave the mixture on high for 30 seconds.

Stir thoroughly to make sure all the gelatin has dissolved, then add the tequila, triple sec, and food coloring (if desired). Stir thoroughly again and pour the mixture into a mold. Refrigerate for at least 1 hour or, preferably, overnight.

MARTINEZ

FAMILY: **FRENCH-ITALIAN: GIN, RUM, GENEVER, VODKA, AND TEQUILA** || Adapted from the recipe in Jerry Thomas's 1887 book *The Bar-Tender's Guide, or How to Mix All Kinds of Plain and Fancy Drinks*. Thomas used more vermouth than gin in his Martinez, and his choice of bitters was Boker's, which is now made by Dr. Adam Elmegirab. This drink, I believe, was born of the Manhattan, and is the mother—or perhaps grandmother—of the Dry Gin Martini. It tastes nothing like a Dry Gin Martini, of course, mainly because it calls for sweet vermouth, but this is a glorious drink that's well worth trying.

To make a version of the Martinez that's more in line with modern tastes but still sticks to Thomas's ingredients, just reverse the amounts of gin and vermouth, using 2 ounces of Old Tom and 1 ounce of vermouth. I highly recommend the Ransom Old Tom, which is slightly aged in oak, and for the vermouth, I usually use Noilly Prat.

2 ounces Noilly Prat sweet vermouth
1 ounce Old Tom gin (preferably Ransom)
2 dashes maraschino liqueur
1 dash Boker's bitters
¼ lemon slice, for garnish

M

STIR AND STRAIN into a chilled cocktail glass. Add the garnish.

MARTINEZ BY PERRONE

FAMILY: **FRENCH-ITALIAN: GIN, RUM, GENEVER, VODKA, AND TEQUILA** || In 2006, I tasted the very best Martinez I have ever had. It was made at Montgomery Place, in London, by Italian bartender Ago Perrone, who was working at Montgomery Place at the time. So in 2017 I went to Ago, who is now director of mixology at the Connaught Hotel in London, for his recipe.

As is the case with most of the world, Ago works in milliliters rather than ounces, and I've tried to translate the amounts as closely as possible, but in this instance, that has meant working in teaspoons as well as ounces. I just want you to taste the incredible balance in Ago's offering.

1¾ ounces Carpano Punt e Mes
¾ ounce plus 2 teaspoons Plymouth Navy Strength gin or Sipsmith VJOP gin
1½ teaspoons orange curaçao
1 teaspoon maraschino liqueur
2 dashes Abbott's bitters

STIR AND STRAIN into a chilled cocktail glass.

MARTINI

FAMILY: FRENCH-ITALIAN: GIN, RUM, GENEVER, VODKA, AND TEQUILA || We'll never know with absolute certainty when the Martini was born or who its creator was, but my research points toward the drink being a direct descendant of the Manhattan. Recipes for the Martini started to appear in cocktail books in the late 1800s, and many of them were very similar, and sometimes identical, to recipes for the Martinez, a cocktail that appeared in print in the 1880s and was often described as "a Manhattan, substituting gin for the whiskey." Thus, theoretically at least, the Martinez was a variation on the Manhattan, and the Martini is, for all intents and purposes, a Martinez.

The first Martinis were made with Old Tom gin, sweet vermouth, bitters, and maraschino liqueur; even when the Dry Martini came into being, circa 1906, it contained bitters, as well as dry gin and dry vermouth. Orange bitters remained an ingredient in Dry Martinis right through to Prohibition and beyond, but by the late 1940s the drink was being made with just dry gin and dry vermouth, and the amount of vermouth used was getting smaller and smaller.

Many of the first Dry Martinis were made with equal amounts of gin and vermouth, but by the early 1950s some bartenders had already started to use atomizers to dispense the vermouth into the drink, and bitters had been dropped from the recipe.

In my opinion, Martinis should be stirred and not shaken, simply because the sight of a bartender lovingly stirring this drink for at least twenty to thirty seconds is something that people enjoy. Stirring for approximately thirty seconds will yield a drink that's just as cold as one that has been shaken for about ten seconds—it's worth the time. Shake it if you must, and if a customer requests that the drink be shaken, then that's how it should be made. Never use gin or vodka from the fridge or the freezer, since the spirit will be too cold to melt enough ice to properly dilute the cocktail.

I have included a few recipes here, culled from various books in my library, so you can see how the drink evolved, devolved, and evolved once more to rise victorious from the shadow of her former splendor in the latter half of the twentieth century.

MARTINI 1906

This is the first formula I can find that calls for dry gin and dry vermouth.

2 ounces dry gin
1 ounce dry vermouth
1 dash orange curaçao
2 dashes orange bitters
1 lemon twist, for garnish

STIR AND STRAIN into a chilled cocktail glass. Add the garnish.

MARTINI 1912

Back to Old Tom gin for this one.

1 ounce Old Tom gin
1 ounce vermouth (style not mentioned)
1 dash curaçao or absinthe
2 dashes gum syrup
1 lemon twist, for garnish

STIR AND STRAIN into a chilled cocktail glass. Add the garnish.

MARTINI 1930

1 ounce dry gin
1 ounce dry vermouth
1 dash orange bitters
1 lemon twist, for garnish

STIR AND STRAIN into a chilled cocktail glass. Add the garnish.

MARTINI 1948

1¾ ounces dry gin
¼ ounce dry vermouth
1 olive, for garnish

STIR AND STRAIN into a chilled cocktail glass. Add the garnish.

MARTINI 1960

2 ounces dry gin or vodka
1–2 drops dry vermouth
1 olive or 1 lemon twist, for garnish

STIR AND STRAIN into a chilled cocktail glass. Add the garnish.

MARTINI 2016

This formula is a generalization that's meant to be representative of the style of Martini generally enjoyed by folks today. Proportions should be altered to suit the individual.

2 ounces dry gin
1 ounce dry vermouth
1–2 dashes orange bitters
1 olive or 1 lemon twist, for garnish

STIR AND STRAIN into a chilled cocktail glass. Add the garnish.

MARY PICKFORD COCKTAIL

FAMILY: INTERNATIONAL SOURS || The drink, named for the early twentieth-century movie star who was once known as America's Sweetheart, was created by Eddie Woelke, an American bartender who worked in Havana, Cuba, during Prohibition. The formula here is the one reportedly used by famed Cuban bartender Juan Coronado in Washington, D.C.

1½ ounces light rum
1½ ounces pineapple juice
1 barspoon maraschino liqueur
¼ ounce grenadine

SHAKE AND STRAIN into a chilled cocktail glass.

MIMOSA

FAMILY: CHAMPAGNE COCKTAILS || This drink can be varied by the addition of a splash of grenadine, in which case it's sometimes known as a Buck's Fizz. Or try adding a little cognac or substituting Grand Marnier for the triple sec. Many people omit the triple sec altogether; it's a big mistake.

½ ounce triple sec
1½ ounces fresh orange juice
3½ ounces chilled champagne
1 orange slice, for garnish

BUILD in the order given in a champagne flute. Add the garnish.

MINT JULEP

FAMILY: JULEPS || Here's a drink worthy of much debate. It dates back, in its present form of spirit, mint, and sugar, to around the late 1700s, although according to *The Mint Julep*, by Richard Barksdale Harwell, the first printed mention of mint as an ingredient in a Julep didn't appear until 1803. The English used the term "julep" to describe simple syrup as far back as 1400, and the word, according to various sources, appears to have been derived from the Persian *gul-ab* or the Arabic *julab*, meaning "rose water."

Many people drink Mint Juleps only on Kentucky Derby day (when, at Churchill Downs, they serve premixed Juleps hardly worthy of the name), but hidden in Harwell's book you can find other dates suitable for serving this wonderful drink: May 28 marks the opening of Julep season as celebrated by members of the General P.G.T. Beauregard Marching and Burial Society. No mention is given of the closing date of the season, so we must presume that it lasts—well, as long as you would like. In 1837, English captain Frederick Marryat wrote that during New York's Independence Day celebrations, Mint Juleps were served (along with porter, ale, cider, mead, brandy, wine, ginger beer, pop, soda water, whiskey, rum, punch, cocktails and "many other compounds to name which nothing but the luxuriance of American-English could invent a word"), so July Fourth seems as though it, too, is an appropriate date on which to drink Juleps.

My all-time favorite story about the Mint Julep, though, involves a South Carolinian by the name of William Heyward Trapier, who is said to have taken several casks of bourbon with him when visiting England in 1845. Harwell states that the casks of bourbon were "pure assumption" on the part of the original reporter of this event, but he does agree that the following took place.

While visiting England, Trapier went to New College, Oxford (formally named the College of the Blessed Virgin Mary of Winchester), and was there entertained by the "warden and fellows." He was surprised to find out that nobody at New College knew how to make a Mint Julep and took it on himself to demonstrate. The drinks were so well received that ever since, on June 1, Mint Juleps are served at New College, and a seat there remains empty in case Trapier returns to join in the festivities. So now you can add June 1 to your Julep calendar.

May 15 marks the anniversary of the founding of the Old Dominion Society of New York City, which, in 1860, was given a poem about the Mint Julep to be read at its annual banquet by John Reuben Thompson, a poet from Richmond. The end of the first verse states, "A whiskey julep is the drink that typifies the nation!" So now you can pick any of these dates on which to serve a Mint Julep. Or, as long as the weather is warm, serve it whenever you like.

The major issue concerning the Mint Julep is whether or not the mint leaves should be crushed to release their essential oils, and I've previously taken a stand on this, maintaining that the mint should serve only as an aromatic garnish. I must admit, however, that a Julep that tastes of mint is also a thing of beauty; but rather than crushing mint leaves with sugar and water in the bottom of a julep cup, I prefer to infuse the mint into simple syrup, and use that as the sweetener for the drink. And I still believe that an abundance of mint should be placed atop the drink in order that the drinker's nose be buried in the garnish while he sips it through short straws.

Of primary importance when preparing a Mint Julep is making sure that a thin layer of ice forms on the outside of the julep cup (preferably made of silver) or the glass in which it is served. To achieve this, the bartender must use the finest crushed ice available and stir the drink until the ice forms. Then the drink must be topped with mint, and straws should be inserted into the drink—straws short enough to ensure that the customer gets the full benefit of the mint aroma. Always serve a Mint Julep with a coaster of some sort, since the condensation from the ice on the glass can be a problem.

Silver julep cups can be prohibitively expensive, and although they are the proper vessel for this drink, I don't think that regular glasses—collins glasses are preferable—should be considered improper.

The first Mint Juleps were probably not made with bourbon. Rum, peach brandy, and regular brandy have all been cited in recipes dating back to 1787, and at that time bourbon was only just coming to be known by that name. The recipes here call for straight bourbon, but you should feel free to experiment with other spirits, though brown goods (whiskey, brandy, and the like) are far preferable in this drink to their lighter cousins.

3 ounces bourbon
1 to 2 ounces simple syrup or Minted Simple Syrup (**recipe follows**)
5 or 6 stems of fresh mint, for garnish

Cut straws so they are approximately 2 inches taller than the serving glass. Add crushed ice to a julep cup or collins glass until it is two-thirds full. Add the bourbon and simple syrup and stir for 10 to 20 seconds. Add more crushed ice and stir again until a thin layer of ice forms on the outside of the glass; then add more crushed ice so that it domes slightly over the rim of the glass. Garnish with the fresh mint stems and insert the straws. Serve with a cocktail napkin to catch the condensation.

MINTED SIMPLE SYRUP

1 cup water
1 cup granulated sugar
1 bunch fresh mint

Combine the ingredients in a small saucepan over medium heat. Stir frequently until the mixture reaches a simmer; then cover the pan, turn the heat down to low, and allow it to simmer for 5 minutes. Remove the pan from the heat and let the mixture come down to room temperature, approximately 1 hour. Remove the mint before storing the syrup in the refrigerator.

MINT JULEP BY KEELER

Ian Hall, the president of BRAND Hospitality Group in New Albany, Indiana, included the following note along with this spectacular variation on the Mint Julep: "Our former beverage director, Brian Keeler, developed this recipe just before Derby last year. Brian is now a general manager at one of our restaurants, but is still very much involved in our cocktail programs at both of our restaurants."

4 to 6 fresh mint leaves
1 ounce simple syrup
1 dash Angostura bitters
2 ounces Old Forester bourbon
½ ounce fresh lemon juice
½ ounce fresh peach puree
1 fresh mint sprig, for garnish

Lightly MUDDLE the mint leaves with the simple syrup and the Angostura bitters in a mixing glass. Add ice and the remaining ingredients, and shake well. Strain into a crushed-ice filled collins glass, and add the garnish.

MINT JULEP BY MARRYAT

This recipe is loosely based on a formula detailed in Jerry Thomas's 1862 book *How to Mix Drinks, or The Bon Vivant's Companion*. Thomas states that it was a recipe taken to England by Captain Frederick Marryat (1792–1848), a British naval officer who wrote books about his seafaring adventures after he retired from the navy. Marryat related that he had overheard an American woman saying, "Well, if I have a weakness for any one thing, it is for a mint julep!" He remarked that the drink was, "like the American ladies, irresistible."

1½ ounces brandy
1½ ounces peach brandy
1 to 2 ounces simple syrup or Minted Simple Syrup (page 250)
5 or 6 stems of fresh mint, for garnish
1 pineapple spear, for garnish

Cut straws so they are approximately 2 inches taller than the serving glass. Add crushed ice to a julep cup or collins glass until it is two-thirds full. Add the brandy, peach brandy, and simple syrup and stir for 10 to 20 seconds. Add more crushed ice and stir again until a thin layer of ice forms on the outside of the glass; then add more crushed ice so that it domes slightly over the rim of the glass. Garnish with the fresh mint stems and the pineapple spear, and insert the straws. Serve with a cocktail napkin to catch the condensation.

MOJITO

FAMILY: JULEPS || Although you can use simple syrup in the Mojito, granulated sugar makes a far better cocktail, since, as with the Caipirinha, the sugar abrades the zest of the limes and releases their essential oils into the drink.

4 lime wedges
2 to 3 teaspoons granulated sugar
8 to 10 fresh mint leaves
2 ounces light rum
Club soda
2 or 3 mint sprigs, for garnish

MUDDLE the lime wedges, sugar, and mint leaves in a mixing glass until the sugar is completely dissolved, all the juice is extracted from the limes, and the mint is thoroughly integrated into the juice. Add ice and the rum to the mixing glass, shake briefly, and strain into a collins glass filled with crushed ice. Top with club soda, and add the garnish.

MONKEY GLAND COCKTAIL

FAMILY: INTERNATIONAL SOURS || There are two legitimate Monkey Gland Cocktails, one of which takes absinthe as an accent and the other calls for Bénédictine. I discovered this in 1997, when Dale DeGroff made this drink for me at the Rainbow Room and I saw him reaching for an absinthe substitute (this happened before absinthe became legal again in the twenty-first century), whereas I had always used Bénédictine. It turned out that Dale followed Harry Craddock's recipe from the 1930 *Savoy Cocktail Book*, whereas I had learned the drink from Patrick Gavin Duffy's *The Official Mixer's Guide* (1934). Craddock, based in London, had access to absinthe, but Duffy changed the recipe to make it easier on American bartenders. Both versions are well worth trying.

2 ounces gin
1 ounce fresh orange juice
1 to 2 dashes Bénédictine or absinthe
1 dash grenadine

SHAKE AND STRAIN into a chilled cocktail glass.

MOSCOW MULE

FAMILY: HIGHBALLS || Created in 1941 by Jack Morgan, owner of the Cock 'n' Bull Tavern in Los Angeles, and John G. Martin of the Heublein company. Morgan had a surplus of ginger beer, and Heublein's executives were trying to get Americans to drink their newly acquired Smirnoff vodka. This drink is traditionally served in a small copper tankard.

2 ounces vodka
3 ounces ginger beer
2 lime wedges, for garnish

BUILD in an ice-filled highball glass. Add the garnish.

MUDSLIDE

FAMILY: DUOS AND TRIOS || A very simple and effective twist on the Black Russian theme, this adds a little Baileys instead of fresh cream to the vodka–Kahlúa marriage.

2 ounces vodka
1 ounce Kahlúa
1 ounce Baileys Irish Cream

SHAKE AND STRAIN into an ice-filled old-fashioned glass.

MY WAY MANHATTAN

FAMILY: FRENCH-ITALIAN: WHISKEY AND BRANDY || It took Daniel-Grigore Mostenaru to really nail a drink called the My Way Manhattan, so I sort of think of him as being the Sid Vicious—the only person to nail the Sinatra song, in my honest opinion—of classic cocktails. I do hope he approves.

I'd hate to give my Romanian "Sid Vicious" a big head, but I'd be wrong if I didn't point out that the combination of curaçao and Branca Menta as a rinse is a stroke of genius. Little things mean a lot.

¼ ounce orange curaçao
¼ ounce Branca Menta
2 ounces Four Roses bourbon
1 ounce Dubonnet Rouge
1 lemon twist, for garnish

Pour the curaçao and Branca Menta into an empty mixing glass, and swirl the liquids around so as to coat the interior of the glass. Add ice and the remaining ingredients. STIR AND STRAIN into a chilled champagne coupe. Add the garnish.

NEGRONI

FAMILY: FRENCH-ITALIAN: GIN, RUM, GENEVER, VODKA, AND TEQUILA || An Italian count by the name of Camillo Negroni created this drink, circa 1919, when he asked Fosco Scarselli, barman at the Cafe Casoni in Florence, Italy, to substitute gin for the club soda in his Americano (page 174); The first printed recipes I can find for the Negroni, however, are in two books, both printed in 1955: *The U.K.B.G. Guide to Drinks*, a British book compiled by the United Kingdom Bartenders' Guild, and Oscar Haimo's *Cocktail and Wine Digest*, published in New York.

I also point you to a book I penned in 2015 called *The Negroni: Drinking to La Dolce Vita, with Recipes & Lore* if you'd like to learn more about the fascinating history of this spectacular drink (spoiler alert: Italian-born Count Negroni was a cowboy in the United States prior to creating the drink), and its many variations.

1½ ounces Campari
1½ ounces sweet vermouth
1½ ounces gin
1 orange twist, for garnish

BUILD in any order in an ice-filled rocks glass. Add the garnish.

NEGRONI D'OR

FAMILY: FRENCH-ITALIAN: GIN, RUM, GENEVER, VODKA, AND TEQUILA || Adapted from a recipe by Brian MacGregor, San Francisco. Brian made this for the finals of the G'Vine Best Gin Bartender Competition in Paris in June 2010, where I was a judge alongside the intrepid Phillip Duff and Jean-Sebastian Robicquet. Using the Dolin Blanc vermouth was a good idea here, but it's the Grand Classico bitters, an infusion of numerous herbs and roots including bitter orange peel, wormwood, gentian, rhubarb, and other aromatic plants, that steals the limelight here. It makes for an interesting variation on the classic Negroni.

1½ ounces G'vine Nouasion gin
½ ounce Dolin Blanc vermouth
½ ounce Grand Classico bitters

STIR AND STRAIN into a chilled sherry copita glass.

NORANGE FOR MY NUNCLE

FAMILY: ORPHANS || Recipe by Phoebe Esmon, Night Bell, Asheville, North Carolina. Phoebe stands out in a crowd. One is never quite sure which decade would best suit her and her partner, Christian R. Gaal. I'm happy, though, that they chose to live around the same time as me. We've become friends over the years, and their drinks never fail to impress.

2 ounces Ketel One vodka
1 ounce Don Zoilo manzanilla sherry
¼ ounce Pierre Ferrand dry curaçao
2 dashes Regan's Orange Bitters No. 6
1 small pinch salt
1 orange twist, for an aromatic garnish

STIR AND STRAIN into a chilled cocktail glass. Squeeze the twist over the drink, then discard.

NUCLEAR DAIQUIRI

N

FAMILY: INTERNATIONAL SOURS || Adapted from a recipe by Gregor De Gruyther, London. Gregor De Gruyther, a fabulous bartender who died in 2009 and is greatly missed by his brother and sister bartenders all over the world, created this drink and declared that he didn't call for a garnish because "no garnish can withstand the awesome power of the Nuclear Daiquiri."

¾ ounce plus 1 teaspoon Wray & Nephew overproof rum
¾ ounce plus 1 teaspoon Green Chartreuse
½ ounce velvet falernum
¾ ounce plus 1 teaspoon fresh lime juice
1 dash simple syrup

SHAKE AND STRAIN into a chilled cocktail glass.

OLD BAY RIDGE

FAMILY: OLD-FASHIONEDS || Created by David Wondrich, 2005. Here's a Dave Wondrich drink named for a New York neighborhood. It has a whiskey base, and of course the Professor has historical context for using aquavit in his drink. The menu at 5 Ninth in New York in 2005 states, "Back in the day, Bay Ridge [Brooklyn] used to be peopled with Irish folks, who drank rye, and Scandinavians, who drank aquavit. This smooth and spicy variation on the venerable Old-Fashioned splits the difference." Sometimes one must take liberties, for the good of the cocktail.

1½ ounces Rittenhouse Rye whiskey
1½ ounces Linie aquavit
1 teaspoon brown sugar simple syrup (page 125) or Rich Demerara Syrup (page 126)
2 dashes Angostura bitters
1 lemon twist, for garnish

BUILD over ice in a double old-fashioned glass. Add the garnish.

OLD CUBAN COCKTAIL

FAMILY: SPARKLING SOURS AND JULEPS || Adapted from a recipe by Audrey Saunders. Audrey makes her own sugared vanilla-bean garnishes. If you don't have a vanilla bean, it's better to omit the garnish than to miss out on this fabulous drink.

O

½ ounce fresh lime juice
¾ to 1 ounce simple syrup
6 fresh mint leaves
1½ ounces Bacardi 8 añejo rum
2 dashes Angostura bitters
Moët & Chandon champagne
1 Sugared Vanilla Bean, for garnish (recipe follows)

MUDDLE the lime juice, simple syrup, and mint leaves in the bottom of a mixing glass. Add the rum, bitters, and ice. SHAKE AND STRAIN into a chilled cocktail glass, and top with a little champagne. Add the garnish, if using.

SUGARED VANILLA BEAN

Slice a vanilla bean lengthwise, remove the seeds, and reserve the seeds for another use. Sprinkle granulated sugar over the bean, and press lightly so the sugar adheres to the bean. (If you want to make these garnishes in a larger quantity, simply prepare more of them in a similar manner, then store the beans in a container of granulated sugar; you'll end up with both sugared vanilla beans for garnishes and vanilla sugar for dessert recipes.

OLD-FASHIONED WHISKEY COCKTAIL

FAMILY: OLD-FASHIONEDS || This drink was old-fashioned way back in 1895, when Kappeler detailed it in his book *Modern American Drinks: How to Mix and Serve All Kinds of Cups and Drinks.* He made the drink by dissolving a lump of sugar with a little water, then adding two dashes of Angostura bitters, a small piece of ice, lemon peel, and a jigger of whiskey. Seven years prior to that, Harry Johnson had made a similar drink with the addition of a couple of dashes of curaçao. His recipe was titled the Whiskey Cocktail, so presumably those seven years seemed like a generation to Kappeler.

The Old-Fashioned can be a controversial drink on more than one front. Some bartenders add a splash of club soda, either before muddling or after mixing the drink, and others add a little water. Neither of these ingredients should be in there, as far as I'm concerned. But the thing that really raises the hackles of many cocktailians is the question of fruit. Is it correct to muddle, say, a slice of orange and a maraschino cherry with the bitters and sugar before adding the ice and whiskey?

Historically, this is not the prescribed method—most vintage recipes call only for a twist of lemon to be added to the drink, the way in which President Eisenhower sipped the drink at New York's 21 Club, according to a 1973 *Playboy* article by Emanuel Greenberg. And in 1945, Crosby Gaige, a playboy himself, wrote, "Serious-minded persons omit fruit salad from 'Old-Fashioneds,' while the frivolous window-dress the brew with slices of orange, sticks of pineapple, and a couple of turnips."

So when did the fruit find its way into this drink? It could have been during Prohibition, if you listen to Ted Saucier, who said as much in his 1951 book *Bottoms Up.* Be that as it may, the fruit question is a serious one, and although many people in the twenty-first century expect a small fruit salad to be muddled into the drink, a good bartender will always ask before proceeding.

Personally, I like the fruit-salad Old-Fashioned, but both have their merits. Here, I detail an old-fashioned Old-Fashioned, as well as a fruity Old-Fashioned. You should also experiment with very small quantities—a couple of dashes at most—of liqueurs such as curaçao and maraschino, both of which have been previously recorded as ingredients, to fashion your own Old-Fashioned.

Although whiskey was the base in the world's first Old-Fashioned, you can also experiment with other spirits, such as brandy, genever, or dark rum, to make this style of drink.

OLD-FASHIONED OLD-FASHIONED

1 sugar cube
3 dashes Angostura bitters
3 ounces bourbon or straight rye whiskey
1 lemon twist, for garnish

MUDDLE the sugar cube and bitters in an old-fashioned glass. Add ice and the whiskey. Add the garnish. Stir briefly.

THE OLD-FASHIONED

This was brought to the Old Waldorf in the days of its "sit-down" Bar, and was introduced by, or in honor of, Col. James E. Pepper, of Kentucky, proprietor of a celebrated whiskey of the period. It was said to have been the invention of a bartender at the famous Pendennis Club in Louisville, of which Col. Pepper was a member.

—Albert Stevens Crockett,
The Old Waldorf-Astoria Bar Book, 1935

I once entered the bar of the Drake Hotel in Chicago where an ancient presided over a veritable American wing of glasses and bottles, and tried to explain that I wanted an Old Fashioned without fruit except the lemon. The Nestor of the decanters waxed as livid as a Marxist on May Day, smashed a champagne glass he was polishing and danced up and down on the duck-boards in an ecstasy of rage. "Young impudent sir," he screamed, "my hair is hoary-with eld," he added as an afterthought. "Man and boy I've built Old Fashioned cocktails these sixty years. Yes sir, since

> *the first Armour was pushing a wheelbarrow in a slaughterhouse, and I have never yet had the perverted nastiness of mind to put fruit in an Old Fashioned. Get out, scram, go over to the Palmer House and drink."*
>
> —LUCIUS BEBE, introduction to Crosby Gaige's *Cocktail Guide and Ladies' Companion*, 1945

FRUITY OLD-FASHIONED

Here's the way I was taught to make the drink at Drake's Drum, New York City, circa 1973.

1 sugar cube
3 dashes Angostura bitters
1 maraschino cherry
½ orange wheel
3 ounces bourbon or straight rye whiskey

MUDDLE the sugar, bitters, cherry, and orange in an old-fashioned glass. Add ice and the whiskey. Stir briefly.

ORIENTAL COCKTAIL

FAMILY: NEW ORLEANS SOURS AND ENHANCED SOURS || Adapted from a recipe in *The Savoy Cocktail Book* (1930), which also notes that an American man desperately ill with fever in the Philippines in 1924 gave the doctor who saved his life the recipe for this drink by way of thanks.

Take away the lime juice and you have yet another variation on the Manhattan, this one with a lovely orange glow.

1½ ounces straight rye whiskey
¾ ounce sweet vermouth
¾ ounce triple sec
½ ounce fresh lime juice

SHAKE AND STRAIN into a chilled cocktail glass.

PADDY COCKTAIL

FAMILY: FRENCH-ITALIAN: WHISKEY AND BRANDY || This is an Irish Manhattan. Play with the ratios to suit the Irish whiskey you use, although the following formula works well with most bottlings. The 1930 recipe called for no garnish, but I find that a twist of lemon works well here—it brings a wonderful aromatic dimension not present in the original.

Although this isn't my drink, I'd like to dedicate this printing of the recipe to Irishman Kevin Noone, one of my mentors from "back in the day," and a man who went ballistic if anyone had the gall to call him Paddy. Sláinte, Kevin, I learned much from you!

2 ounces Irish whiskey
1 ounce sweet vermouth
Angostura bitters to taste
1 lemon twist, for garnish

STIR AND STRAIN into a chilled cocktail glass. Add the garnish.

PASSION OF DALÍ

FAMILY: FRENCH-ITALIAN: WHISKEY AND BRANDY || This Rob Roy variation is adapted from a recipe by Erwin W. Trykowski, a man who at the time of this writing was the Scotch Whisky Ambassador at Diageo. Note that by calling for specific brands of scotch and vermouth (or *aperitivo* wine), plus bringing both aromatic and chocolate bitters into the mix, the drink is transformed into a very special version of the Rob Roy.

1 ounce Johnnie Walker Gold Label blended scotch
1 ounce Caol Ila Moch Islay single-malt scotch
1 ounce Cocchi Rosa Americano Aperitivo
1 dash Angostura bitters
1 dash chocolate bitters
1 orange twist, for garnish

STIR AND STRAIN into a chilled cocktail glass. Add the garnish.

PEGU CLUB COCKTAIL

FAMILY: NEW ORLEANS SOURS || In Harry Craddock's *The Savoy Cocktail Book* (1930), Craddock notes that this drink is "the favourite cocktail of the Pegu Club, Burma, and one that has traveled, and is asked for, round the world." And I note, with great pride, that my friend Chris "PUG! Muddler" Gallagher and I were the first people to sip Pegu Club Cocktails in Manhattan's fabulous Pegu Club when it opened its doors in 2005.

Audrey Saunders, Queen of the Pegu Club, donated her specific recipe to this book (thanks, Aud!). She notes that "Tanqueray's juniper-forward base works in tandem with lime juice," and says that she has "tried other curaçaos over time, but Brizard is still the ideal. [This is] an extremely calibrated recipe—you just won't achieve the degree of magic with another combination. I put dozens and dozens of hours into this recipe." For Audrey's thoughts on orange bitters, see the Note.

2 ounces Tanqueray gin
¾ ounces Marie Brizard orange curaçao
¾ ounce fresh lime juice
1 to 2 dashes Angostura bitters
1 dash Pegu House orange bitters (see Note)
1 carved lime wedge, for garnish (see Note)

SHAKE AND STRAIN into a chilled cocktail glass.

NOTE: In 2016, when Audrey and I had a conversation about her bitters, she said, "I created the recipe for Pegu's House orange bitters in 2005. At that point in time Regan's Orange Bitters No. 6 was just released onto the market, and Mark Brown had agreed to allow Pegu to become a distributor of your bitters, along with Peychaud's. I discovered that 50 percent of your bitters combined with 50 percent of Fee's orange bitters was the perfect balance—the cardamom-forward profile of yours combined with Joe Fee's orange base had the angels singing. At this point in time you'll find many of the New York bars still using this blend. They are simply referred to as House orange bitters, or Feegan's [or New York orange bitters]. I know such things can't be controlled, but I think this blend should be referred to Pegu's House orange bitters, since it was originally proprietary to Pegu."

At the Pegu Club, you'll get a lime wedge that has pretty patterns carved into its skin, but a regular lime wedge will suffice here.

PENICILLIN

FAMILY: **SIMPLE SOURS** || Created by Sam Ross, Attaboy, New York. This drink, which pairs scotch and ginger very nicely indeed, has been around since 2005, when it was created by Sam Ross at New York's Milk and Honey speakeasy. It's known throughout the cocktailian world as one of the new classics of the twenty-first century.

Sam explains to me how his version came about: "We had just received a shipment of the Compass Box line of scotches, and we were playing around with some of their malts. I riffed on a Gold Rush by subbing out the bourbon for Compass Box's Asyla bottling, and added a little ginger for heat. The result was great but it needed another level, so I picked up the Peat Monster [another Compass Box scotch] and splashed a little on top of the drink for a big whiff of ocean air. It seemed to work out pretty well."

2 ounces lightly peated single-malt or blended scotch (go with your favorite bottling)
¼ ounce good Islay malted scotch (such as Peat Monster or Laphroaig)
¾ ounce fresh lemon juice
¾ ounce Honey-Ginger Syrup (recipe follows)
1 piece candied ginger on a skewer, for garnish

SHAKE AND STRAIN into an ice-filled old-fashioned glass. Add the garnish.

HONEY-GINGER SYRUP

P

3 medium knobs of fresh ginger (about 2 inches long)
2-ounce jigger of granulated sugar
3 ounces honey
2 tablespoons water

Use a centrifugal juicer to make 3 ounces fresh ginger juice, then dissolve the sugar in the juice to make the ginger syrup. (You can also make ginger juice by grating the unpeeled fresh ginger and adding it to a double layer of dampened cheesecloth, then squeeze hard to get 3 ounces of juice.) Gently heat the honey and water, stirring frequently, to make a thin syrup. Combine with the ginger syrup, mix well, and refrigerate before serving.

PERFECT 10

FAMILY: FRENCH-ITALIAN: WHISKEY AND BRANDY || This Manhattan variation is from Josh Powell, Somerset House, Bristol, England. Josh notes, "I wanted to make a fruity twist on a Manhattan with great body and depth. In my recipe I used Slider, which is cider infused with the 'highly alcoholic sloes' that Bramley and Gage used to make sloe gin. It's a bit of a local ingredient so sloe gin works just as well if you can't get hold of it." In this variation, Josh has used the Bitter Truth Elixier, a bitter herbal liqueur, instead of bitters. Look at this product, and other amari-type products, for more inspiration.

1¾ ounces Bulleit rye whiskey
⅓ ounce Punt e Mes
⅓ ounce Bramley and Gage Slider or sloe gin
1 teaspoon Bitter Truth Elixier (sold as EX**R in the U.S.)**
1 orange twist, for aromatic garnish

STIR AND STRAIN into a chilled coupe. Release the oils from the orange twist on top of the drink, and discard the twist.

PHOEBE SNOW COCKTAIL

FAMILY: FRENCH-ITALIAN: WHISKEY AND BRANDY || A curveball in the French-Italian family, since it calls for Dubonnet rather than sweet vermouth, but it's a great drink nevertheless. You'll be tempted to think that this one was named for the singer, probably best known for her 1974 hit "Poetry Man," but actually both the drink and the singer borrowed their names from a fictitious character, first seen circa 1900, who always dressed in a spotless white dress and gloves to promote the Lackawanna and Western Railroad's use of anthracite, a clean-burning form of coal. Here's one of the jingles used in the campaign:

I won my fame and wide acclaim
For Lackawanna's splendid name
By keeping white and snowy bright
Upon the Road of Anthracite.

1½ ounces brandy
1½ ounces Dubonnet Rouge
1 dash absinthe

STIR AND STRAIN into a chilled cocktail glass.

PIMM'S CUP

FAMILY: **ORPHANS** || This is a marvelously refreshing summertime quaff that's not too high in alcohol. James Pimm opened his first London restaurant in 1823, and by 1840 he had a chain of five establishments. Pimm himself is said to have created this gin-based aperitif, flavored with fruit liqueurs and herbs; it was traditionally served in tankards. Pimm's Cup became so successful that it was exported throughout the British Empire, and eventually five more bottlings were released, each with a different base: Pimm's No. 2 Cup was made with scotch, No. 3 with brandy, No. 4 with rum, No. 5 with rye, and No. 6 with vodka.

In the north of England, Pimm's is usually served in a highball glass, topped off with club soda or ginger ale and an abundance of fruit—a wedge of apple, a slice of orange, a maraschino cherry, and maybe a small slice of lemon. On the Thames, however, drinkers look down their noses at this fruit salad, preferring to take their Pimm's in the more traditional fashion with just a sliver of cucumber rind. Another great way to garnish the drink is with a huge bunch of basil on top. Serve it, like a Julep, with straws cut short enough so that the drinker must bury his nose in the basil while sipping through the straw.

2 ounces Pimm's No. 1 Cup
5 to 7 ounces ginger ale, lemon-lime soda, or club soda
1 sliver cucumber rind, for garnish

BUILD in a 16-ounce mixing glass. Add the garnish.

PIÑA COLADA

FAMILY: **ORPHANS** || There's nothing wrong with my recipe for the Piña Colada, but there's nothing astoundingly special about it, either—unless you count the fact that I call for a huge slug of rum. For this book, though, I sought out the best of the best, and I knew exactly who to go to for an extraordinary Piña Colada recipe. Dean Callan, the Irish-born, Australian-bred, London-based bartender—and one of the most brilliant marketers I've ever met—is, shall we say, a Piña Colada freak. Here's what he wrote to me when I asked him for his thoughts on the drink: "The Piña Colada to me represents all hospitality. A lot of people hate the drink. But mostly those who hate it can't make a good one; they don't like it themselves so they choose not to bother learning to make a good one. In hospitality the focus is and always will be the guest; if they like it, then you should very well have done your best to learn how to make it so that you can give them what they desire," says Dean. And given the fact that the pineapple is an international symbol of hospitality, this makes complete sense.

This recipe is somewhat exacting. And it's worth every second it takes you to make it properly.

2 ounces rum (Plantation 3-Stars, Bacardi Light, or Havana Club Silver)
4½ ounces (weight) super-ripe fresh pineapple chunks
¾ ounce Coco Lopez coconut cream
3 ounces (weight) ice, fresh from freezer

Add the ingredients to a blender. Blend and pour into a chilled hurricane glass.

PISCO SOUR

FAMILY: SIMPLE SOURS || Modern-day drinkers owe a debt of gratitude to Dale DeGroff for bringing this incredible drink to our attention. Dale, in turn, credits the late Joe Baum for featuring the Pisco Sour on his cocktail menu at La Fonda Del Sol, New York, in the late 1960s, and says that the drink can be found on other drinks lists from the 1930s.

The Pisco Sour is detailed by Charles H. Baker Jr. in *The South American Gentleman's Companion*, where he wrote that the Angostura bitters, which are dashed on top of the drink rather than being shaken with the other ingredients, were "the finishing touch put on by the talented bar-maestro at the wonderful and luxurious Lima Country Club, before they served them to your pastor and Limenian good friends on our suite balcony overlooking the polo fields and possibly the handsomest swimming pool you'll find in the world."

2 ounces Pisco brandy
1 ounce fresh lime juice
½ ounce simple syrup
1 small egg white (see page 128)
Angostura bitters, for an aromatic garnish

SHAKE AND STRAIN into a chilled champagne flute. Dash some bitters on top.

PLANTER'S PUNCH

FAMILY: PUNCHES || This is the official International Bartender's Association (IBA) formula for the drink. Personally, I like some grapefruit juice in there, too. The choice is yours.

1½ ounces dark rum
1 ounce fresh orange juice
1 ounce fresh pineapple juice
⅔ ounce fresh lemon juice
⅓ ounce grenadine
⅓ ounce simple syrup
3 to 4 dashes Angostura bitters, for an aromatic garnish

SHAKE AND STRAIN into an ice-filled collins glass. Add the garnish by dashing the bitters on top of the drink.

POMPIER COCKTAIL

FAMILY: ORPHANS || Based on the Pompier Highball found in Charles Baker Jr.'s *The Gentleman's Companion.* I came up with this variation for a cocktail dinner at Painter's Tavern, in Cornwall-on-Hudson, New York, in 2001.

The gin in this recipe isn't present in the Pompier Highball, but in order to turn the drink into a cocktail of sorts, a spirit had to be added. I opted to use only a very small amount of gin here, simply because the drink was created to accompany food and I wanted to keep the alcohol level down. Nevertheless, the spirit does its job and adds a dry quality to the drink, which balances the fruitiness of the cassis and makes this cocktail perfect to sip alongside a salad course.

2½ ounces dry vermouth
¼ ounce crème de cassis
¼ ounce gin
1 lemon twist, for garnish

STIR AND STRAIN into a chilled cocktail glass. Add the garnish.

PREAKNESS COCKTAIL

FAMILY: FRENCH-ITALIAN: WHISKEY AND BRANDY || I believe that this drink was formulated in the 1940s; later recipes call for blended whiskey as a base. Bourbon or straight rye work best in this one. Of course, it's the addition of Bénédictine herbal liqueur that makes this cocktail stand apart from a regular Manhattan, and the lemon twist goes a long way, too.

2 ounces bourbon or straight rye whiskey
1 ounce sweet vermouth
2 dashes Bénédictine
2 dashes Angostura bitters
1 lemon twist, for garnish

STIR AND STRAIN into a chilled cocktail glass. Add the garnish.

RAMOS GIN FIZZ

FAMILY: SPARKLING SOURS || Henry Ramos, creator of this Fizz, had his own methods of making sure that the drink was prepared correctly: He hired a bevy of bartenders, who passed the shaker from one to the next until the drink reached the desired consistency. In *Famous New Orleans Drinks & How to Mix 'em*, author Stanley Clisby Arthur states that at Mardi Gras in 1915 "35 shaker boys nearly shook their arms off, but still were unable to keep up with the demand."

Ramos, a native of Baton Rouge, owned the Imperial Cabinet Saloon in New Orleans from 1888 until 1907. At that point he took over the Stag Saloon, which served his special Gin Fizzes until 1920, when Prohibition was enacted. Here, it is said, customers would wait as long as an hour to get their hands on an authentic Ramos Fizz.

Following the directions of various old masters, a couple of friends and I once shook three shakers of this drink for a full five minutes, at which point it was hard to pry our hands from the shakers—we were as one with them. The point of the long shake is to achieve a "ropy" consistency. This is somewhat hard to describe, but "silky" also fits the bill, and once you experience this texture, you'll swear you're in heaven. In *The Gentleman's Companion*, Charles H. Baker Jr. prescribes making the Ramos Gin Fizz in a blender, but with less ice than you would use to make a frozen drink. I've found this to deliver a perfect Fizz, with the correct consistency and without the pain of frozen hands.

An optional ingredient in this drink is vanilla extract, and if you decide to use it (which I don't recommend), you should be very sparing; add only a couple of drops, which will make enough for two champagne flutes. At 1 ounce of gin per drink, the alcohol content is very low, so this is a great brunch drink or something to consider if you're planning on having more than one.

MAKES 2 COCKTAILS

2 ounces gin
1 ounce cream
1 raw egg white (see page 128)
½ ounce simple syrup
½ ounce fresh lime juice
½ ounce fresh lemon juice
¼ ounce orange flower water
Club soda
2 half orange wheels, for garnish

BLEND everything except for the club soda with enough ice to fill one champagne flute. Divide the mixture between two champagne flutes, and top each drink with a splash of club soda. Add the garnishes.

RBS SPECIAL COCKTAIL

FAMILY: INTERNATIONAL SOURS || Adapted from a recipe created by David Wondrich in 2001 for New York's *RBS Gazette*, a paper published for the Rubber Band Society, a New York–based partnership of writers and artists, many of whom happen to be Russian. Wondrich notes, "The rye combines with the caraway notes of the kümmel (a liqueur formerly quite popular in Russia) to give the drink a faint and (I hope) [not unpleasant] flavor of rye bread, which New Yorkers and Russians are known to be particularly fond of. The grenadine gives the drink a faint red cast, to commemorate the former Soviet Union, from which many of the artists in the Rubber Band Society escaped."

2 ounces Wild Turkey straight rye whiskey
¼ ounce Gilka kümmel liqueur
½ ounce fresh lemon juice
¼ ounce grenadine

SHAKE AND STRAIN into a chilled cocktail glass.

RED SNAPPER

FAMILY: SNAPPERS || Adapted from the recipe donated by Gaston Lauryssen, then manager of the St. Regis Hotel, to the 1945 book *Crosby Gaige's Cocktail Guide and Ladies' Companion.* The St. Regis Hotel is reportedly where the Bloody Mary was first served in the United States (see page 186), and I believe that this is probably the original recipe for the drink, masquerading under a different name.

1½ ounces tomato juice
1½ ounces vodka
2 dashes Worcestershire sauce
2 dashes fresh lemon juice
Salt and cayenne pepper to taste

SHAKE AND STRAIN into a chilled cocktail glass.

REMEMBER THE MAINE

FAMILY: FRENCH-ITALIAN: WHISKEY AND BRANDY || Adapted from a recipe detailed by Charles H. Baker Jr. in his book, *The Gentleman's Companion.* He insists that the drink be stirred in a clockwise direction. In this variation on the Manhattan you can see that, although no bitters are called for, the cocktail has added dimensions of cherry brandy and absinthe. This is one great drink, by the way.

1½ ounces straight rye whiskey
¾ ounce sweet vermouth
⅓ ounce cherry brandy
1 to 2 dashes absinthe
1 lemon twist, for garnish

Stir over ice in a clockwise direction. Strain into a chilled cocktail glass. Add the garnish.

RESURRECTION FLIP

FAMILY: ORPHANS || Adapted from a recipe by Tim Philips, Dead Ringer and Bulletin Place, Sydney, Australia. This is the drink that blew everyone away in Rio de Janeiro, 2012, when Tim Philips presented it as part of his quest to win Diageo's World Class Bartender competition.

Although I'd like to say that the Resurrection Flip is the drink that sealed the deal, the fact is that this competition is multifaceted, and to get that crown, bartenders have to be superlative in many different directions. When Tim presented this cocktail to Hidetsugu Ueno (Ueno-San to his friends) and me in Rio, he blew our socks off—in fact, I gave him a well-deserved standing ovation. Here's what he did:

Tim assembled all the ingredients in a shaker tin while reciting a poem that he'd written especially for the occasion. He then took the tin to the sink to add ice, and he inadvertently spilled the whole drink down the drain. Ueno-San and I gasped. He'd just lost that round. Or so we thought. Tim then took a hen's egg from an egg tray behind the bar, and he dropped it, unbroken shell and all, into the tin. He added ice and shook all heck out of it, and from that tin he strained out the drink that he'd just spilled down the drain.

How did he do that?

It was explained to me, about two days later: Tim had taken a hen's egg, and after pricking holes into each end of it, he had blown the egg out of its shell (a common practice among egg collectors). Then, after putting his pre-made cocktail into a syringe, he injected the drink into the shell, sealing the holes in both ends with glue. The ice cubes then broke the egg shell as Tim shook the drink, and he strained the cocktail effortlessly into the glass, adding a little ground cinnamon as garnish.

What a showman. What a bartender. What a raconteur. Tim Philips is a shining star in the bar world. I'm proud to call him a friend.

1¾ ounces Ron Zacapa Centenario Sistema Solera 23 rum
1 teaspoon Lagavulin 16-year-old single-malt scotch
½ ounce honey
½ ounce fresh lemon juice
1 pinch ground cinnamon
½ fresh fig
1 quail egg
Ground cinnamon, for garnish

SHAKE AND STRAIN into a chilled sherry copita glass, and add the garnish.

RICKEY

FAMILY: ORPHANS || "The Rickey owes its name to Colonel 'Joe' Rickey . . . a lobbyist in Washington, and as such used to buy drinks for members of Congress in the glamorous days before they had come to depend upon the discreet activities of gentlemen in green hats to keep them wet while they voted dry. The drink was invented and named for him at Shoomaker's, famous in Washington as a Congressional hangout," reported Albert Stevens Crockett in *The Old Waldorf-Astoria Bar Book* (1935).

I'm not a fan of this drink, which started life as a whiskey-based quaff, but it is often served these days as a gin cooler. Nevertheless, I have known people who love it. The secret is in the amount of lime juice used, and many bartenders are guilty of serving merely a Highball with a squeeze of juice from just one wedge of lime.

½ ounce fresh lime juice
1½ ounces bourbon, rye, or Old Tom gin
3 to 4 ounces club soda
1 lime wedge, for garnish

BUILD in a wine glass filled with crushed ice. Add the garnish.

THE RITZ COCKTAIL

FAMILY: CHAMPAGNE COCKTAILS || Adapted from a recipe by Dale DeGroff, author of *The Essential Cocktail*, New York. According to an interview in *Foodie* magazine, The Ritz was the first cocktail that Dale DeGroff ever created. "I was bartending at Aurora, a very high-end restaurant on 49th Street, and wanted to create the Ritz of New York cocktails. I chilled Cointreau with lemon juice, a dash of maraschino liqueur, and cognac, poured the mixture into a martini glass and finished it with champagne and a flaming orange peel, which later became a signature of mine. It was written up in *Playboy* magazine," he said.

1 ounce cognac
½ ounce Cointreau
2 dashes maraschino liqueur
½ ounce fresh lemon juice
Chilled champagne or other sparkling wine
1 flamed orange twist, for garnish

SHAKE AND STRAIN into a chilled cocktail glass, and top with the champagne. Add the garnish.

ROB ROY

FAMILY: FRENCH-ITALIAN: WHISKEY AND BRANDY || Crockett's *The Old Waldorf-Astoria Bar Book* states that this drink was named after a Broadway show of the same name, so it's possible that it dates back to 1894, when *Rob Roy*, an operetta by Reginald De Koven, opened on the Great White Way. Given that bartenders of that period were using more and more vermouth in their drinks than had their predecessors, there's a fair chance that the date is close to being correct. Rob Roy, of course, is a fictional character detailed in Sir Walter Scott's book of the same name, and is best described as a sort of Scottish Robin Hood who stole from the rich to give to the poor in the late seventeenth and early eighteenth centuries.

The Rob Roy is always made with sweet vermouth, unless otherwise requested. A Dry Rob Roy (sometimes referred to as the Beadlestone Cocktail) is made by substituting dry vermouth for the sweet; and a Perfect Rob Roy calls for half sweet and half dry vermouths. Classically, the basic Rob Roy calls for a cherry garnish, whereas the other two variations are usually served with twists of lemon. Personally, I prefer to use lemon twists in all three versions.

Few people these days add bitters to the Rob Roy. Angostura bitters doesn't work well in this drink, although orange bitters does a graceful tango with the scotch and vermouth. However, as David Embury suggested in the 1950s, Peychaud's bitters marries very well with the scotch in the Rob Roy, and I highly recommend that you try using that.

2 ounces scotch
1 ounce sweet vermouth
2 dashes Peychaud's bitters
1 maraschino cherry, or 1 lemon twist, for garnish

STIR AND STRAIN into a chilled cocktail glass. Add the garnish.

RUBY CAN'T FAIL

FAMILY: ENHANCED SOURS || Adapted from a recipe by Julian de Feral, London. With this recipe, Julian taught me that there are better ways to marry gin and port than the slapdash way I put them together in Athens, 2010, when I stole a bottle of port from him and used it to serve Tanqueray No. 10 and Port cocktails. He won't let me forget this . . .

1 ounce plus 1 teaspoon gin
½ ounce ruby port
½ ounce fresh lemon juice
⅓ ounce fino sherry
⅓ ounce simple syrup
1 dash Regan's Orange Bitters No. 6
1 lemon twist, for garnish
1 pink grapefruit twist, for garnish

SHAKE AND STRAIN into a chilled fancy wine glass. Squeeze the twists over the drink, then discard.

RUSTY NAIL

FAMILY: DUOS AND TRIOS || This is a good recipe for experimentation, since by using different bottlings of scotch and altering the ratios of base spirit to liqueur, the cocktailian bartender can learn much about ingredients. Blended scotch is normally used in this drink, but to display wiles of the craft, try using different bottlings of single malt, tasting each one before adding the Drambuie (which should also be tasted prior to experimentation). You'll find that you need far less Drambuie if you use a lightly peated single malt, such as Glenmorangie, than with a pungent single malt from Islay, such as Ardbeg. The Macallan and Aberlour have much character of their own, without being heavily peated, but it's imperative that you add only enough Drambuie to either of these bottlings to flavor the scotch without completely destroying its personality.

2½ ounces scotch
½ ounce Drambuie

STIR AND STRAIN into an ice-filled old-fashioned glass.

SALTY DOG

|| FAMILY: HIGHBALLS ||

2 ounces vodka
3 ounces fresh grapefruit juice
Salt for glass

BUILD in an ice-filled, salt-rimmed highball glass.

SATAN'S WHISKERS

FAMILY: FRENCH-ITALIAN: GIN, RUM, GENEVER, VODKA, AND TEQUILA || There are two formulas for Satan's Whiskers. This one, known as "straight," calls for Grand Marnier, whereas the "curled" potion takes orange curaçao. This formula is adapted from *Jones' Complete Barguide.*

½ ounce gin
½ ounce dry vermouth
½ ounce sweet vermouth
½ ounce fresh orange juice
¼ ounce Grand Marnier
1 to 2 dashes orange bitters

SHAKE AND STRAIN into a chilled cocktail glass.

SAZERAC

FAMILY: ORPHANS || The Sazerac Company of New Orleans pins down 1850 for the creation of this drink and says it was served at the Sazerac Coffee House in the French Quarter. Stanley Clisby Arthur, author of *Famous New Orleans Drinks & How to Mix 'em*, wrote that Leon Lamothe was the bartender who first made the drink. He suggests that Lamothe merely added the absinthe component to the cocktail of brandy, sugar, and Peychaud's bitters that Peychaud himself is credited with serving as early as 1838. That brandy was the original base liquor is agreed upon by the Sazerac Company, which has a photograph of an early bottling of premixed Sazerac Cocktails. On the label, these words can be found: "Sazerac Cocktail, Prepared and bottled by Thomas H. Handy, Limited, Sole Proprietors. Guaranteed . . . under the food and drugs act, June 30, 1906. Martini." We don't know exactly when this bottle was issued, but we can be sure that it was prior to the onset of Prohibition in 1920; and already, cocktails other than a mixture of gin and vermouth were being referred to as Martinis, a phenomenon that's usually attributed to the 1990s.

We aren't quite sure when straight rye whiskey replaced the brandy in this drink, but it's possible that the phylloxera blight that devastated European vineyards that began just before the 1860s, and continued until the mid-1870s, had something to do with it. The Sazerac Company's records indicate that the change occurred during the 1870s.

The ritual of making this drink involves chilling an old-fashioned glass with crushed ice, muddling sugar into the bitters in another glass, adding ice and whiskey to the bitters, and stirring the mixture to chill and dilute it. The ice is then discarded from the first glass, the glass is rinsed with absinthe and filled with fresh crushed ice, and the chilled whiskey is strained into the absinthe-rinsed glass. Finally, a twist of lemon is added, though some old recipes dictate that the twist not be dropped into the drink—just its oils should be released onto the drink's surface.

Sazerac aficionados have come up with various changes in the methodology of making this classic drink, and not wanting to be left out, I'm going to prescribe that the Sazerac be served straight up in a champagne flute—or a cocktail glass, if you must—simply because newcomers to the drink might be more tempted to try it if the glassware is a little more elegant. If you'd like to sample the original drink made with cognac, select a dryish bottling such as Hennessy or Hine, rather than fruitier brandies like Courvoisier.

3 ounces straight rye whiskey
¾ ounce simple syrup
2 to 3 dashes Peychaud's bitters
Absinthe, to rinse the glass
1 lemon twist, for garnish

STIR AND STRAIN into a chilled, absinthe-rinsed champagne flute. Add the garnish.

SCOFFLAW COCKTAIL

FAMILY: ENHANCED SOURS || According to Michael B. Quinion, publisher of worldwidewords.org, the word *scofflaw* came about in 1923, when the sum of $200 was offered to whoever came up with the best word to describe "a lawless drinker of illegally made or illegally obtained liquor." The prize money was donated by a rich Prohibitionist, who wanted to "stab awake the conscience" of those who drank alcohol during Prohibition.

The following year, it was reported in the *Chicago Tribune* that "Jock," a bartender at Harry's New York Bar in Paris, had created the Scofflaw Cocktail. This recipe calls for bourbon or straight rye, whereas the original drink contained blended Canadian whisky.

2 ounces bourbon or straight rye whiskey
1 ounce dry vermouth
¼ ounce fresh lemon juice
1 to 2 dashes grenadine
1 dash orange bitters

SHAKE AND STRAIN into a chilled cocktail glass.

SCORPION

FAMILY: SIMPLE SOURS AND TIKI || Adapted from a recipe in Jeff Berry's Total Tiki app (well worth the price of admission).

2 ounces light rum
1 ounce brandy
2 ounces fresh orange juice
1½ ounces fresh lemon juice
½ ounce orgeat syrup

SHAKE AND STRAIN into an ice-filled double old-fashioned glass.

SEELBACH COCKTAIL

FAMILY: CHAMPAGNE COCKTAILS || Here's a drink with a great backstory—two great backstories, as a matter of fact. The recipe for the Seelbach Cocktail was given to me in the mid-1990s by a certain Adam Seger, then beverage manager at the Seelbach Hotel in Louisville, Kentucky. He told me that he had found the formula in the hotel's archives, and handed me a tale about a bartender making a Manhattan and a Champagne Cocktail, and getting confused along the way. The Seelbach, he said, was the result of this man's mistakes.

I must admit that I didn't buy the story hook, line, and sinker, but the drink was really good, so I featured it in *New Classic Cocktails*, which I was working on at the time.

Cut to 2016, when Robert Simonson of the *New York Times* interviewed Adam—by this time Adam had become a very successful entrepreneur—who confessed to having made up both the drink and the story, just to get press for the hotel. So, the drink received lots of press back in the 1990s, and it got even more coverage in 2016. Adam Seger is quite the marketer, huh? He makes a damned fine drink, too!

¾ ounce bourbon
½ ounce triple sec
7 dashes Angostura bitters
7 dashes Peychaud's bitters
4 ounces chilled brut champagne
1 orange twist, for garnish

BUILD in the order given in a champagne flute. Add the garnish.

SHANDY

FAMILY: ORPHANS || Originally known as a Shandy Gaff, this drink has been around since at least the 1880s, when it was usually made with ginger ale rather than lemon-lime soda. The old ginger ale version is superior to today's lemon-lime drink. But to make it better than that, build a Shandy with Jamaican ginger beer—it's a crisp, mouth-puckering treat. However you make this drink, be sure to pour the soda into the glass first; otherwise, it will foam over the top before you can finish pouring.

8 ounces lemon-lime soda, ginger ale, or ginger beer
8 ounces amber ale

BUILD in the order given in a pilsner glass.

SIDECAR

FAMILY: NEW ORLEANS SOURS || In *The Fine Art of Mixing Drinks*, David Embury claims that the Sidecar was created during the First World War by a friend who traveled to his favorite "little bistro" in Paris in the sidecar of a motorbike. Popular legend has it that the bistro was Harry's New York Bar, but Embury doesn't mention this fact. Other accounts claim that it was created by Frank Meier at the Paris Ritz, but that account was challenged by Meier's successor, a man by the name of Bertin.

Whoever made the world's first Sidecar had probably never heard of the Brandy Crusta, and he can't have been aware of what would become of the formula he used—that this combination of a spirit, an orange-flavored liqueur, and a citrus juice eventually spawned the Margarita, the Kamikaze, and the Cosmopolitan, to name just a few. The original drink, claims Embury, "contained six or seven ingredients," but his recipe calls for just cognac or armagnac, triple sec, and lemon juice—the ingredients we still use today. Embury used eight parts brandy to one of triple sec and two of lemon juice, but that formula doesn't work well for me—it's far too sour.

I usually use my old 3:2:1 ratios to make all New Orleans Sour drinks like this one, and it's worth trying it here using three parts cognac, two parts Cointreau, and one part lemon juice. For fun, though, I asked Colin Field, head bartender at The Ritz, Paris, for the recipe they use there, and although Colin writes his recipes in *parts* rather than ounces or milliliters, it turns out that we're using very similar proportions.

For fun, Colin also gave me the recipe for their 1923 Ritz Sidecar, using 8/10 Ritz Grand Fine Champagne 1854 cognac, 1/10 Cointreau, and a drop of lemon juice. It will set you back €1,500 at Colin's bar.

1½ ounces cognac
1 ounce Cointreau
½ ounce fresh lemon juice
Sugar, for glass (optional)
1 lemon twist, for garnish

SHAKE AND STRAIN into a chilled, sugar-rimmed (if using) cocktail glass. Add the garnish.

SIDECAR DELUXE (BOTTLED)

MAKES 24 OUNCES

12 ounces cognac
3 ounces Grand Marnier
3 ounces fresh lemon juice
6 ounces bottled water
Lemon twists, for garnish

MIX AND CHILL for a minimum of 6 hours. Serve in chilled cocktail glasses with lemon twists for garnish.

SINGAPORE SLING

FAMILY: **SPARKLING SOURS** || The discussions about the original recipe for this drink are endless, and although the truth may never be known, the Raffles Hotel in Singapore, where the drink is said to have been created by bartender Ngiam Tong Boon, in 1915, puts forth a recipe, and there are also a couple of other formulas worthy of note.

The Ngiam Tong Boon/Raffles story cannot be true since, according to *Imbibe!*, by Dave Wondrich, the drink was already well known in Singapore in the late 1890s. And Wondrich, who for all intents and purposes is the God of Cocktail History, uncovered another recipe for the Singapore Sling. This is the real deal.

You'll have to buy *Imbibe!* to get the whole story of this version of the Singapore Sling, and if you haven't read this book already, you'll thank me for this. What follows, then, is a result of taking the recipe that Wondrich found for the original drink, pondering his thoughts on the ingredients, and coming up with this fairly simple, and utterly delightful, drink.

SINGAPORE SLING Á LA *IMBIBE!*

1½ ounces gin
1 ounce Cherry Heering
½ ounce Bénédictine
¾ ounce fresh lime juice
2 to 3 dashes Angostura bitters
Club soda
1 spiral of lime peel, for garnish (optional)

SHAKE AND STRAIN all ingredients except for the club soda into an ice-filled collins glass. Top with club soda, stir briefly, and add the garnish, if using.

SINGAPORE SLING AS THE STRAIGHTS SLING

FAMILY: **SPARKLING SOURS** || Ted "Dr. Cocktail" Haigh discovered the recipe here in a 1922 book, *Cocktails: How to Mix Them*, by Robert Vermeire, a highly regarded Belgian bartender who also worked in London and other places in Europe. It was called Straights Sling, but was referred to as a "well-known Singapore drink." Since it calls for dry cherry brandy, Doc surmises that a cherry eau-de-vie, such as kirsch, was used in this version. This recipe is adapted from the one in Doc's book, *Vintage Spirits and Forgotten Cocktails*, and is included chiefly for historical interest, although it's not a bad drink at all.

2 ounces gin
½ ounce Bénédictine
½ ounce kirsch
¾ ounce fresh lemon juice
2 dashes orange bitters
2 dashes Angostura bitters
Club soda

SHAKE AND STRAIN all ingredients except the club soda into an ice-filled collins glass. Top with club soda.

Just looking around the terrace porch we've seen Frank Buck, the Sultan of Johore, Aimee Semple McPherson, Somerset Maugham, Dick Halliburton, Doug Fairbanks, Bob Ripley, Ruth Elder and Walter Camp. . . . When our soft footed Malay boy brings the 4th Sling and finds us peering over the window sill at the cobra-handling snake charmers tootling their confounding flutes below he murmurs "jaga baik-baik Tuan"—"jaga bye-bye too-wan," as it is in English—or "take care master" as it means in English. The Singapore Sling is a delicious, slow-acting, insidious thing.

—CHARLES H. BAKER JR., *The Gentleman's Companion,* 1946

SINGAPORE SLING AT RAFFLES HOTEL

The ingredients in this version are listed on a coaster from Raffles Hotel in Singapore, but no measurements were given, and club soda wasn't mentioned, either.

S

2 ounces Beefeater gin
½ ounce Cherry Heering
¼ ounce Bénédictine
¼ ounce Cointreau
2 ounces pineapple juice
¼ ounce fresh lime juice
1 to 2 dashes Angostura bitters
Club soda

SHAKE AND STRAIN all ingredients except the club soda into an ice-filled collins glass. Top with club soda.

THE SLOPE

FAMILY: FRENCH-ITALIAN: WHISKEY AND BRANDY || Adapted from a recipe by Julie Reiner, Clover Club, New York. It's tough to go wrong with a Julie Reiner drink, especially when the drink is totally serious, like this one. The Punt e Mes comes with its own brand of bitterness, and the scant ¼ ounce of apricot brandy adds a subtle fruitiness to the drink. Because Julie left the Angostura bitters in this one, though, that fruitiness is incredibly well balanced.

2 ounces Rittenhouse rye
¾ ounce Punt e Mes
¼ ounce apricot brandy
2 dashes Angostura bitters
1 fresh cherry, for garnish

STIR AND STRAIN into a chilled cocktail glass. Add the garnish.

SOUTHSIDE COCKTAIL

FAMILY: SIMPLE SOURS AND JULEPS || The Southside is, more or less, a gin-based Mojito calling for lemon as the citrus rather than lime (though some recipes do call for limes). I like to use granulated sugar in this drink since, when muddling the lemon wedges with the mint and sugar, the sugar abrades the zest of the fruit, capturing their wonderfully aromatic oils.

4 lemon wedges
2 to 3 teaspoons granulated sugar
4 or 5 fresh mint leaves
2½ ounces gin
1 mint sprig, for garnish

MUDDLE the lemon wedges, sugar, and mint leaves in a mixing glass until the sugar is completely dissolved, all the juice is extracted from the lemons, and the mint is thoroughly integrated into the juice. Add ice and the gin to the mixing glass, and SHAKE AND STRAIN into a chilled cocktail glass. Add the garnish.

SOUTHSIDE FIZZ

FAMILY: **SPARKLING SOURS AND JULEPS** || As you can see, this is just a Southside Cocktail with a splash of club soda.

4 lemon wedges
2 to 3 teaspoons granulated sugar
6 to 8 fresh mint leaves
2½ ounces gin
Club soda
3 mint sprigs, for garnish

MUDDLE the lemon wedges, sugar, and mint leaves in a mixing glass until the sugar is completely dissolved, all the juice is extracted from the lemons, and the mint is thoroughly integrated into the juice. Add ice and the gin to the mixing glass, and SHAKE AND STRAIN into an ice-filled collins glass. Add the soda and the garnish.

STINGER

FAMILY: **DUOS AND TRIOS** || The combination of brandy and crème de menthe dates back to at least 1892, when William Schmidt detailed a drink called the Judge in his book *The Flowing Bowl.* "Shake to the freezing-point," he instructed, and his words have stayed with us, for the Stinger is the only drink I can name that will be shaken by the most professional bartenders, even though it contains no fruit juices, eggs, or dairy products.

The Stinger can be served straight up or over ice, but it's more often served over crushed ice. Be wary of the ratios here, since the crème de menthe can easily overpower the brandy, especially if you choose a dry-ish brandy such as Hennessy or Hine rather than a fruitier bottling like Courvoisier. And dry brandy *is* the best way to go with this drink.

3 ounces cognac
¼ to ½ ounce white crème de menthe

SHAKE AND STRAIN into a large brandy snifter filled with crushed ice.

A TALE OF TWO ROBERTS

FAMILY: FRENCH-ITALIAN: WHISKEY AND BRANDY || This Rob Roy variation is adapted from a 2013 recipe by Frank Caiafa, Peacock Alley, The Waldorf Astoria, New York City. When Frank sent me this recipe, it arrived with a lovely note that explains how he put this drink together: "At Peacock Alley, we have debuted our Robert Burns Cocktail. It's a hybrid of the *Old Waldorf Bar Book* recipe which is essentially a Rob Roy with Absinthe, and the Bobby Burns, from the *Old Savoy Cocktail Book,* which is equal parts scotch, sweet vermouth, and a bit of Bénédictine. . . . I did not add (orange) bitters to this version as I feel the drink is complex enough and the bitters helped to muddy up the mix. To happily confuse things more, I asked the Waldorf Astoria pastry kitchen to make shortbread cookies as a garnish (thanks, guys!). . . . I think the small changes make big differences (and the finish is awesome!). Enjoy!"

2¼ ounces Sheep Dip 8-year-old blended scotch
1¼ ounces sweet vermouth
⅓ ounce Bénédictine
6 dashes Pernod/absinthe mix (see Note)
1 lemon twist, for garnish
2 shortbread cookies, for serving

STIR AND STRAIN into a chilled cocktail glass. Add the lemon garnish, serving the cookies on a plate on the side.

NOTE: Mix 2 ounces Pernod and 1 ounce La Muse Verte absinthe.

TART GIN COOLER

FAMILY: HIGHBALLS || Recipe by gaz regan, 1998. This drink came into being as a result of experimentation with tonic water, which when mixed with a little lemon juice tastes like bitter lemon soda. I tried it with grapefruit juice, and the rest of the drink just evolved. The Tart Gin Cooler is simple—it's certainly not a creative masterpiece—but I go back to it time after time after time. It's great served for brunch, too.

2 ounces gin
2 ounces fresh pink grapefruit juice
2 ounces tonic water
Peychaud's bitters to taste

BUILD in an ice-filled collins glass.

T

THRUST AND PARRY COCKTAIL

FAMILY: DUOS AND TRIOS || It's about time I updated the Debonair (page 204), a good drink for its day that still stands tall on its own, but I've learned so much more about mixology since I came up with the original that I wanted young millennial bartenders to see how far I've come!

¼ ounce Del Maguey Vida mezcal, as a rinse
2 ounces Highland Park 12-year-old single-malt scotch
¾ ounce Domain de Canton ginger liqueur
3 small pieces candied ginger on a cocktail skewer, for garnish

Pour the mezcal into a chilled cocktail glass, and swirl the glass to coat the interior with the spirit. Discard any excess. STIR AND STRAIN the scotch and the ginger liqueur into the prepared glass, and add the garnish.

TOM COLLINS

FAMILY: SPARKLING SOURS || "This is a long drink, to be consumed slowly with reverence and meditation," wrote cocktailian David Embury in the 1950s, and the Tom Collins is certainly a drink worthy of more respect than it gets. It isn't a complex drink, and neither is it made from a formula that required genius to figure it out—it's no more than a carbonated Gin Sour—but this refreshing quaff can be delightful in hot weather.

Old Tom, a sweetened gin, was first used as the base for this drink, but dry gin is also commonly used. The recipe here calls for fresh lemon juice and simple syrup, but if you would like to experiment with the Tom Collins, try muddling fresh lemon wedges with granulated sugar instead. The sugar will abrade the zest of the fruit and add a sparkle to the drink.

2½ ounces gin
1 ounce fresh lemon juice
¾ ounce simple syrup
Club soda
1 maraschino cherry, for garnish
1 half orange wheel, for garnish

SHAKE AND STRAIN all ingredients except the club soda into an ice-filled collins glass. Top with club soda. Add the garnishes.

TOMMY'S MARGARITA

FAMILY: **SIMPLE SOURS** || Julio Bermejo, Tequila Ambassador to the United States and the man who put San Francisco's Tommy's Mexican Restaurant on the map, created this Margarita variation, circa 1990, and it can now be found on the best cocktail lists all over the world.

The agave fructose that Julio uses in his formula was pretty new to America back when he created the drink. The recipe detailed here, which came straight from Mr. Bermejo himself, reveals a little-known fact about how the drink comes together so well at his family's restaurant: "We actually dilute our agave fructose in order to pour it more effectively: not leaving any on the bar spoon if that is used or in the jigger because of the viscosity," he says.

2 ounces 100% agave tequila (see Note)
1 ounce fresh lime juice
1 ounce diluted agave fructose (see Note)
1 lime wedge, for garnish
Salt, for the glass (optional)

SHAKE AND STRAIN into an ice-filled double old-fashioned glass with a salted rim (see Note). Add the garnish.

NOTE: Julio doesn't mind if you use blanco, reposado, añejo, or even extra añejo tequila. To make the diluted agave fructose, mix a few ounces of agave fructose with an equal amount of purified water, stirring thoroughly to combine.

The salted rim is optional. You might want to put salt on just half the rim of the glass so the drinker can make his or her own decision.

TREACLE

FAMILY: **OLD-FASHIONEDS** || Adapted from a recipe by the late, great Dick Bradsell, London. Bradsell is known as the man who (almost) single-handedly changed the face of the cocktail scene in London in the 1980s. I knew him only slightly, but I was lucky enough to spend a couple of hours in the now defunct Colony Room Club when he was behind the bar there, and afterwards he and I had a good chinwag at Groucho, the London Club that boasts many celebrity members. To say that Dick Bradsell was a quirky character doesn't do him justice.

Bradsell was known for creating a number of cocktails, and my favorite is the Treacle. It's so darned simple. And it's so darned fabulous.

2 ounces dark rum
½ ounce simple syrup
2 dashes Angostura bitters
½ ounce apple juice

Stir the rum, simple syrup, and bitters together in an ice-filled old-fashioned glass for at least 20 seconds. FLOAT the apple juice on top of the drink.

TREMBLEMENT DE TERRE (EARTHQUAKE)

FAMILY: DUOS AND TRIOS || A drink mentioned in *Absinthe: History in a Bottle*, by Barnaby Conrad III, but without measurements. This was apparently a cocktail favored by Henri de Toulouse-Lautrec, the French artist who died in 1901 at the age of thirty-six. Consider yourself forewarned.

I dedicate this drink to Roy Finamore, the brilliant man who edited the first edition of this book. Roy is a great friend, and he and I spent one glorious evening drinking very high-quality bootleg absinthe back in the nineties, when absinthe was still illegal. (Thanks, Ted!)

2½ ounces cognac
¼ to ½ ounce absinthe
1 lemon twist, for garnish

STIR AND STRAIN into a chilled cocktail glass. Add the garnish.

TRINIDAD SOUR

FAMILY: SIMPLE SOURS || Recipe by Giuseppe Gonzalez, Suffolk Arms, New York. The *Washington Post* called this an oddball because of the pretty huge amount of Angostura bitters in there. What the heck do you expect from Giuseppe Gonzalez? I ask them. He's pretty much an oddball his own self.

I have sipped this delightful potion at Giuseppe's Suffolk Arms—two of them, as a matter of fact. It's a fabulous creation, and Giuseppe Gonzalez is one of my new favorite bartenders. I've known him for quite some time now, but it's only since Suffolk Arms opened, I believe, that he has blossomed into one of the most wonderful characters in the business. Time spent with Giuseppe Gonzalez is time that's very well spent indeed.

1½ ounces Angostura bitters
½ ounce rye whiskey
1 ounce orgeat syrup
¾ ounce fresh lemon juice

SHAKE AND STRAIN into a chilled coupe.

TWENTIETH-CENTURY COCKTAIL

FAMILY: INTERNATIONAL SOURS || Detailed in Tarling's *Café Royal Cocktail Book* (1937), this drink was created by C. A. Tuck. Dr. Cocktail (Ted Haigh) brought it to my attention many years ago, and I've been mixing and drinking it ever since.

The citrus juice acts as a foil for the sweet liqueur in this delightful drink, but it's the mixture of gin and chocolate that intrigues me. Did Tuck envisage these flavors before he put the drink together? We'll never know, but however he came up with the formula, nobody can argue with the fact that this drink is a masterpiece. The measurements here reflect the original formula laid down in the Café Royal book.

1½ ounces gin
¾ ounce Lillet Blonde
¾ ounce white crème de cacao
¾ ounce fresh lemon juice

SHAKE AND STRAIN into a chilled cocktail glass.

U.S.S. WONDRICH

FAMILY: TIKI || Created by Jeff "Beachbum" Berry, Latitude 29, New Orleans, 2016. Berry told me that this drink is named for the first guest at his bar who asked for a sherry-based drink. The guest, of course, was none other than cocktail scholar David Wondrich, author of *Imbibe!*

1½ ounces amontillado sherry
¾ ounce sweet vermouth
¾ ounce Sabra chocolate-orange liqueur
¾ ounce pineapple juice
1 dash Angostura bitters
1 pineapple cube on a bamboo cocktail pick, for garnish

SHAKE AND STRAIN into a chilled cocktail coupe. Add the garnish.

VESPER

FAMILY: **FRENCH-ITALIAN: GIN, RUM, GENEVER, VODKA, AND TEQUILA** || This drink is named for Vesper Lynd, a character in Ian Fleming's *Casino Royale.* James Bond insisted that his Martini be shaken, he preferred Lillet to vermouth, and he suggested that a grain-based vodka worked better than a potato vodka. The cocktailian bartender might pause to wonder why somebody would add vodka to this gin-based drink, and in this instance the vodka acts as a diluting agent, taking the edge off the gin. If you use a softer gin, such as Bombay, you'll find that this drink has little character. Far better to employ a sturdier bottling, like Tanqueray, lest the gin get completely lost in the mix.

2 ounces gin
½ ounce vodka
¼ ounce Lillet Blonde
1 lemon twist, for garnish

SHAKE AND STRAIN into a chilled cocktail glass. Add the garnish.

VIEUX CARRÉ

FAMILY: **FRENCH-ITALIAN: WHISKEY AND BRANDY** || This classic drink was invented in the 1930s by Walter Bergeron, then the head bartender at the Monteleone Hotel in New Orleans, and the cocktail is named after the French term for what we call "The French Quarter." Literally translated, *le vieux carré* means "the old square."

¾ ounce rye whiskey
¾ ounce brandy
¾ ounce sweet vermouth
¼ ounce Bénédictine
1 to 2 dashes Peychaud's bitters
1 to 2 dashes Angostura bitters

BUILD over ice in an old-fashioned glass.

WARD EIGHT

FAMILY: **SIMPLE SOURS** || Although politician Martin M. Lomasney was known to many as "the Boston Mahatma," others called him "the Czar of Ward Eight." It has generally been accepted that this drink was created at the Locke-Ober Café in Boston, circa 1898, to celebrate his victory in a race for the state legislature. The twist to the story, though, is that the drink was made before the election results were in.

True to form, David Wondrich debunked this myth in his book *Imbibe!*, God bless his little cotton socks! Citing a 1934 letter in the *New York Sun*, Wondrich says that Charlie Carter, a "veteran Boston Bartender," lay claim to having created the drink in 1903 at Boston's Puritan Club, and the occasion for which he came up with this drink was, once again, to celebrate a political victory for Lomasney. As always, my money is on Wondrich when it comes to historical truth, and I'm pinching his formula from *Esquire* for this recipe.

2 ounces straight rye whiskey
¾ ounce fresh orange juice
¾ ounce fresh lemon juice
1 teaspoon grenadine

SHAKE AND STRAIN into a chilled cocktail glass.

WEESKI

FAMILY: **FRENCH ITALIAN: WHISKEY AND BRANDY** || Created by David Wondrich at the home of Mike and Cynthia D'Aprix Sweeney, Halloween, 2003.

It's interesting, I think, to hear Wondrich's musing on putting this drink together, and notes such as this serve us well by giving us a glimpse into the thought processes that went through his head during creation. Here's what he said about this one in the December 2003 issue of *Drinks* magazine:

> *Irish whiskey is one of those otherwise-charming tipples that becomes withdrawn and uncommunicative when introduced to its peers. Mix it with almost anything and it wanders into the other room and stares out the window. As a result, it turns up in very few classic cocktails. I've always been kinda fond of the Emerald: Irish whiskey, red vermouth and orange bitters (basically, an Irish*

Manhattan). It's not bad, even if the vermouth rolls right over the whiskey. But what if you replace the bold, red vermouth with Lillet, the quiet, blonde French apéritif? Before you know it, the two wallflowers are deep in conversation, over there by the window. Add a splash of Cointreau to help them mix and voilà! If the French made whiskey, this is what it would taste like: elegant, subtle, delightful. So let's call it the "weeski"—that's French for whiskey, right?

2 ounces Irish whiskey (preferably Jameson 12)
1 ounce Lillet Blanc
1 teaspoon Cointreau
2 dashes orange bitters
1 lemon twist, for garnish

STIR AND STRAIN into a chilled cocktail glass. Add the garnish.

WHISKEY SOUR

|| FAMILY: SIMPLE SOURS ||

2 ounces bourbon or rye whiskey
1 ounce fresh lemon juice
½ ounce simple syrup
1 maraschino cherry, for garnish
½ orange wheel, for garnish

SHAKE AND STRAIN into a chilled sour glass or an ice-filled rocks glass. Add the garnishes.

WHISKEY SOUR JELLY SHOT

|| FAMILY: JELLY SHOTS ||

2 ounces fresh lemon juice
1 ounce simple syrup
1 ounce water
1 package unflavored gelatin (¼ ounce)
4 ounces whiskey
Food coloring (optional)

Place the lemon juice, simple syrup, and water in a small glass measuring cup, and add the gelatin. Allow this to sit for 1 minute, then microwave the mixture on high for 30 seconds. Stir thoroughly to make sure all the gelatin has dissolved, then add the whiskey and food coloring (if desired). Stir thoroughly again and pour the mixture into a mold. Refrigerate for at least 1 hour or preferably overnight.

WHITE RUSSIAN

FAMILY: **DUOS AND TRIOS** || I've no idea who added milk or cream to the Black Russian in order to turn it into a White Russian, but it happened in the mid-1960s as far as I can ascertain, and the drink was immortalized in 1998 when Jeff Bridges, playing The Dude in *The Big Lebowski*, quaffed eight of them during the course of the movie (he dropped the ninth one on the floor).

2 ounces vodka
1 ounce Kahlúa
1 ounce cream

SHAKE AND STRAIN into an ice-filled old-fashioned glass.

WHITE WALKER

FAMILY: **FRENCH-ITALIAN: GIN, RUM, GENEVER, VODKA, AND TEQUILA** || From Sky Huo, Earl's Juke Joint, Sydney, New South Wales, Australia. When Sky Huo, a good friend of mine, submitted this recipe for consideration in this book, here's the note she wrote to accompany it: "Basically, it's a white tequila Martinez. Dolin Blanc works as a connection of blanco tequila and maraschino liqueur. This drink is simple and easy to make. But different variations of tequila or mezcal could be used."

1½ ounces Don Julio blanco tequila
⅔ ounce Dolin Blanc vermouth
⅓ ounce Luxardo maraschino liqueur
1 dash Fee Brothers lemon bitters
1 lemon twist, for garnish

STIR AND STRAIN into a chilled sour glass or Nick & Nora glass. Add the garnish.

THE WILLIAMSBURG

FAMILY: **FRENCH-ITALIAN: WHISKEY AND BRANDY** || This Manhattan variation is adapted from a recipe by Clif Travers, Bar Celona, Brooklyn, New York. It's the Chartreuse that transports this drink across the bridge from Manhattan to Williamsburg, and the nice balance of Punt e Mes and Dolin dry vermouth helps, too. "I crossed the Greenpoint with the Red Hook (location, location) and changed the rye to bourbon in a nod to the Williamsburg hipster culture," Clif Travers wrote when he sent me this recipe.

2½ ounces W. L. Weller bourbon
¾ ounce Punt e Mes
¾ ounce Dolin dry vermouth
¾ ounce Yellow Chartreuse
1 orange twist, for garnish

STIR AND STRAIN into a chilled coupe. Add the garnish.

ZOMBIE

FAMILY: **SIMPLE SOURS AND TIKI** || The Zombie was created by Ernest Raymond Beaumont Gantt, a.k.a. "Donn Beach," a native of New Orleans who opened his Hollywood bar, Don's Beachcomber, in 1933. It wasn't long before other bars started to copy his faux-Polynesian décor, food, and cocktails. To prevent others from stealing his drink recipes, Donn emptied his ingredients into numbered bottles—not even the bartenders knew what was being poured into his cocktails.

Ernest Raymond Beaumont Gantt, however, didn't know that, some eighty-odd years later, a certain Jeff "Beachbum" Berry, of Latitude 29 in New Orleans, would perform some sleuthing worthy of Sherlock himself, eventually uncovering the original recipe for the Zombie, the drink that launched the whole tiki movement. The story behind Beachbum's pursuance of this formula can be found on his website, beachbumberry.com—it's a fascinating tale.

Here's how the recipe is detailed on the Beachbum's site: "Combine ¾ ounce fresh lime juice, ½ ounce falernum, 1½ ounces each gold Puerto Rican rum and gold or dark Jamaican rum, 1 ounce 151-proof Lemon Hart Demerara rum, 1 teaspoon grenadine, 6 drops Pernod, a dash of Angostura bitters, and ½ ounce Don's mix (2 parts grapefruit juice to 1 part cinnamon-infused sugar syrup. Put this mix in an electric blender with 6 ounces (¾ cup) crushed ice, then blend at high speed for no more than 5 seconds. Pour into a Beachbum Berry Zombie Glass or other tall Glass. Add ice cubes to fill. Garnish with a mint sprig."

Luckily for us, the Beachbum has a huge heart, so if this formula seems to be beyond your grasp, here's his simplified version of the drink—it's a version that Jeff came up with in 2007.

¾ ounce fresh lime juice
1 ounce white grapefruit juice
½ ounce Cinnamon Syrup (recipe follows)
½ ounce 151-proof gold Puerto Rican rum (such as Bacardi or Don Q)
1 ounce dark Jamaican rum
1 mint sprig, for garnish

Shake well with ice cubes. Pour unstrained into a tall glass, adding more ice to fill if necessary, and add the garnish.

CINNAMON SYRUP

3 cinnamon sticks, crushed
1 cup water
1 cup granulated sugar

In a nonreactive pan, combine the cinnamon sticks, water, and sugar. Bring the mixture to a boil, lower the heat, cover the pan, and simmer for 2 minutes. Allow the syrup to stand for 2 hours. Strain the mixture through a double layer of dampened cheesecloth. Bottle the syrup, and refrigerate.

TABLES AND CHARTS

Minim.—There are 60 minims in a dram or teaspoon; 120 in a dessertspoon; 240 in a tablespoon; 480 in an ounce; 960 in a wineglass; 1,920 in a teacup or gill; 3,840 in a breakfast-cup or tumbler; 7,680 in a pint; 15,360 in a quart; 61,440 in a gallon; 2,935,360 in a barrel; 3,970,720 in a hogshead. Its equivalent weight is .9493 grams. A Minim is equal to a drop.

—Cuyler Reynolds, *The Banquet Book*, 1902

BOTTLE SIZES

375 MILLILITERS: half a standard spirit or wine bottle
750 MILLILITERS: standard spirit or wine bottle
MAGNUM: 1.5 liters
DOUBLE MAGNUM: 3 liters
JEROBOAM: 3 liters
REHOBOAM: 4.5 liters
IMPERIAL: 6 liters
METHUSELAH: 6 liters
SALMANAZAR: 8 to 9 liters
BALTHAZAR: 12.3 liters
NEBUCHADNEZZAR: 15.4 liters

FRESH FRUIT JUICE YIELDS

The following yields are a result of some five years of noting how much juice I squeezed from each fruit, then arriving at an average.

1 GRAPEFRUIT yields 6 ounces juice
1 LEMON yields 1½ ounces juice
1 LIME yields 1 ounce juice
1 ORANGE yields 2½ to 3 ounces juice

FLUID MEASUREMENT CONVERSIONS

There is much confusion about the term *gill*, and I believe this arises because of the confusion between British and American pints. Although British and American fluid ounces are slightly different (the British measurement containing four-hundredths of an ounce more than the American ounce), it's generally accepted that a British pint contains 20 ounces and a pint in the States contains 16 ounces—the difference in ounce size being disregarded.

A gill, which is a more or less arcane measurement, *usually* referred to one-fourth of a pint; so in Britain, a gill would be 5 ounces, and in the States, it would contain 4 ounces.

BARSPEAK	U.S.	U.K.	METRIC
1 pony	1 ounce	1.04 ounces	2.96 centiliters
1 jigger	1.5 ounces	1.56 ounces	4.44 centiliters
1 gill	4 ounces	5 ounces	14.19 centiliters

U.S.	U.K.	METRIC
1 ounce	1.04 ounces	2.96 centiliters
1.5 ounces	1.56 ounces	4.44 centiliters
1 pint	0.83 pint	47.32 centiliters
1 gallon	0.83 gallon	3.79 liters

U.K.	U.S.	METRIC
1 ounce	0.961 ounce	2.841 centiliters
1 pint	1.201 pints	56.825 centiliters
1 gallon	1.201 gallons	4.546 liters

METRIC	U.S.	U.K.
1 liter	33.82 ounces	35.195 ounces
750 milliliters	25.36 ounces	26.396 ounces
1 milliliter	0.034 ounce	0.035 ounce
1 centiliter	0.338 ounce	0.352 ounce

HOW MANY SHOTS ARE IN THAT BOTTLE?

BOTTLE SIZE	SHOT SIZE	NUMBER OF SHOTS
750 milliliters	1 ounce	25.36
750 milliliters	1¼ ounces	20.29
750 milliliters	1½ ounces	16.91
750 milliliters	2 ounces	12.68
750 milliliters	2½ ounces	10.14
1 liter	1 ounce	33.82
1 liter	1¼ ounces	27.01
1 liter	1½ ounces	22.55
1 liter	2 ounces	16.91
1 liter	2½ ounces	13.53

HOW MUCH ALCOHOL IS IN THAT BOTTLE?

Thankfully, most producers of alcoholic beverages have started to steer away from using *proof* as an indicator of the amount of alcohol in any one product and now use *abv*, "alcohol by volume," to show strength. Therefore, a bottle of liquor at 40 percent abv contains 40 percent pure alcohol by volume (as opposed to by weight, which would get very confusing).

Britain, which used to use the Sikes scale to display proof, now uses the European scale set down by the International Organization of Legal Metrology (IOLM). This scale, for all intents and purposes the same as the Gay-Lussac scale, which was previously used by much of mainland Europe, was adopted by all the countries in the European Community in 1980. Using the IOLM scale or the Gay-Lussac scale is essentially the same as measuring alcohol by volume, except that their figures are expressed as degrees, not percentages.

ALCOHOL BY VOLUME	U.S. PROOF	IOLM
40%	80°	40°
43%	86°	43°
50%	100°	50°

GLOSSARY

ABSINTHE A high-proof spirit with a predominant anise flavor. Absinthe was declared illegal in the United States in 1912, because the wormwood used in its production was deemed to be harmful.

ABRICOTINE An apricot-flavored liqueur from France.

ADVOCAAT A brandy-based liqueur made with eggs, vanilla, and various other flavorings.

AGED SPIRITS Spirits labeled with a specific age statement have spent the indicated number of years aging in wooden barrels. The contents of the bottle can contain spirits older than the given age, but not younger.

AGING DISTILLED SPIRITS Some spirits, such as whiskey, aged brandy, and aged rum, require time in oak barrels before being bottled. During that time, the congeners, which are basically impurities in the liquor, oxidize, forming acids that react with other congeners to produce pleasant-tasting esters. The alcohol also reacts with the wood, extracting vanillins, wood sugars, tannins, and color.

ALE A style of beer made with a top-fermenting yeast. Subcategories of ales include amber ales, barley wines, India pale ales, lambics, porters, stouts, and wheat beers.

ALIZÉ A proprietary passionfruit-flavored liqueur from France.

ALIZÉ RED PASSION A proprietary passionfruit- and cranberry-flavored liqueur from France.

AMARETTO An almond-flavored liqueur, usually made in Italy. Disaronno is a great example of this liqueur, but at the time of this writing, the company is considering taking the word *amaretto* off its label. This will leave it in the same boat as Cointreau, and future generations might not realize that Disaronno *is* an amaretto, just as there are people today who don't realize that Cointreau is a triple sec.

AMER PICON A hard-to-find French aperitif with orange notes and a bitter herbal backdrop.

AMERICAN BRANDY Primarily produced on the West Coast and usually distilled from a fermented mash of grapes. The less expensive bottlings can be overly sweet, but some of the newer artisanal American brandies rank among the finest in the world. American brandy makers are not restricted as to which variety of grape may be used, so a few distilleries, using traditional French-style *alembique* stills and employing varietals such as chardonnay, chenin blanc, meunière, muscat, and pinot noir grapes, produce great aged brandies.

ANISETTE An anise-flavored liqueur.
APERITIF A beverage designed to whet the appetite.
APPLEJACK An American product, currently available only from Laird's in New Jersey, made from a blend of distilled cider, neutral spirits, and "apple wine," which is produced from hard cider and apple brandy. I'd like to see applejack back behind every bar in America, as it was just a few decades ago—it's a very versatile spirit and can be of great use to the cocktailian bartender.
APRICOT BRANDY An apricot-flavored liqueur.
APRY A proprietary apricot-flavored liqueur from France.
ARDENT SPIRITS 1. From the Latin *adere,* meaning "to burn," this term was used to describe the first distilled spirits, simply because they could be ignited. The word *spirit,* in all probability, referred to the vapors that rose from the liquid being distilled. 2. An email newsletter free to anyone sending their email address to gary@ardentspirits.com.
ARMAGNAC A brandy distilled from a fermented mash of grapes, made in the Gascony region of France. Armagnac is made from ugni blanc (Saint-Émilion), colombard, and/or folle blanche grapes, and although this practice is starting to wane, it is traditionally aged in Monlezun oak. Like cognac, much Armagnac is aged for longer than the law requires, but the following guidelines were set in 1994: 3 stars, 3 years; V.O., 5 years; V.S.O.P., 5 years; Réserve, 5 years; Extra, 6 years; Napoléon, 6 years; X.O., 6 years; Vielle Reserve, 6 years, and Hors d'Age, 10 years.
AROMATIZED WINES Wines flavored with botanicals such as herbs and spices and slightly fortified by the addition of brandy.
AURUM A proprietary orange-flavored liqueur from Italy.
B & B A proprietary bottling of Bénédictine and cognac.
BAILEYS IRISH CREAM A cream-based liqueur flavored with Irish whiskey.
BEER A beverage made by fermenting grains. There are two groups: ales and lagers.
BÉNÉDICTINE A French herbal liqueur developed in 1510 by the Bénédictine monk Dom Bernardo Vincelli.
BITTERS 1. A nonpotable high-proof infusion of various botanicals used as an accent in many cocktails. 2. A potable spirit, emanating mainly from Italy, where it is known as *amaro* and is flavored with bitter botanicals and, sometimes, fruits and other flavorings. Campari and Averna are two good examples, and if you compare these two bottlings, you'll get a grasp of how diverse this category can be. Since the Bureau of Alcohol, Tobacco, and Firearms doesn't have a category for potable bitters, they are often labeled as liqueurs.
BLACKBERRY BRANDY A blackberry-flavored liqueur.
BLUE CURAÇAO An blue-colored, orange-flavored liqueur; it is similar to triple sec, but usually sweeter.
BOTANICALS A collection of flavoring agents that can be made up of a variety of barks, fruits, herbs, spices, and various other ingredients. Juniper, for example, is one botanical used to flavor gin, and orange peel is

a botanical employed in the flavoring of Cointreau.

BOURBON A whiskey made in the United States from a fermented mash of grains; corn must make up at least 51 percent, but no more than 79 percent, of the mash. Bourbon must be aged in new charred-oak barrels for at least two years, but if it is bottled at less than four years of age, its age must be noted on the label.

BRANDY A spirit distilled from a fermented mash of fruit. Usually when we think of brandy we think of a grape-based spirit that has been aged in wood, but that isn't always the case. *See also* American brandy, armagnac, brandy de Jerez, cognac, eau-de-vie, grappa, marc.

BRANDY DE JEREZ An aged grape-based brandy made in the Jerez region of Spain. The liquor is aged using the solera system of adding young spirits to older spirits in a pyramid fashion: The top row of a solera holds new distillates, and the bottom row holds the oldest brandies, with barrels full of ascending ages in between. Airén or palomino grapes are the usually used varietals, and the brandy can be sweeter than most other grape brandies. Bottlings of brandy de Jerez that use the word *Solera* on the label have been aged for about one year; *Solera Reserva* brandies spend around twenty-four months in the wood, and *Solera Gran Reserva* bottlings can be over seven years old.

CALVADOS A spirit distilled from a fermented mash of apples, usually with a small percentage of pears. Made in the Calvados region of Normandy, France, it is aged in oak.

CAMPARI An Italian form of potable bitters.

CANADIAN BLENDED WHISKY Many people erroneously think of Canadian whisky as being rye whisky, but that's just not true unless you see the words *rye whisky* on the label. The vast majority of Canadian blended whisky is made in continuous stills from a base of corn and is mixed with neutral grain whisky after aging. Flavorings are commonly added to the end product. Bourbon, cognac, rum, and sherry are all employed by one distillery or another to flavor Canadian whiskies, and even a product known as prune wine can be an additive. By law, the distillers are allowed to add 9.09 percent flavoring to their products, but in practice a far smaller percentage is actually used.

CHAMBORD A black-raspberry-flavored liqueur from France.

CHAMPAGNE A French sparkling wine from the Champagne district of northeastern France. Although sparkling wines from the United States are sometimes labeled "champagne," they are not recognized as such by the knowledgeable.

CHARCOAL FILTRATION In most cases, these words refer to filtration with activated carbon, a process used on many spirits, after they have been aged, to eliminate impurities that can cause them to develop a chill haze when cold. (This is not to be confused with the charcoal filtration used in the production of Tennessee whiskey.) The problem with filtration is that the impurities that are removed during the process are flavorful, and if the spirit is chilled before filtration, even more impurities are lost. The alternative is to bottle spirits at high proof—around 50 percent alcohol by volume—since these spirits won't easily develop a chill haze.

CHARTREUSE An herbal liqueur from France said to have been created by Carthusian monks in 1737, though the recipe supposedly dates back to 1605. Available in green and yellow bottlings. Yellow Chartreuse, introduced in 1838, is the sweeter variety.

CHERI SUISSE A proprietary chocolate- and cherry-flavored liqueur from Switzerland.

CHERRY BRANDY A cherry-flavored liqueur.

CHERRY HEERING A proprietary cherry-flavored liqueur from Denmark.

CHERRY MARNIER A cherry-flavored, cognac-based liqueur from France.

COGNAC An aged grape-based spirit from the Cognac region of France. Cognac must be made from at least 90 percent ugni blanc (also known as Saint-Émilion), folle blanche, and/or colombard grapes, and is usually aged in Limousin oak barrels. Much cognac is aged for longer than the law requires; however, in order to put the following codes on the bottle, it must spend the time noted in wood: V.S. (Very Special), 2.5 years; V.S.O.P. (Very Special Old Pale), 4.5 years; V.O. (Very Old), 4.5 years; Réserve, 4.5 years; X.O. (Extra Old), 6 years; and Napoléon, 6 years.

COINTREAU A highly recommendable proprietary brand of triple sec from France.

CONTINUOUS STILL A type of still patented by Aeneas Coffey, circa 1860, that's sometimes referred to as a Coffey still, a column still, or a patent still. The still contains a series of perforated metal plates; the fermented mash is entered at the top of the still, and steam is piped into the bottom. The steam strips the mash of its alcohol, and the alcohol-laden vapors are collected at the top. It's possible to attain a spirit with around 96 percent alcohol in a single distillation in this type of still. Similar stills were in use in France in the late 1700s.

CORDIAL A sweetened and flavored low-alcohol beverage usually referred to as a liqueur.

CORN WHISKEY A spirit distilled from a grain mash, a minimum of 80 percent of which must be corn. If aged, it must rest in previously used barrels.

CRÈME DE ANANAS A pineapple-flavored liqueur.

CRÈME DE BANANE A banana-flavored liqueur.

CRÈME DE CACAO A chocolate-flavored liqueur available in both white and dark bottlings.

CRÈME DE CASSIS A black-currant–flavored liqueur.

CRÈME DE MENTHE A mint-flavored liqueur available in both green and white bottlings.

CRÈME DE NOYAU An almond-flavored liqueur.

CRÈME YVETTE A now unavailable proprietary violet-flavored liqueur. At the time of this writing, you can order a violet liqueur at www.sallyclarke.com.

CUARENTA Y TRES A Spanish herbal liqueur with a predominance of vanilla.

CURAÇAO An orange-flavored liqueur similar to triple sec but usually sweeter. Curaçao comes in different colors, but they all taste of orange.

DANZIGER GOLDWASSER A proprietary aniseed- and caraway-flavored liqueur flecked with gold flakes, from Germany.

DIGESTIF A beverage, such as Underberg bitters, designed to aid digestion.

DISTILLATION The distillation of beverage alcohol, as far as we know, dates back to the century between 1050 and 1150 and most probably occurred at the University of Salerno, in Italy. The word *distillation* is derived from the Latin *dis* or *des,* which implies separation, and *stilla,* which translates to "drop." In a literal sense, therefore, it means "separation drop by drop." In the case of distilled spirits, the object is to separate alcohol from water using heat. Since beverage alcohol evaporates at a little under 173°F, whereas water turns to steam at 212°F, if a liquid containing both water and alcohol is heated to a point above the boiling point of alcohol but below that of water, the resultant vapors can be condensed into a liquid that contains more alcohol than the original liquid.

DISTILLED SPIRITS Beverages distilled from fermented food products, such as grains, fruits, or vegetables, that are bottled at a minimum of 40 percent alcohol by volume.

DRAMBUIE A scotch-based herbal liqueur flavored with honey. The word *Drambuie* is derived from the Gaelic *an dram buidheach,* meaning "the drink that satisfies."

DUBONNET An aromatized wine, similar to vermouth, available in rouge and blanc.

EAU-DE-VIE A generic French term meaning "water of life" that can be applied to all unaged fruit brandies.

FERMENTATION This term refers to the process that occurs when yeast feeds on sugar, producing carbon dioxide, heat, and alcohol. In the case of fruit-based spirits, such as brandy, this is easy: The sugar is ready, willing, and able. But grain-based spirits like whiskey are a little trickier. Grains contain starches, though, and starches are merely complex forms of sugar, so they can be broken down to yield fermentable sugars.

FORBIDDEN FRUIT A proprietary American brandy–based, fruit-flavored liqueur. Very hard to find.

FORTIFIED WINE A wine such as madeira, port, or sherry that has been fortified by the addition of brandy.

FRAMBOISE 1. An eau-de-vie made from a fermented mash of raspberries. 2. A raspberry-flavored liqueur.

FRANGELICO A proprietary hazelnut-flavored Italian liqueur.

GALLIANO A proprietary Italian vanilla-herbal liqueur with orange notes.

GIN A spirit distilled from a fermented mash of grains and flavored with a number of botanicals, of which juniper must be predominant. Having written that, I must now say that some gins on the market these days do not show a predominance of juniper. These bottlings seem to be very popular, and some vodka drinkers have been converted to gin as a result of experimentation with these products.

London dry gin need not be produced in London—the phrase is used to describe a dry style of gin. *Plymouth gin,* on the other hand, although it displays characteristics similar to London dry bottlings, must be made in Plymouth, England. *Old Tom gin* is a slightly sweetened gin that was very popular during the latter decades of the 1800s, right through to the onset of Prohibition in 1920; it has experienced a resurgence in recent years. *Hollands* or *geneva gin,* made in Holland, can be fairly sweet, although some bottlings are similar in style to the lightly junipered gins favored by vodka drinkers.

GLAYVA A proprietary scotch-based herbal-honey liqueur.

GRAND MARNIER A proprietary orange-flavored, aged cognac-based liqueur from France. Available in three bottlings: Grand Marnier Cordon Rouge; Grand Marnier Cuvée du Centenaire, made with ten-year-old cognac; and Grand Marnier Cuvée du Cent-Cinquantenaire, made with X.O. cognac.

GRAPPA An Italian eau-de-vie distilled from a fermented mash of grape pomace, the leftovers from the winemaking process.

IRISH MIST A proprietary Irish-whiskey-based liqueur flavored with herbs and honey.

IRISH WHISKEY A spirit distilled in Ireland from a fermented mash of grains and aged in wooden barrels for a minimum of three years. There are some fine single-malt Irish whiskeys distilled in pot stills, and their number is growing. Most Irish whiskeys, though, are blended products. The Irish Distillers company, which owns many of the major brands, has a policy to not bottle any of its whiskeys, blended or single malt, until all the whiskey used has been aged for a minimum of five years. I'd wager that the same could be said of the independent Irish whiskeymakers.

One of the major differences between Irish whiskey and scotch is that the Irish rarely use peat fires to dry their malt. Another is that Irish whiskeymakers usually distill their whiskey three times, whereas scotch is normally distilled only twice. The benefits of triple distillation have been described to me time and again, but they never quite seem to make sense. If you can attain the desired proof by double distillation, which is fairly easy, why bother distilling again?

IZARRA A proprietary brandy-based herbal liqueur from the Basque region of France. Like Chartreuse, Izarra is available in both yellow and green bottlings.

JÄGERMEISTER A proprietary herbal liqueur from Germany that tastes somewhat medicinal.

KAHLÚA A proprietary coffee-flavored liqueur from Mexico.

KIRSCH Sometimes called *kirschwasser*; an eau-de-vie made from a fermented mash of cherries.

KÜMMEL A predominantly caraway-flavored herbal liqueur, usually from Holland or Germany

LAGER A style of beer made with a bottom-fermenting yeast. Subcategories of lager include pilsners, Vienna lagers, and bocks.

LIMONCELLO An Italian liqueur flavored with lemon zest. There's an excellent recipe for homemade Limoncello on page 234. The best proprietary bottlings I've tasted are Massa and Giori—many others are far too sweet.

LIQUEUR A sweetened and flavored

low-alcohol beverage sometimes referred to as a cordial.

MADEIRA A fortified wine from the island of Madeira.

MALIBU A proprietary rum-based, coconut-flavored liqueur.

MANDARINE NAPOLÉON A proprietary cognac-based, tangerine-flavored French liqueur.

MARASCHINO A European liqueur flavored with whole Dalmatian marasca cherries.

MARC A French eau-de-vie distilled from a fermented mash of grape pomace, the leftovers from the winemaking process.

MASH A "soup" that can be made up of fruits, fruit juices, grains, vegetables, sugars, or any other edible material and can be fermented by the addition of yeast to produce alcohol.

METAXA Commonly thought of as a brandy, Metaxa is actually Greek brandy mixed with aged muscat wine, blended with a secret mix of botanicals, and aged in oak casks.

MEZCAL A spirit distilled in Mexico from a fermented mash of agave, mezcal is to tequila what brandy is to cognac: All tequilas are forms of mezcal, but not all mezcals can be called tequila.

MIDORI A proprietary melon-flavored liqueur.

NEUTRAL GRAIN ALCOHOL Distilled at high proof from a fermented mash of any grains, this is basically high-proof vodka that is never aged. Neutral grain alcohol can be used in gin production, and it's sometimes diluted to make vodka. It also has many other uses in the liquor business, especially when flavors need to be extracted from raw materials, such as for liqueurs.

NEUTRAL GRAIN WHISKEY A spirit distilled from grains that leaves the still containing few impurities and much alcohol, and therefore it doesn't develop much flavor, even if it is aged. Neutral grain whiskey is used in blended whiskeys, along with other, more flavorful spirits. The age statement on any bottle of blended whiskey refers to the number of years of aging of the neutral whiskey, or the other components, whichever is smaller.

OUZO A Greek anise-flavored liqueur.

PEACH BRANDY A peach-flavored liqueur.

PEACH SCHNAPPS A peach-flavored liqueur, usually drier than peach brandy.

PEAT REEK The smoky odor found in scotch whisky, a result of the barley being dried over peat fires.

PEPPERMINT SCHNAPPS A peppermint-flavored liqueur, usually drier than crème de menthe.

PISCO BRANDY A Peruvian grape brandy also made in other South American countries. Aged for a few months in clay containers, pisco is more of an eau-de-vie than an aged brandy.

PORT A fortified Portuguese wine produced in the Douro region of Portugal. Other countries also produce fortified wines that are labeled as ports; although this practice has been scoffed at in the past, there are now some good bottlings on the market, and the practice is gaining legitimacy.

POT STILL Pot stills come in many styles; most people automatically think of the Scottish or Irish pot still, a beautiful, bulbous, onion-shaped copper vessel with a graceful tall swan's neck sprouting from it. The French, too, have very elegant pot stills, known as *alembiques;* these are somewhat more elaborate affairs, with a tank that holds wine waiting to be distilled that is warmed by the vapors from the wines *being* distilled, thus making use of the heat. Quite simply, though, pot stills are more labor-intensive than continuous stills. They require at least two distillations to attain a high enough proof in the spirit, but they tend to produce spirits with a character that's specific to the individual still.

POT-STILLED A term found on some liquor bottles, most notably Irish whiskey, that describes the method of distillation but not the grains used to make the product. Pot-stilled does not imply single malt.

ROCK AND RYE A whiskey-based liqueur flavored with fruit juices and horehound.

RUM A spirit distilled from a fermented mash of molasses or sugarcane juice. Rum is almost impossible to define, since it emanates from so many countries, each of which has its own regulatory laws. Styles include dark, amber, añejo (aged), and white, or light, rum. Various bottlings are made in pot stills, though most come from continuous stills. There are some fabulous rums on the market, and these are well suited to be sipping rums. Almost any rum can be successfully employed as a cocktail ingredient, as long as you remember, of course, that better-quality products will yield superior cocktails and mixed drinks.

RYE WHISKEY Although legally this product can be made anywhere, at the time of this writing the term refers to a whiskey produced in the United States from a fermented mash of grains including at least 51 percent rye. Straight rye whiskey made in America must be aged in new charred-oak barrels for at least two years, and if it is bottled at less than four years of age, its age must be noted on the label. Many people refer to Canadian blended whiskies as ryes; this practice began during and right after Prohibition, when American whiskey stocks were depleted and much of the bootleg trade came from our northern neighbors, who, at that time, used a great deal of rye in their whisky.

SAMBUCA An Italian anise-based liqueur. Available in white and black bottlings; black Sambuca has notes of lemon zest.

SCOTCH (BLENDED) A whisky made in Scotland from a blend of single-malt scotches and neutral grain whisky and aged for a minimum of three years. More expensive bottlings usually contain a higher percentage of single malts than those sold at bargain prices.

SCOTCH (SINGLE MALT) A whisky made in Scotland, distilled from a fermented mash of malted barley that, traditionally, is dried over peat fires. Single-malt scotches are aged for a minimum of three years and are always the product of a single distillery. Single-malt scotches emanate from different areas of Scotland. They bear regional characteristics due, in part, to the climate where they are aged, and also to various other idiosyncrasies, such as the height of the still and the amount of time the barley spends over peat fires in the malting process.

Traditionally, descriptions of single-malt scotches from different areas divide Scotland into five regions—the following characteristics attributed to malts from those regions are gross generalizations: *Islay (EYE-luh):* Single-malt scotches from this small island just off the western coast of Scotland are usually characterized by their peaty-seaweed-iodine-medicinal tones. *Lowland:* This southern part of Scotland usually produces single-malt scotches that are lighter and somewhat "cleaner" than all others. *Campbeltown:* This small town on Scotland's western coast is primarily known for single-malt scotches bearing a briny character, along with some peaty-iodine notes. *Highlands:* The northern areas of Scotland tend to produce fresh, heathery, medium-bodied malts. But since this is where most single-malt scotches are made, bottlings can differ tremendously, and not all of them fit this description accurately. *Speyside:* The Speyside region is actually a subregion of the Highlands that is home to over fifty distilleries, each with its own style. Although Speyside produces light-, medium-, and heavy-bodied malts, all of these single-malt scotches can be loosely characterized as complex and mellow, with hints of peat.

SCOTCH (VATTED) Usually labeled "Pure Malt Scotch" in the United States, vatted malts contain a blend of single-malt scotches from different distilleries.

SHERRY A fortified wine from the region of Spain around the city of Jerez.

SINGLE-BARREL WHISKEY These whiskeys come from one specific barrel of whiskey that the blender or distiller has deemed good enough to bottle without the addition of whiskeys from any other barrels.

SINGLE-MALT AMERICAN WHISKEY A few single-malt American whiskeys are now on the market, and I have no doubt that at some point in the future we'll see some great bottlings. The distillers producing them—most notably Jorg Rupf at the St. George Distillery in California and Steve McCarthy at the Clear Creek distillery in Oregon—are very skilled at their craft, so watch out for new releases.

SLOE GIN A liqueur flavored with the fruit of the blackthorn and sometimes, though seldom, made with a gin base.

SMALL BATCH A term used by many spirits companies to describe superior bottlings of their products. Each company has its own definition of the term; although you might be tempted to think that the spirit was produced in small batches, this isn't always the case. Sometimes it refers to, say, whiskey taken from a small batch of casks, for instance. I don't know of a company that uses the term *small batch* on inferior products, but personally, I put greater stock in age statements.

SOUTHERN COMFORT A proprietary fruit-flavored liqueur.

SPARKLING WINE Wine, such as champagne or prosecco, that is carbonated by a secondary fermentation.

STRAWBERRY BRANDY A strawberry-flavored liqueur.

STREGA A proprietary Italian herbal liqueur. *Strega* translates from the Italian to "witch."

TENNESSEE WHISKEY A spirit distilled in Tennessee from a fermented mash of grains that is filtered through large vats of sugar-maple charcoal before being aged in new, charred oak barrels. The charcoal filtration adds a sooty sweetness to the whiskey not found in bourbons or straight ryes.

TEQUILA A spirit distilled in demarcated regions of Mexico from a fermented mash of cooked *Agave tequilana Weber,* otherwise known as blue agave. Most tequila falls under the category of *mixto* (MEES-toh); that word denotes that the spirit can be made with as little as 51 percent blue agave—the rest of the distillate is usually made from sugar in one form or another.

Tequilas made entirely from blue agave are known as "100 percent blue agave," and those words appear on the label of such bottlings. These are the finest tequilas, and some are suitable as an after-dinner drink, being taken neat at room temperature. *Blanco* ("silver" or "white") tequilas are unaged and bear the vegetal, sharp, and peppery notes that I love in tequila. *Gold* tequilas must, by law, contain a small percentage of *reposado* tequila (see below), but the amount is not specified. *Reposado,* or "rested," tequilas are, by law, aged in oak barrels—usually used bourbon casks—for a minimum of two months. They can be more complex than *blanco* bottlings, and many, especially 100 percent agave bottlings, can be successfully used in mixed drinks. *Añejo,* or "aged," tequilas are, again by law, aged in oak for a minimum of one year. These are the sipping tequilas, especially the 100 percent agave bottlings, but although they can be delightful, like aged gin, most have lost their delightful vegetal bite. Among the exceptions to this rule are the Don Julio and Herradura tequilas, which retain their character even after being aged. *Muy añejo,* or "extra-aged," tequilas, are aged for longer than one year, and the amount of time they have spent in wood is usually noted on the label.

TIA MARIA A proprietary rum-based, coffee-flavored Jamaican liqueur.

TRIPLE SEC A generic orange-flavored liqueur. Many bottlings are fairly sweet and low in alcohol. The best bottlings on the market are Cointreau and Van Gogh O'Magnifique, both of which, at 80 proof, are dry, sophisticated, and perfect for cocktailian bartenders.

TUACA A proprietary herbal liqueur from Italy with predominant orange and vanilla notes.

USQUEBAUGH or **UISGA BEATHA** Both are Gaelic terms meaning "water of life"; they were later anglicized to "whiskey."

VERMOUTH An aromatized wine that's slightly fortified by the addition of a little brandy. Available in sweet (red), also known as Italian vermouth, and dry (white), also known as French vermouth.

VINTAGE-DATED SPIRITS Aged spirits that were distilled in the specific year noted as the vintage. These are different from other aged spirits, which bear an age statement but no vintage year since they might contain a percentage of spirits distilled earlier than the age statement indicates.

VODKA A spirit distilled from almost any vegetal matter, although most are grain based and there are quite a few potato vodkas available. The rest—some made from beets or molasses—are less expensive, and producers of these vodkas rarely boast about the base of their products. Although by American legal definition, vodka should have no distinctive flavor, if you taste different bottlings, side by side and at room temperature, it's easy to find nuances from one label to the next. In the vast majority of mixed drinks, however, it's virtually impossible to distinguish which brand is in the glass.

VODKA (FLAVORED) Many flavored vodkas are now available, and new ones are released regularly. These products can be wonderful bases on which new cocktails can be built.

WHISKEY, WHISKY A spirit distilled from a mash of fermented grains. The *e* is usually, but not always, included when the word refers to Irish or American whiskeys, whereas Scottish and Canadian products leave the *e* out.

WOOD FINISHES Some whiskeys are aged in one barrel for, say, twelve years, then are transferred to another cask for "finishing," which usually takes between six and eighteen months. The time the whiskey spends in the secondary barrel is usually left to the distiller's discretion. He will sample the whiskey regularly until he thinks it is perfect. The finishing process usually takes place in barrels that previously held products such as sherry, madeira, or port, each of which adds its own nuance to the final product.

BIBLIOGRAPHY

BOOKS

ABC of Cocktails, The. New York: Peter Pauper Press, 1953.

Ade, George. *The Old-Time Saloon.* New York: Old Town Books, 1993.

Amis, Kingsley. *Kingsley Amis on Drink.* New York: Harcourt Brace Jovanovich, 1973.

Angostura Bitters Complete Mixing Guide. New York: J.W. Wupperman, 1913.

Anthology of Cocktails Together with Selected Observations by a Distinguished Gathering and Diverse Thoughts for Great Occasions, An. London: Booth's Distilleries, n.d.

Anthony, Norman, and O. Soglow. *The Drunk's Blue Book.* New York: Frederick A. Stokes, 1933.

Armstrong, John. *VIP's All New Bar Guide.* Greenwich, CT: Fawcett Publications, 1960.

Arthur, Stanley Clisby. *Famous New Orleans Drinks & How to Mix 'em.* 1937. Reprint, Gretna, LA: Pelican Publishing, 1989.

Asbury, Herbert. *The Barbary Coast: An Informal History of the San Francisco Underworld.* New York: Garden City Publishing, 1933.

———. *The French Quarter: An Informal History of the New Orleans Underworld.* New York: Garden City Publishing, 1938.

———. *The Gangs of New York.* New York: Thunder's Mouth Press, 2001.

———. *The Great Illusion: An Informal History of Prohibition.* New York: Doubleday, 1950; New York: Greenwood Press, 1968.

Baker, Charles H., Jr. *The Gentleman's Companion: An Exotic Drinking Book.* New York: Crown Publishers, 1946.

———. *The South American Gentleman's Companion.* New York: Crown Publishers, 1951.

Barr, Andrew. *Drink.* London: Bantam Press, 1995.

———. *Drink: A Social History of America.* New York: Carroll & Graf Publishers, 1999.

Barrett, E. R. *The Truth About Intoxicating Drinks.* London: Ideal Publishing, 1899.

Batterberry, Michael, and Ariane Batterberry. *On the Town in New York.* New York: Routledge, 1999.

Bayley, Stephen. *Gin.* England: Balding & Mansell, 1994.

Beebe, Lucius. *The Stork Club Bar Book.* New York: Rinehart, 1946.

Behr, Edward. *Prohibition: Thirteen Years That Changed America.* New York: Arcade Publishing, 1996.

Behrendt, Axel, and Bibiana Behrendt. *Cognac.* New York: Abbeville Press, 1997.

Bernard [pseud.]. *100 Cocktails: How to Mix Them.* London: W. Foulsham, [n.d.].

Berry, Jeff, and Annene Kaye. *Beachbum Berry's Grog Log.* San Jose, CA: SLG Publishing, 1998.

Bishop, George. *The Booze Reader: A Soggy Saga of a Man in His Cups.* Los Angeles: Sherbourne Press, 1965.

Blochman, Lawrence. *Here's How*. New York: New American Library, 1957.
Brinnin, John Malcolm. *Dylan Thomas in America*. London: Harborough Publishing, 1957.
Brock, H. I., and J. W. Golinkin. *New York Is Like This*. New York: Dodd, Mead, 1929.
Broom, Dave. *Spirits and Cocktails*. London: Carlton, 1998.
Brown, Charles. *The Gun Club Drink Book*. New York: Charles Scribner's Sons, 1939.
Brown, Gordon. *Classic Spirits of the World*. New York: Abbeville Press, 1996.
Brown, Henry Collins. *In the Golden Nineties*. Hastings-on-Hudson, NY: Valentines's Manual, 1928.
Brown, John Hull. *Early American Beverages*. New York: Bonanza Books, 1966.
Bryson, Bill. *Made in America*. London: Martin Secker & Warburg, 1994.
Bullock, Tom. *The Ideal Bartender*. St. Louis, MO: Buxton & Skinner, 1917.
Bullock, Tom, and D. J. Frienz. *173 Pre-Prohibition Cocktails*. Oklahoma: Howling at the Moon Press, 2001.
Burke, Harman Burney. *Burke's Complete Cocktail and Drinking Recipes*. New York: Books, 1936.
Carling, T. E. *The Complete Book of Drink*. London: Practical Press, 1951.
Carson, Johnny. *Happiness Is a Dry Martini*. New York: Doubleday, 1965.
Charles and Carlos [pseuds.]. *The Cocktail Bar*. London: W. Foulsham, 1977.
Charles of Delmonicos. *Punches and Cocktails*. New York: Arden Books, 1930.
Cipriani, Arrigo. *Harry's Bar: The Life and Times of the Legendary Venice Landmark*. New York: Arcade Publishing, 1996.
Cocktail Book: A Sideboard Manual for Gentlemen, The. 1900. Reprint, Boston: Colonial Press, C. H. Simonds, 1926.
Conrad, Barnaby, III. *Absinthe: History in a Bottle*. San Francisco: Chronicle Books, 1988.
Cotton, Leo, comp. and ed. *Old Mr. Boston De Luxe Official Bartender's Guide*, various editions. Boston: Ben Burke, 1935; Boston: Berke Brothers Distilleries, 1949, 1953; Boston: Mr. Boston Distiller, 1966, 1970.
Craddock, Harry. *The Savoy Cocktail Book*. New York: Richard R. Smith, 1930.
Craig, Charles H. *The Scotch Whisky Industry Record*. Scotland: Index Publishing, 1994.
Crewe, Quentin. *Quentin Crewe's International Pocket Food Book*. London: Mitchell Beazley International, 1980.
Crockett, Albert Stevens. *The Old Waldorf-Astoria Bar Book*. New York: A. S. Crockett, 1935.
Culver, John Breckenridge. *The Gentle Art of Drinking*. New York: Ready Reference Publishing, [1934].
Daiches, David. *Scotch Whisky: Its Past and Present*. London: Macmillan, 1969.
Davies, Frederick, and Seymour Davies. *Drinks of All Kinds*. London: John Hogg, [n.d.].
DeVoto, Bernard. *The Hour*. Cambridge, MA: Riverside Press, 1948.
Dickens, Cedric. *Drinking with Dickens*. Goring-on-Thames, England: Elvendon Press, 1980.
Dickson, Paul. *Toasts*. New York: Crown Publishers, 1991.
Downard, William L. *Dictionary of the History of the American Brewing and Distilling Industries*. Westport, CT: Greenwood Press, 1980.
Doxat, John. *The Book of Drinking*. London: Triune Books, 1973.
——. *Stirred—Not Shaken: The Dry Martini*. London: Hutchinson Benham, 1976.
Duffy, Patrick Gavin. *The Official Mixer's Manual*. New York: Alta Publications, 1934.
——. *The Official Mixer's Manual*. New York: Blue Ribbon Books,

1948. Revised and enlarged by James A. Beard. New York: Garden City Books, 1956; New York: Permabooks, 1948, 1958, 1959.
Earle, Alice Morse. *Customs and Fashions in Old New England.* New York: Charles Scribner's Sons, 1913.
Edmunds, Lowell. *Martini, Straight Up: The Classic American Cocktail.* Baltimore: Johns Hopkins University Press, 1998.
Edwards, Bill. *How to Mix Drinks.* Philadelphia: David McKay, 1936.
Elliot, Virginia, and Phil D. Stong. *Shake 'Em Up: A Practical Handbook of Polite Drinking.* [n.p.]: Brewer and Warren, 1932.
Embury, David A. *The Fine Art of Mixing Drinks*, 2nd ed. New York: Garden City Books, 1952; revised edition, 1958.
Emmons, Bob. *The Book of Tequila: A Complete Guide.* Chicago: Open Court Publishing, 1997.
Engel, Leo. *American and Other Drinks.* London: Tinsley Brothers, [1883].
Erdoes, Richard. *Saloons of the Old West.* New York: Gramercy Books, 1997.
Erenberg, Lewis A. *Steppin' Out: New York Nightlife and the Transformation of American Culture, 1890–1930.* Chicago: University of Chicago Press, 1981.
Faith, Nicholas, and Ian Wisniewski. *Classic Vodka.* London: Prion Books, 1997.
Feery, William C. *Wet Drinks for Dry People.* Chicago: Bazner Press, 1932.
Fields, W. C. *W. C. Fields by Himself: His Intended Biography.* Commentary by Ronald J. Fields. Englewood Cliffs, NJ: Prentice-Hall, 1973.
Gaige, Crosby. *Crosby Gaige's Cocktail Guide and Ladies' Companion.* New York: M. Barrows, 1945.
———. *The Standard Cocktail Guide.* New York: M. Barrows, 1944.
Gale, Hyman, and Gerald F. Marco. *The How and When.* Chicago: Marco's, 1940.
Gordon, Harry Jerrold. *Gordon's Cocktail and Food Recipes.* Boston: C. H. Simonds, 1934.
Gorman, Marion, and Felipe de Alba. *The Tequila Book.* Chicago: Contemporary Books, 1978.
Gregory, Conal R. *The Cognac Companion: A Connoisseur's Guide.* Philadelphia: Running Press, 1997.
Grimes, William. *Straight Up or On the Rocks: A Cultural History of American Drink.* New York: Simon & Schuster, 1993.
———. *Straight Up or On the Rocks: The Story of the American Cocktail.* New York: North Point Press, 2001.
Grossman, Harold J. *Grossman's Guide to Wines, Beers, and Spirits*, 6th ed. Revised by Harriet Lembeck. New York: Charles Scribner's Sons, 1977.
Haimo, Oscar. *Cocktail and Wine Digest.* New York: International Cocktail, Wine, and Spirits Digest, 1955.
Hamilton, Edward. *The Complete Guide to Rum.* Chicago: Triumph Books, 1997.
Harrington, Paul, and Laura Moorhead. *Cocktail: The Drinks Bible for the Twenty-first Century.* New York: Viking, 1998.
Harwell, Richard Barksdale. *The Mint Julep.* Charlottesville: University Press of Virginia, 1985.
Haskin, Frederic J. *Recipes for Mixed Drinks, Wines: How to Serve Them.* Hartford, CT: [n.p.], 1934; circulated by the *Hartford Courant.*
Hastings, Derek. *Spirits and Liqueurs of the World.* Consulting editor, Constance Gordon Wiener. London: Footnote Productions, 1984.
Hewett, Edward, and Axton, W. F. *Convivial Dickens: The Drinks of Dickens and His Times.* Athens: Ohio University Press, 1983.
Holden, Jan. *Hell's Best Friend: The True Story of the Old-Time Saloon.* Stillwater, OK: New Forums Press, 1998.
Holmes, Jack D. L. *New Orleans Drinks and How to Mix Them.* New Orleans, LA: Hope Publications, 1973.

Hunt, Ridgely, and George S. Chappell, comp. *The Saloon in the Home, or A Garland of Rumblossoms.* New York: Coward-McCann, 1930.
Hutson, Lucinda. *Tequila! Cooking with the Spirit of Mexico.* Berkeley, CA: Ten Speed Press, 1995.
Jackson, Michael. *Michael Jackson's Complete Guide to Single Malt Scotch.* Philadelphia: Running Press, 1999.
Jeffs, Julian. *Sherry.* London: Faber and Faber, 1992.
Johnson, Byron A., and Sharon Peregrine Johnson. *The Wild West Bartenders' Bible.* Austin: Texas Monthly Press, 1986.
Johnson, Harry. *New and Improved Illustrated Bartender's Manual.* New York: Harry Johnson, 1900.
Jones, Andrew. *The Apéritif Companion.* London: Quintet Publishing, 1998.
Jones, Stanley M. *Jones' Complete Barguide.* Los Angeles: Barguide Enterprises, 1977.
Judge Jr. *Here's How.* New York: Leslie-Judge Company, 1927.
———. *Here's How Again!* New York: John Day Company, 1929.
Kappeler, George J. *Modern American Drinks: How to Mix and Serve All Kinds of Cups and Drinks.* New York: Merriam, 1895.
Kinross, Lord. *The Kindred Spirit: A History of Gin and the House of Booth.* London: Newman Neame, 1959.
Lawlor, C. F. *The Mixicologist, or How to Mix All Kinds of Fancy Drinks.* Cleveland, OH: Burrow Brothers, 1897.
Lass, William, ed. *I. W. Harper Hospitality Tour of the United States.* New York: Popular Library, 1970.
Lewis, V. B. *The Complete Buffet Guide, or How to Mix Drinks of All Kinds.* Chicago: M. A. Donahue, 1903.
London, Robert, and Anne London. *Cocktails and Snacks.* Cleveland, OH: World Publishing, 1953.
Lord, Tony. *The World Guide to Spirits, Aperitifs and Cocktails.* New York: Sovereign Books, 1979.
Lowe, Paul E. *Drinks: How to Mix and How to Serve.* Toronto: Gordon & Gotch, 1927.
Mahoney, Charles S. *Hoffman House Bartender's Guide: How to Open a Saloon and Make It Pay.* New York: Richard K. Fox Publishing, 1912.
Mamma's Recipes for Keeping Papa Home. Texas: Martin Casey, 1901.
Mario, Thomas. *Playboy's Bar Guide.* Chicago: Playboy Press, 1971.
———. *Playboy's Host and Bar Book.* Chicago: Playboy Press, 1971.
Marquis, Don. *The Old Soak's History of the World.* New York: Doubleday, Page, 1925.
Marrison, L. W. *Wines and Spirits.* Baltimore: Penguin Books, 1957.
Martin, Paul. *World Encyclopedia of Cocktails.* London: Constable, 1997.
Mason, Dexter. *The Art of Drinking.* New York: Farrar & Rinehart, 1930.
McNulty, Henry. *The Vogue Cocktail Book.* New York: Harmony Books, 1982.
Mencken, H. L. *Heathen Days.* New York: Alfred A. Knopf, 1943.
———. *Newspaper Days.* New York: Alfred A. Knopf, 1963.
———. *The Young Mencken: The Best of His Work.* Collected by Carl Bode. New York: Dial Press, 1973.
Mendelsohn, Oscar A. *The Dictionary of Drink and Drinking.* New York: Hawthorne Books, 1965.
———. *Drinking with Pepys.* London: Macmillan, 1963.
Mew, James, and John Ashton. *Drinks of the World.* London: Leadenhall Press, 1892.
Miller, Anistasia, Jared Brown, and Don Gatterdam. *Champagne Cocktails.* New York: Regan Books, 1999.
Mitchell, Joseph. *McSorley's Wonderful Saloon.* New York: Grosset & Dunlap, 1943.
———. *My Ears Are Bent.* New York: Pantheon Books, 2001.

Montague, Harry. *New Bartender's Guide.* Baltimore: I. & M. Ottenheimer, 1914.

Mr. Boston Official Bartender's Guide: Fiftieth Anniversary Edition. New York: Warner Books, 1984.

Muckensturm, Louis. *Louis' Mixed Drinks with Hints for the Care and Service of Wines.* New York: Dodge Publishing, 1906.

Murray, Jim. *Classic Bourbon, Tennessee, and Rye Whiskey.* London: Prion Books, 1998.

———. *Classic Irish Whiskey.* London: Prion Books, 1997.

———. *The Complete Guide to Whiskey.* Chicago: Triumph Books, 1997.

North, Sterling, and Carl Kroch. *So Red the Nose, or Breath in the Afternoon.* New York: Farrar & Rinehart, 1935.

Pace, Marcel. *Selected Drinks.* Paris: Hotel Industry Mutualist Association, 1970.

Phillips, Louis. *Ask Me Anything About the Presidents.* New York: Avon Books, 1992.

Plotkin, Robert. *The Original Guide to American Cocktails and Mixed Drinks.* Tucson, AZ: BarMedia, 2001.

Pokhlebkin, William. *A History of Vodka.* Translated by Renfrey Clarke. London: Verso, 1992.

Powers, Madelon. *Faces Along the Bar: Lore and Order in the Workingman's Saloon, 1870–1920.* Chicago: University of Chicago Press, 1998.

Proskauer, Julien J. *What'll You Have.* New York: A. L. Burt, 1933.

Rae, Simon, ed. *The Farber Book of Drink, Drinkers and Drinking.* London: Farber and Farber, 1991.

Ray, Cyril. *Cognac.* London: Peter Davis, 1973.

Ray, Cyril, ed. *The Compleat Imbiber.* New York: Rinehart, 1957.

———. *The Compleat Imbiber Six: An Entertainment.* New York: Paul S. Eriksson, 1963.

———. *The Compleat Imbiber Twelve.* London: Hutchinson, 1971.

———. *The Gourmet's Companion.* London: Eyre & Spottiswood, 1963.

Red Jay Bartender's Guide. Philadelphia: Dr. D. Jayne and Son, 1934.

Reminder, The. Worcester, MA: [n.p.], 1899; compliments of M. J. Finnegan High Grade Beverages.

Reynolds, Cuyler. *The Banquet Book.* New York: Knickerbocker Press, 1902.

Sante, Luc. *Low Life: Lures and Snares of Old New York.* New York: Farrar, Straus and Giroux, 1991.

Sardi, Vincent, with George Shea. *Sardi's Bar Guide.* New York: Ballantine Books, 1988.

Saucier, Ted. *Ted Saucier's Bottoms Up.* New York: Greystone Press, 1951.

Savoy Cocktail Book, The. London: Pavilion Books, 1999.

Sax, Richard. *Classic Home Desserts.* Vermont: Chapters Publishing, 1994.

Schmidt, William (the Only William). *The Flowing Bowl: When and What to Drink.* New York: Charles L. Webster, 1892.

Schoenstein, Ralph, ed. *The Booze Book.* Chicago: Playboy Press, 1974.

Shane, Ted. *Authentic and Hilarious Bar Guide.* New York: Fawcett Publications, 1950.

Shay, Frank. *Drawn from the Wood: Consolations in Words and Music for Pious Friends and Drunken Companions.* New York: Macaulay, 1929.

Sonnichsen, C. L. *Billy King's Tombstone.* Caldwell, ID: Caxton Printers, 1942.

Southworth, May E., comp. *One Hundred and One Beverages.* San Francisco: Paul Elder, 1906.

Spence, Godfrey. *The Port Companion: A Connoisseur's Guide.* New York: Macmillan, 1997.

Spenser, Edward. *The Flowing Bowl.* New York: Duffield, [1925].

Steedman, M. E., and Cherman Senn, M.B.E. *Summer and Winter Drinks.* London: Ward, Lock, 1924.

Stephen, John, M.D. *A Treatise on the Manufacture, Imitation, Adulteration, and Reduction of Foreign Wines, Brandies, Gins, Rums, Etc.* Philadelphia: Published for the Author, 1860.

Straub, Jacques. *Drinks.* Chicago: Marie L. Straub–Hotel Monthly Press, 1914.

Sullivan, Jere. *The Drinks of Yesteryear: A Mixology.* [n.p.], 1930.

Tarling, W. J., comp. *Café Royal Cocktail Book.* London: Publications from Pall Mall, 1937.

Terrington, William. *Cooling Cups and Dainty Drinks.* London: Routledge and Sons, 1869.

Thomas, Jerry. *The Bar-Tender's Guide, or How to Mix All Kinds of Plain and Fancy Drinks.* New York: Fitzgerald Publishing, 1887.

———. *How to Mix Drinks, or The Bon Vivant's Companion.* New York: Dick & Fitzgerald, 1862; New York: Grosset & Dunlap, 1928.

Tirado, Eddie. *Cocktails and Mixed Drinks Handbook.* Australia: Tradewinds Group, 1976.

Townsend, Jack, and Tom Moore McBride. *The Bartender's Book.* New York: Viking Press, 1951.

Trader Vic [Victor Bergeron]. *Bartender's Guide.* New York: Garden City Books, 1948.

United Kingdom Bartender's Guild, comp. *The U.K.B.G. Guide to Drinks.* London: United Kingdom Bartender's Guild, 1955.

Van Every, Edward. *Sins of New York, as "Exposed" by the Police Gazette.* New York: Frederick A. Stokes, 1930.

Vermeire, Robert. *Cocktails: How to Mix Them.* London: Herbert Jenkins, [1930s?].

Wainwright, David. *Stone's Original Green Ginger Wine: Fortunes of a Family Firm, 1740–1990.* London: Quiller Press, 1990.

Walker, Stanley. *The Night Club Era.* New York: Frederick A. Stokes, 1933.

Whitfield, W. C., comp. and ed. *Just Cocktails.* [n.p.]: Three Mountaineers, 1939.

Williams, H. I. *Three Bottle Bar.* New York: M. S. Mill, 1945.

Wilson, Ross. *Scotch: The Formative Years.* London: Constable, 1970.

MAGAZINES

National Review, December 31, 1996.

Playboy, August 1973.

JOURNALS

Liebmann, A. J. "The History of Distillation." *Journal of Chemical Education* 33 (April 1956): 166.

Underwood, A. J. V., D.Sc., F.I.C. (Member). "The Historical Development of Distilling Plant." *Transactions of the Institute of Chemical Engineers* 13 (1935): 34–61.

WEBSITES

Architectural Record: archrecord.com.
The Atlantic: theatlantic.com.
Babe Ruth: baberuth.com.
Cocktail database: cocktaildb.com.
Cocktail Times: cocktailtimes.com.
Cyber Boxing Zone: cyberboxingzone.com.
DrinkBoy: drinkboy.com.
DrinkBoy MSN community: groups.msn.com/drinkboy.
Paul Sann, Journalism, Letters, Writings: paulsann.org.
State University of New York at Potsdam: www2.potsdam.edu.
Texas State Historical Association: tsha.utexas.edu.
Twain quotes: twainquotes.com.
Webtender: webtender.com.

INDEX

GARY REGAN is the author of *The Negroni, The Bartender's Bible, The Martini Companion, The Cocktailian Chronicles,* and others. A consultant to major spirits producers such as Diageo and Pernod Ricard, he holds workshops, judges cocktail competitions, and lectures around the world. He lives in the Hudson Valley, New York. Visit him at gazregan.com and follow him on social media @gazregan.

NOTES:

NOTES: